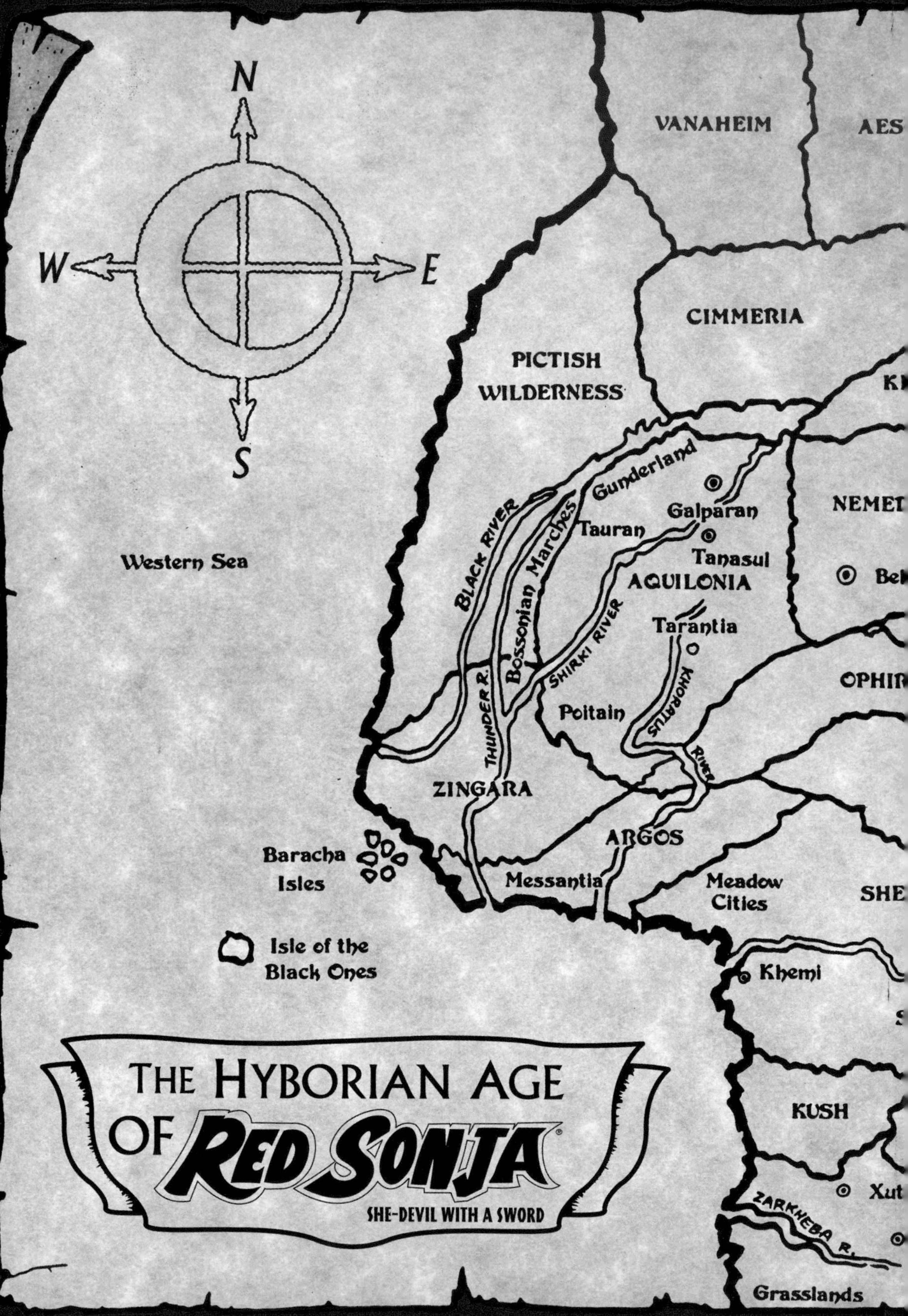
THE HYBORIAN AGE OF RED SONJA
SHE-DEVIL WITH A SWORD
N
S
W
E
VANAHEIM
CIMMERIA
PICTISH WILDERNESS
Western Sea
Gunderland
Galparan
Tauran
Tanasul
AQUILONIA
Bossonian Marches
BLACK RIVER
SHIRKI RIVER
Tarantia
KHORATUS RIVER
THUNDER R.
Poitain
ZINGARA
ARGOS
Messantia
Meadow Cities
Baracha Isles
Isle of the Black Ones
Khemi
KUSH
ZARKHEBA R.
Grasslands

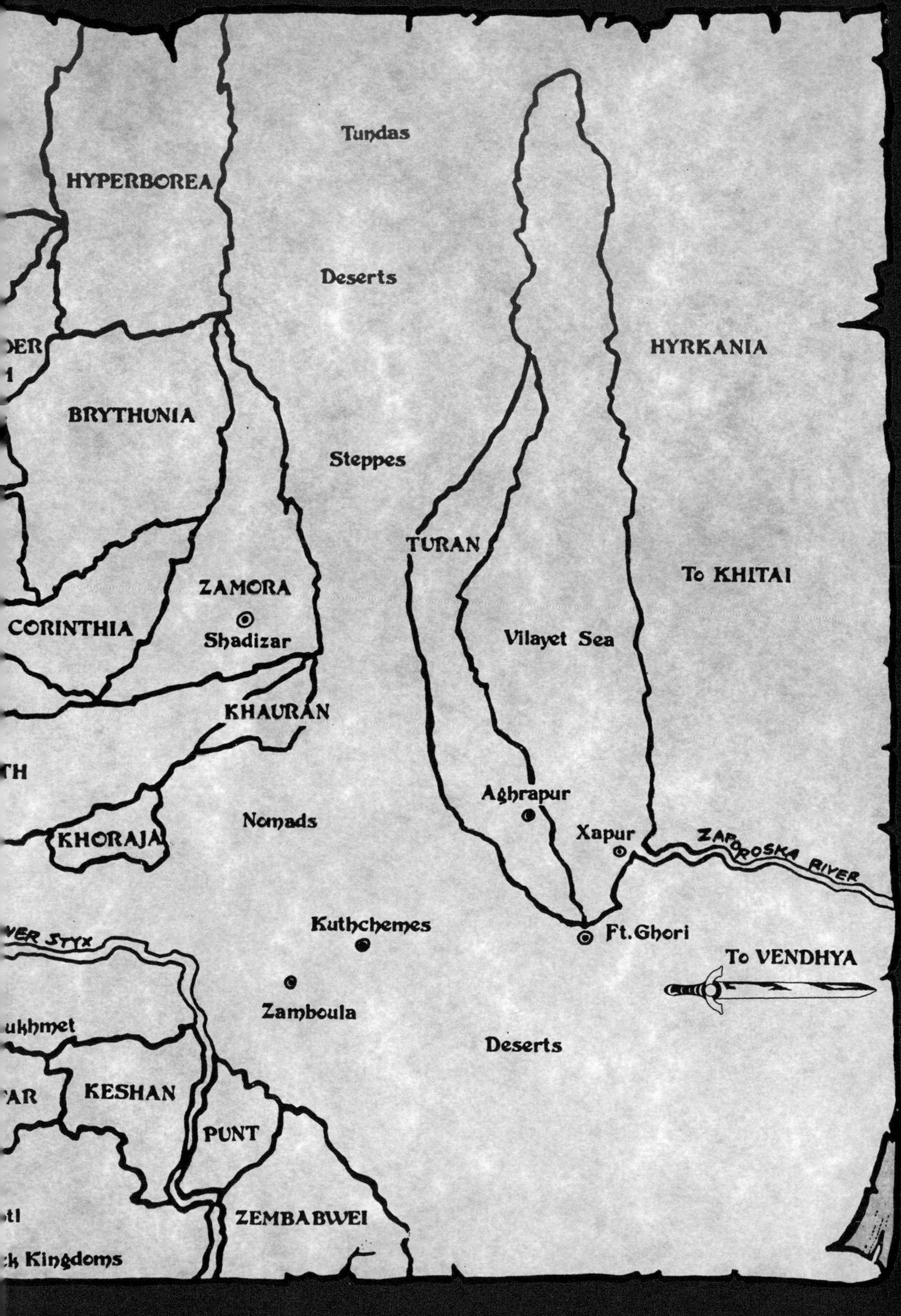

HYPERBOREA
Tundas
Deserts
HYRKANIA
BRYTHUNIA
Steppes
TURAN
To KHITAI
ZAMORA
Shadizar
CORINTHIA
Vilayet Sea
KHAURAN
Aghrapur
Xapur
ZAPOROSKA RIVER
Nomads
KHORAJA
Kuthchemes
Ft. Ghori
To VENDHYA
Zamboula
Deserts
KESHAN
PUNT
ZEMBABWEI

Dynamite Entertainment Presents

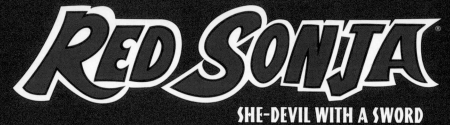

RED SONJA®

SHE-DEVIL WITH A SWORD

Dedicated to Robert E. Howard

Volume IX: War Season

- WRITTEN BY
  ERIC TRAUTMANN
- ART BY
  WALTER GEOVANI (ISSUES 51-54)
  PATRICK BERKENKOTTER (ISSUE 55)
- COLORS BY
  ADRIANO LUCAS (ISSUES 51-54)
  VINICIUS ANDRADE (ISSUES 55)
- LETTERING BY
  TROY PETERI (ISSUES 51)
- COVER BY
  JOSEPH MICHAEL LINSNER
- BASED ON THE HEROINE CREATED BY
  ROBERT E. HOWARD

THIS VOLUME COLLECTS RED SONJA: SHE-DEVIL WITH A SWORD ISSUES FIFTY-ONE THROUGH FIFTY-FIVE BY DYNAMITE ENTERTAINMENT.

EXECUTIVE EDITOR - RED SONJA
LUKE LIEBERMAN

SPECIAL THANKS TO ARTHUR LIEBERMAN
AT RED SONJA LLC.

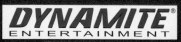

DYNAMITE ENTERTAINMENT
WWW.DYNAMITE.NET

NICK BARRUCCI PRESIDENT
JUAN COLLADO CHIEF OPERATING OFFICER
JOSEPH RYBANDT EDITOR
RICH YOUNG DIRECTOR BUSINESS DEVELOPMENT
JOSH JOHNSON CREATIVE DIRECTOR
JASON ULLMEYER SENIOR DESIGNER
JOSH GREEN TRAFFIC COORDINATOR
CHRIS CANIANO PRODUCTION ASSISTANT

For information regarding press, media rights, foreign rights, licensing, promotions, and advertising e-mail: marketing@dynamite.net

Printed in Canada

First Edition
ISBN-10: 1-60690-112-5 ISBN-13: 978-1-60690-112-0
10 9 8 7 6 5 4 3 2 1

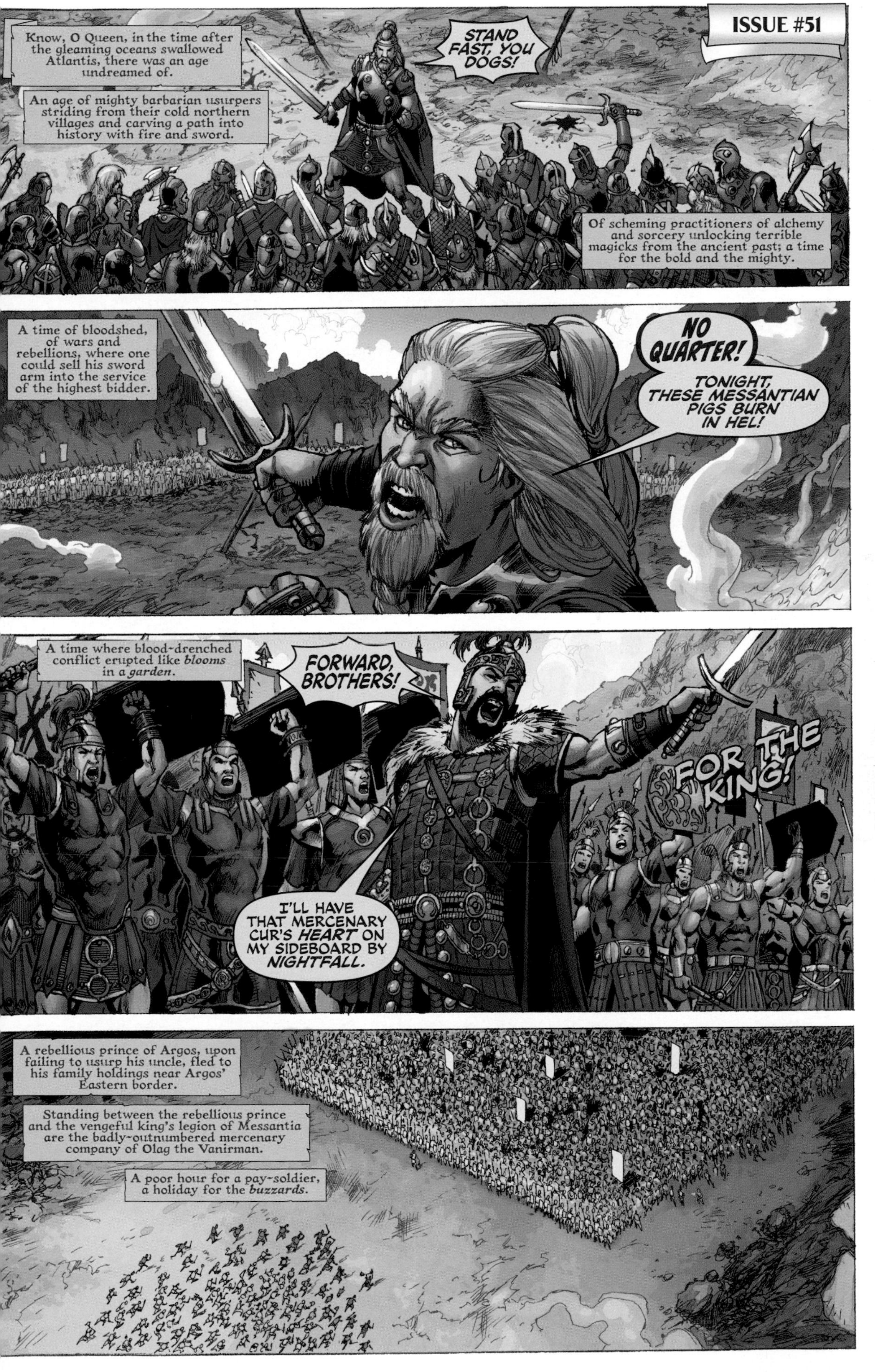
ISSUE #51
Know, O Queen, in the time after the gleaming oceans swallowed Atlantis, there was an age undreamed of.
STAND FAST, YOU DOGS!
An age of mighty barbarian usurpers striding from their cold northern villages and carving a path into history with fire and sword.
Of scheming practitioners of alchemy and sorcery unlocking terrible magicks from the ancient past; a time for the bold and the mighty.
A time of bloodshed, of wars and rebellions, where one could sell his sword arm into the service of the highest bidder.
NO QUARTER!
TONIGHT, THESE MESSANTIAN PIGS BURN IN HEL!
A time where blood-drenched conflict erupted like *blooms* in a *garden*.
FORWARD, BROTHERS!
FOR THE KING!
I'LL HAVE THAT MERCENARY CUR'S *HEART* ON MY SIDEBOARD BY *NIGHTFALL*.
A rebellious prince of Argos, upon failing to usurp his uncle, fled to his family holdings near Argos' Eastern border.
Standing between the rebellious prince and the vengeful king's legion of Messantia are the badly-outnumbered mercenary company of Olag the Vanirman.
A poor hour for a pay-soldier, a holiday for the *buzzards*.

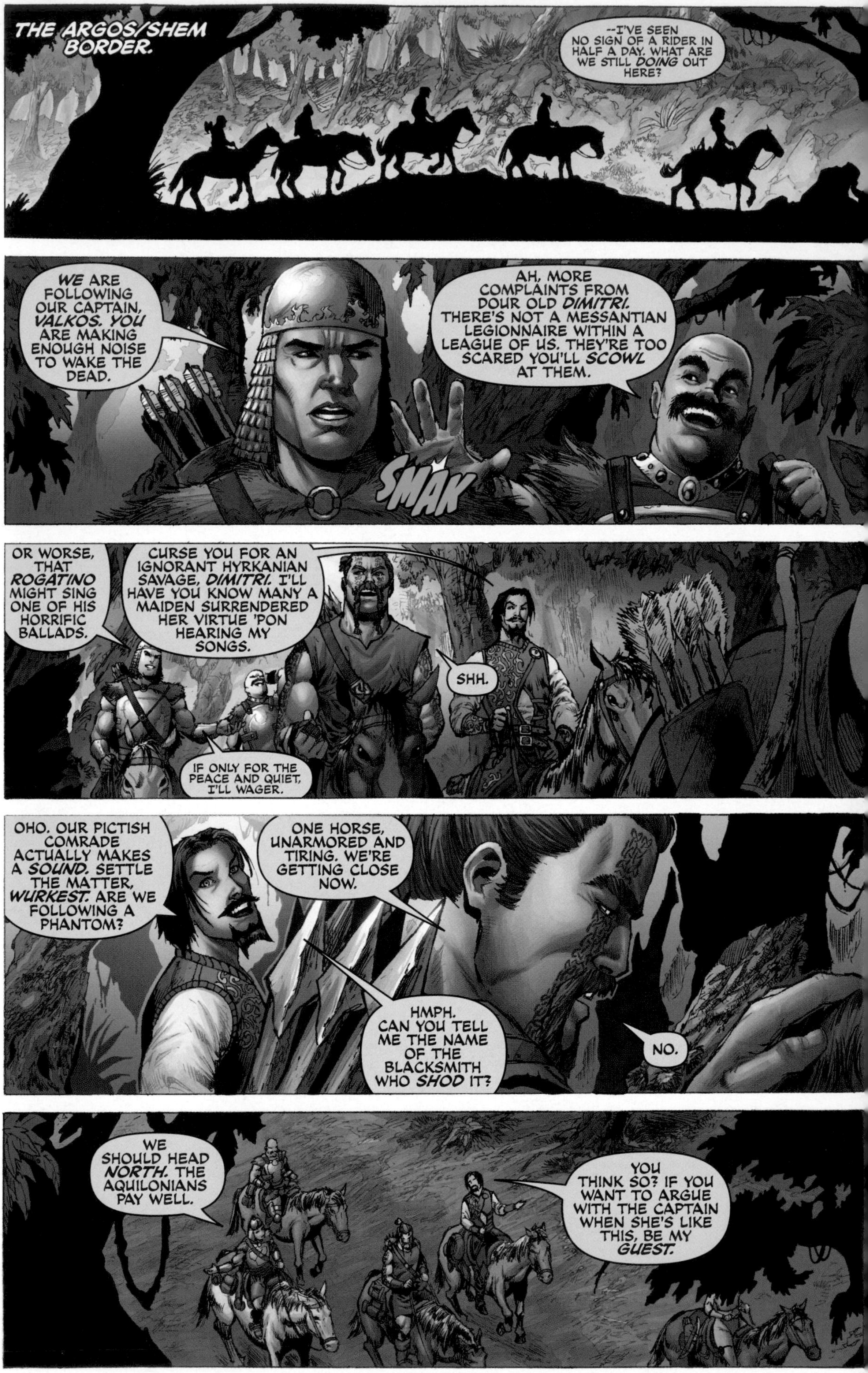
THE ARGOS/SHEM BORDER.
--I'VE SEEN NO SIGN OF A RIDER IN HALF A DAY. WHAT ARE WE STILL DOING OUT HERE?
WE ARE FOLLOWING OUR CAPTAIN, VALKOS. YOU ARE MAKING ENOUGH NOISE TO WAKE THE DEAD.
AH, MORE COMPLAINTS FROM DOUR OLD DIMITRI. THERE'S NOT A MESSANTIAN LEGIONNAIRE WITHIN A LEAGUE OF US. THEY'RE TOO SCARED YOU'LL SCOWL AT THEM.
SMAK
OR WORSE, THAT ROGATINO MIGHT SING ONE OF HIS HORRIFIC BALLADS.
CURSE YOU FOR AN IGNORANT HYRKANIAN SAVAGE, DIMITRI. I'LL HAVE YOU KNOW MANY A MAIDEN SURRENDERED HER VIRTUE 'PON HEARING MY SONGS.
SHH.
IF ONLY FOR THE PEACE AND QUIET, I'LL WAGER.
OHO. OUR PICTISH COMRADE ACTUALLY MAKES A SOUND. SETTLE THE MATTER, WURKEST. ARE WE FOLLOWING A PHANTOM?
ONE HORSE, UNARMORED AND TIRING. WE'RE GETTING CLOSE NOW.
HMPH. CAN YOU TELL ME THE NAME OF THE BLACKSMITH WHO SHOD IT?
NO.
WE SHOULD HEAD NORTH. THE AQUILONIANS PAY WELL.
YOU THINK SO? IF YOU WANT TO ARGUE WITH THE CAPTAIN WHEN SHE'S LIKE THIS, BE MY GUEST.

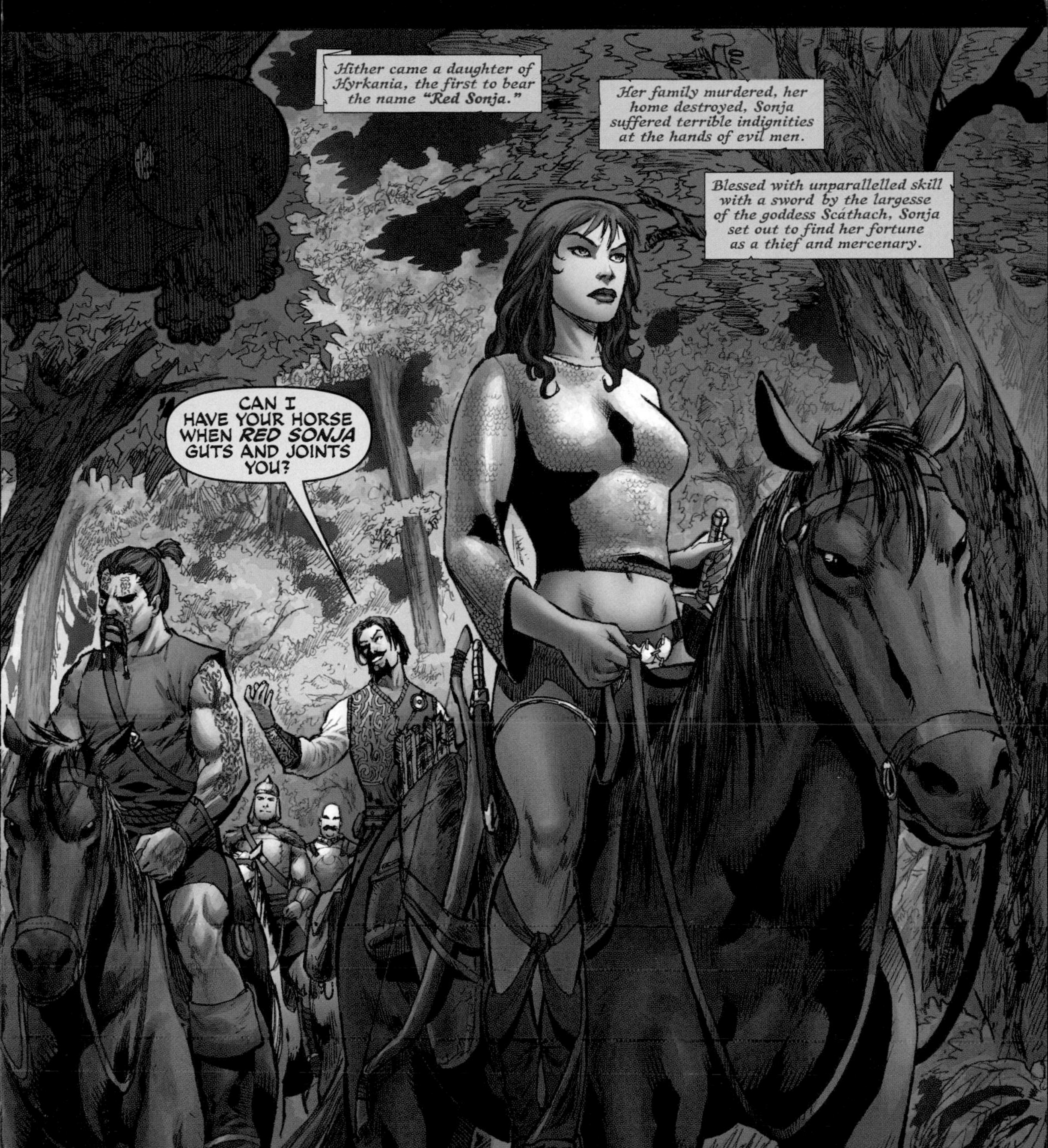
Hither came a daughter of Hyrkania, the first to bear the name "Red Sonja."
Her family murdered, her home destroyed, Sonja suffered terrible indignities at the hands of evil men.
Blessed with unparallelled skill with a sword by the largesse of the goddess Scáthach, Sonja set out to find her fortune as a thief and mercenary.
CAN I HAVE YOUR HORSE WHEN RED SONJA GUTS AND JOINTS YOU?

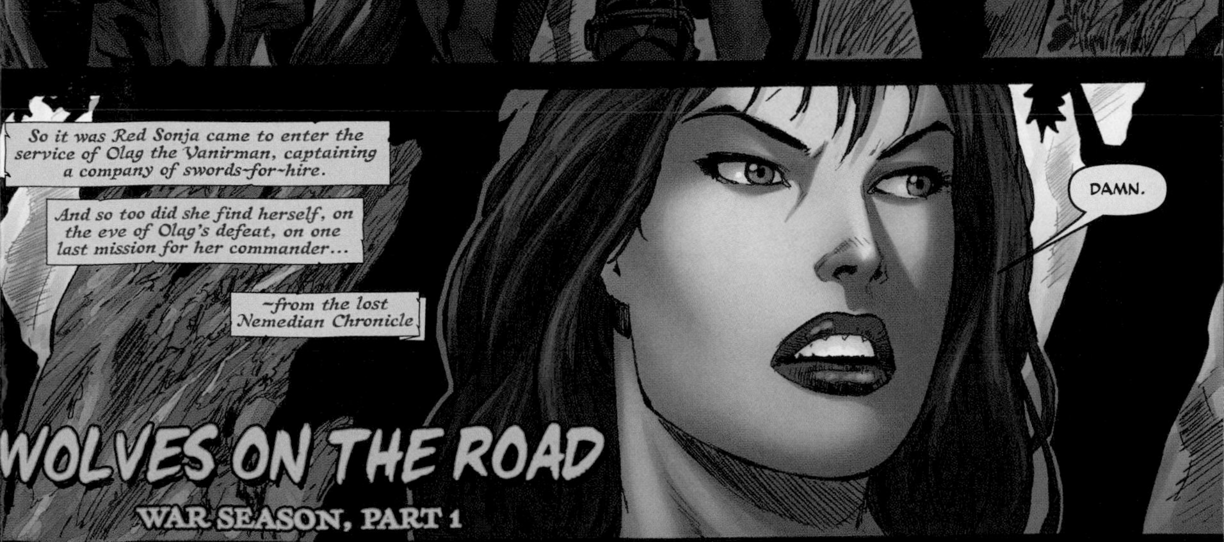
So it was Red Sonja came to enter the service of Olag the Vanirman, captaining a company of swords-for-hire.
And so too did she find herself, on the eve of Olag's defeat, on one last mission for her commander...
~from the lost Nemedian Chronicle
DAMN.
WOLVES ON THE ROAD
WAR SEASON, PART 1

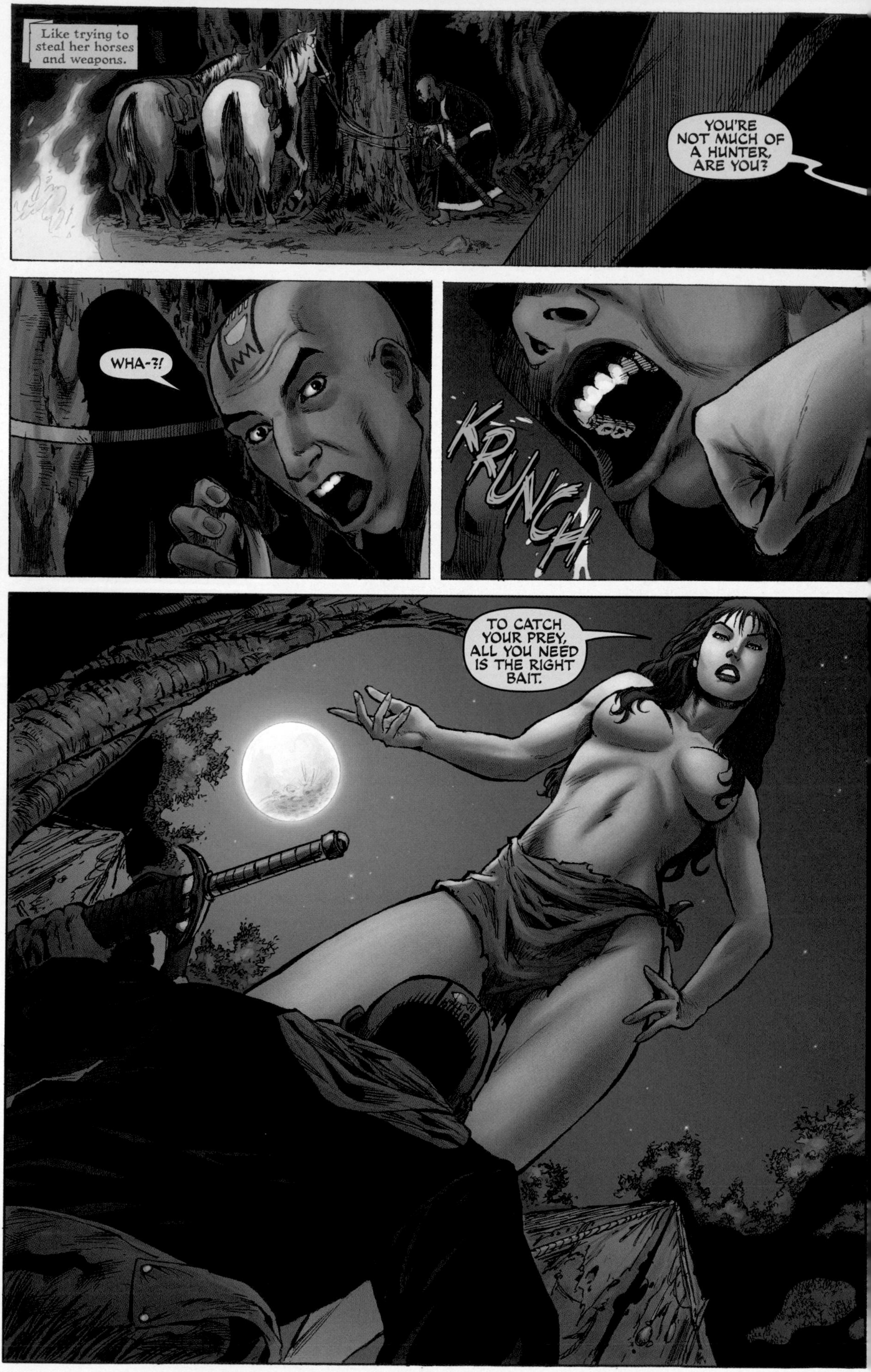

Like trying to steal her horses and weapons.
YOU'RE NOT MUCH OF A HUNTER, ARE YOU?
WHA-?!
KRUNCH
TO CATCH YOUR PREY, ALL YOU NEED IS THE RIGHT BAIT.

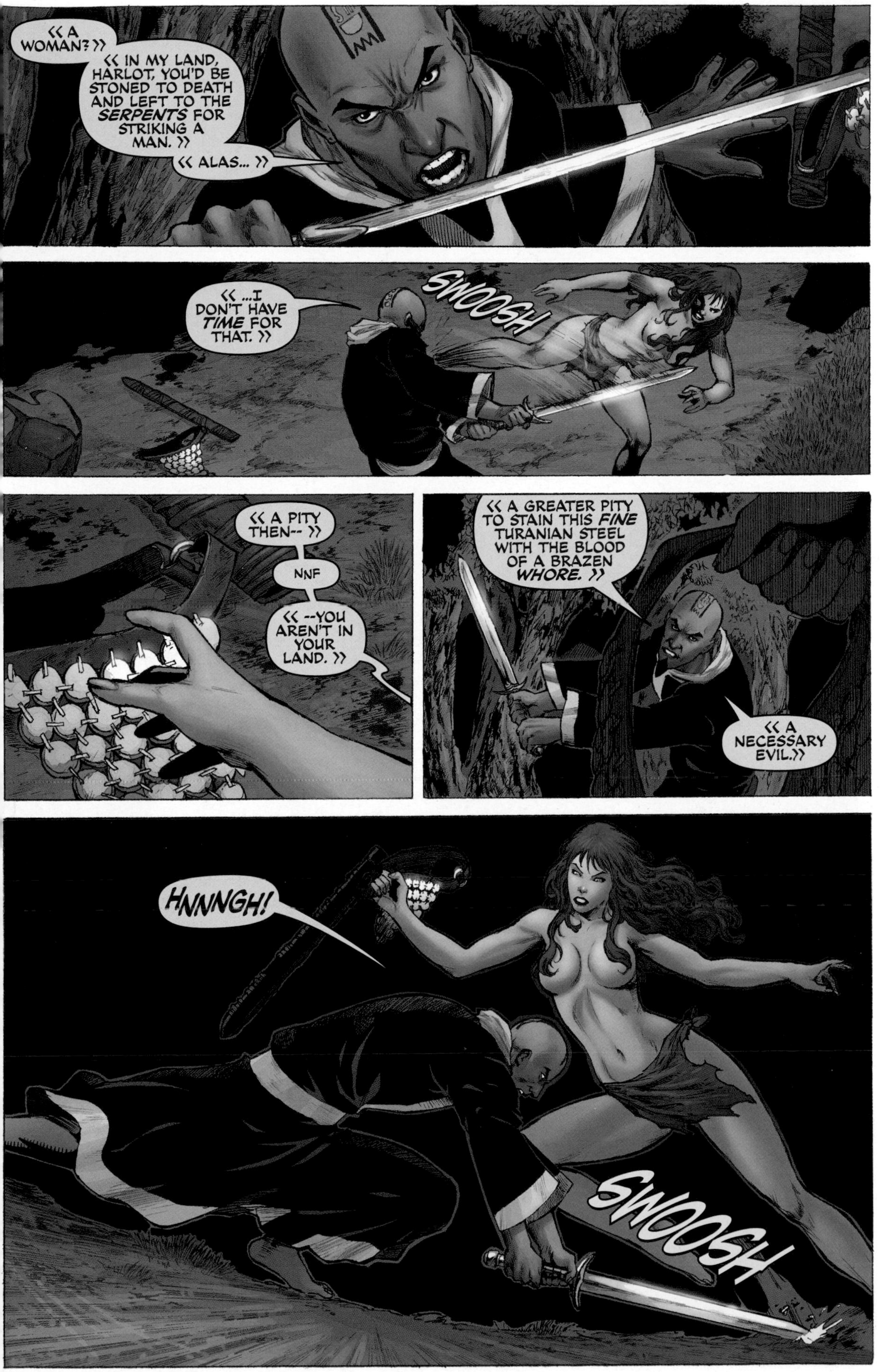

<< A WOMAN? >>
<< IN MY LAND, HARLOT, YOU'D BE STONED TO DEATH AND LEFT TO THE SERPENTS FOR STRIKING A MAN. >>
<< ALAS... >>
<< ...I DON'T HAVE TIME FOR THAT. >>
SWOOSH
<< A PITY THEN-- >>
NNF
<< --YOU AREN'T IN YOUR LAND. >>
<< A GREATER PITY TO STAIN THIS FINE TURANIAN STEEL WITH THE BLOOD OF A BRAZEN WHORE. >>
<< A NECESSARY EVIL. >>
HNNNGH!
SWOOSH

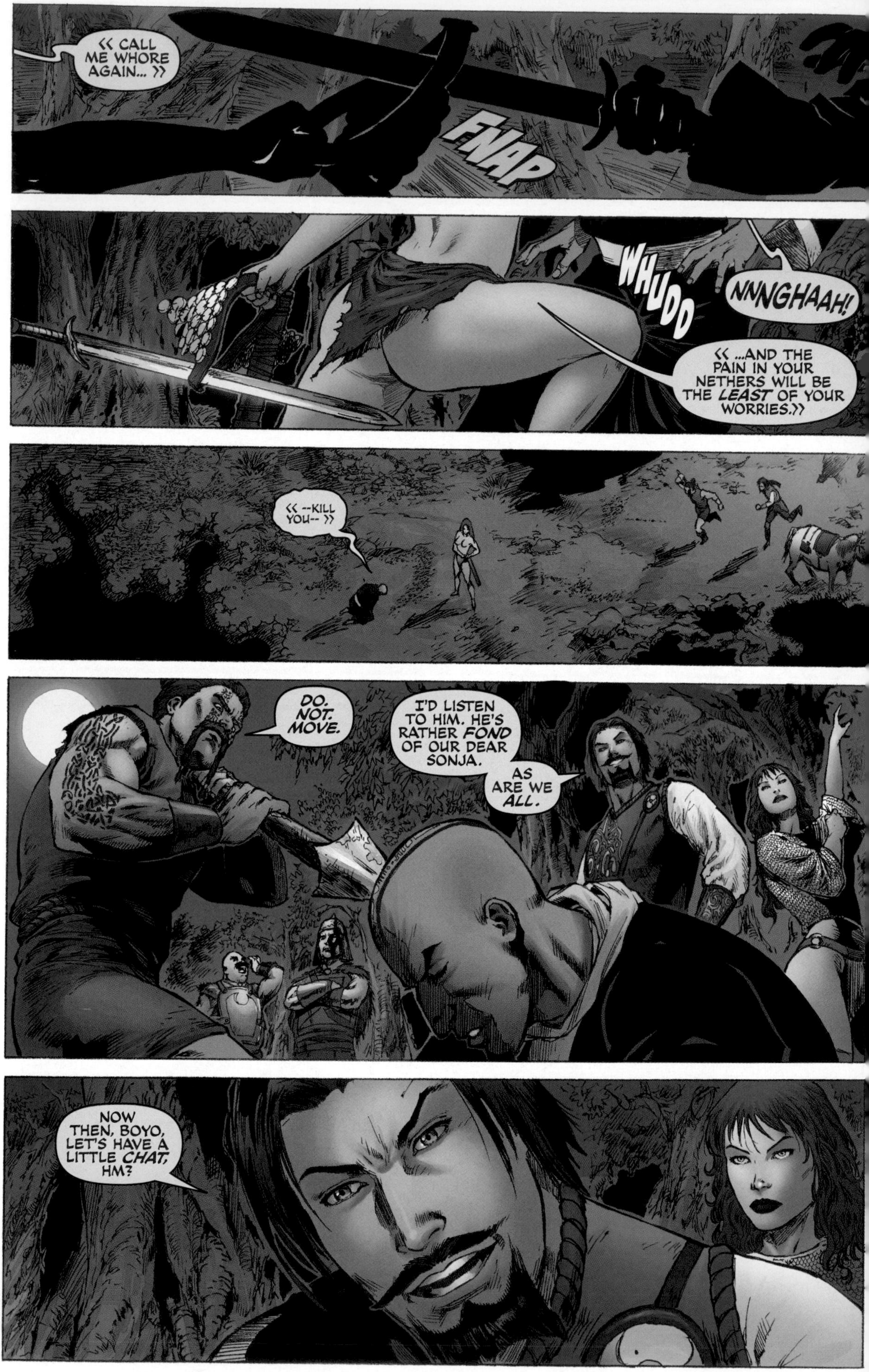
<< CALL ME WHORE AGAIN... >>
FNAP
WHUDD
NNNGHAAH!
<< ...AND THE PAIN IN YOUR NETHERS WILL BE THE *LEAST* OF YOUR WORRIES.>>
<< --KILL YOU-- >>
DO. NOT. MOVE.
I'D LISTEN TO HIM. HE'S RATHER *FOND* OF OUR DEAR SONJA.
AS ARE WE *ALL*.
NOW THEN, BOYO, LET'S HAVE A LITTLE *CHAT,* HM?

IF HE'S AN *ARGOSSIAN,* I'M THE *RAJAH OF AGRAPHUR.*

HE'S A *STYGIAN.* A SCRIBE FROM THE LOOKS OF HIM.

AND *THIS* IS WHO OLAG SENT US HARING OFF AFTER? NOT SOME ARGOSSIAN MESSENGER?

...YES. OLAG BELIEVED THE ARGOSSIANS HAD ARRANGED TO HIRE *STYGIAN SORCERERS,* AND SENT US TO STOP THEM.

SORCERERS? YOU SHOULD HAVE *TOLD* US, CAPTAIN. I'LL FIGHT ANY MAN WITH A SWORD OR AN AXE, BUT NO ONE SAID ANYTHING ABOUT *WIZARDS.*

AND WHAT ARE WE TO *DO* WITH HIM, THEN?

OLAG IS LIKELY DEAD ALREADY, STYGIAN WIZARDS OR NO, AND I DON'T RIDE -- OR *FIGHT* -- FOR FREE.

WE SHOULD JUST *KILL* HIM AND MOVE *NORTH.* THE AQUILONIANS--

"--ALWAYS NEED SWORDS." JUST BECAUSE YOU KEEP REPEATING IT DOESN'T MAKE IT TRUE, DIMITRI.

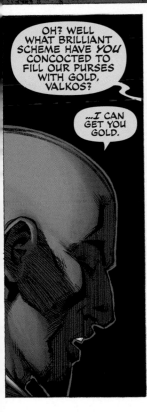

OH? WELL WHAT BRILLIANT SCHEME HAVE *YOU* CONCOCTED TO FILL OUR PURSES WITH GOLD, VALKOS?

...I CAN GET YOU GOLD.

AH. YOU'RE NOT REALLY A SCRIBE, YOU'RE THE *PHAROAH* OF ALL STYGIA. MY *APOLOGIES* FOR NOT RECOGNIZING YOU SOONER, YOUR *ROYALNESS--*

ENOUGH. LET HIM SPEAK.

I'M NO PHAROAH, OPHIRAN, BUT MY FAMILY HAS...SOME STANDING.

I AM TO BE MET BY OUR RETAINERS, IN *SHEM.* THEY WILL PAY MY RANSOM.

IN *GOLD.*

WELL? WHAT SAY YOU?

YOU KNOW ME, SONJA. I *LIKE* MONEY. HELL IS AN EMPTY PURSE...

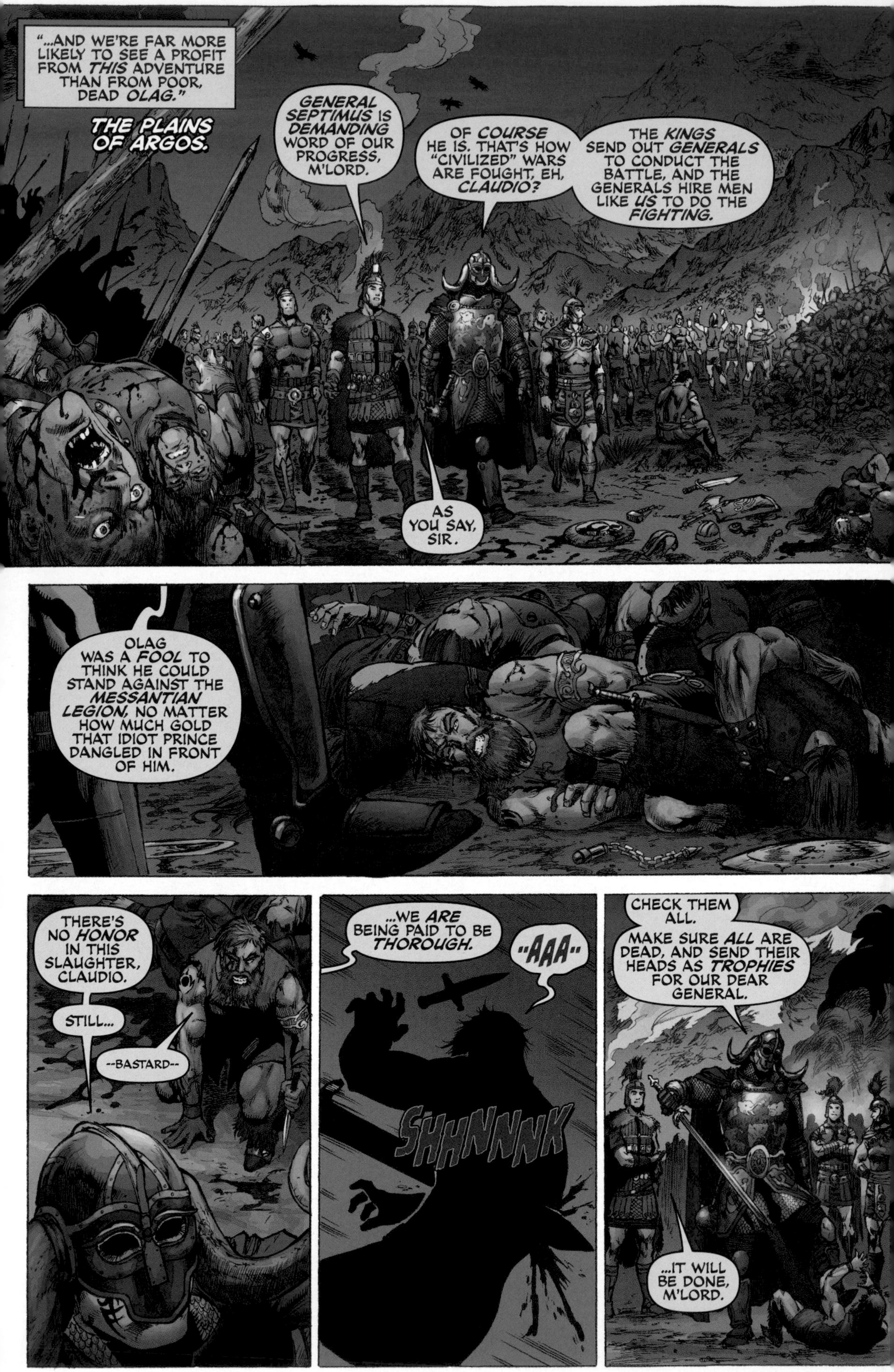
"...AND WE'RE FAR MORE LIKELY TO SEE A PROFIT FROM THIS ADVENTURE THAN FROM POOR, DEAD OLAG."
THE PLAINS OF ARGOS.
GENERAL SEPTIMUS IS DEMANDING WORD OF OUR PROGRESS, M'LORD.
OF COURSE HE IS. THAT'S HOW "CIVILIZED" WARS ARE FOUGHT, EH, CLAUDIO?
THE KINGS SEND OUT GENERALS TO CONDUCT THE BATTLE, AND THE GENERALS HIRE MEN LIKE US TO DO THE FIGHTING.
AS YOU SAY, SIR.
OLAG WAS A FOOL TO THINK HE COULD STAND AGAINST THE MESSANTIAN LEGION, NO MATTER HOW MUCH GOLD THAT IDIOT PRINCE DANGLED IN FRONT OF HIM.
THERE'S NO HONOR IN THIS SLAUGHTER, CLAUDIO.
STILL...
--BASTARD--
...WE ARE BEING PAID TO BE THOROUGH.
-AAA-
SHHNNNK
CHECK THEM ALL.
MAKE SURE ALL ARE DEAD, AND SEND THEIR HEADS AS TROPHIES FOR OUR DEAR GENERAL.
...IT WILL BE DONE, M'LORD.

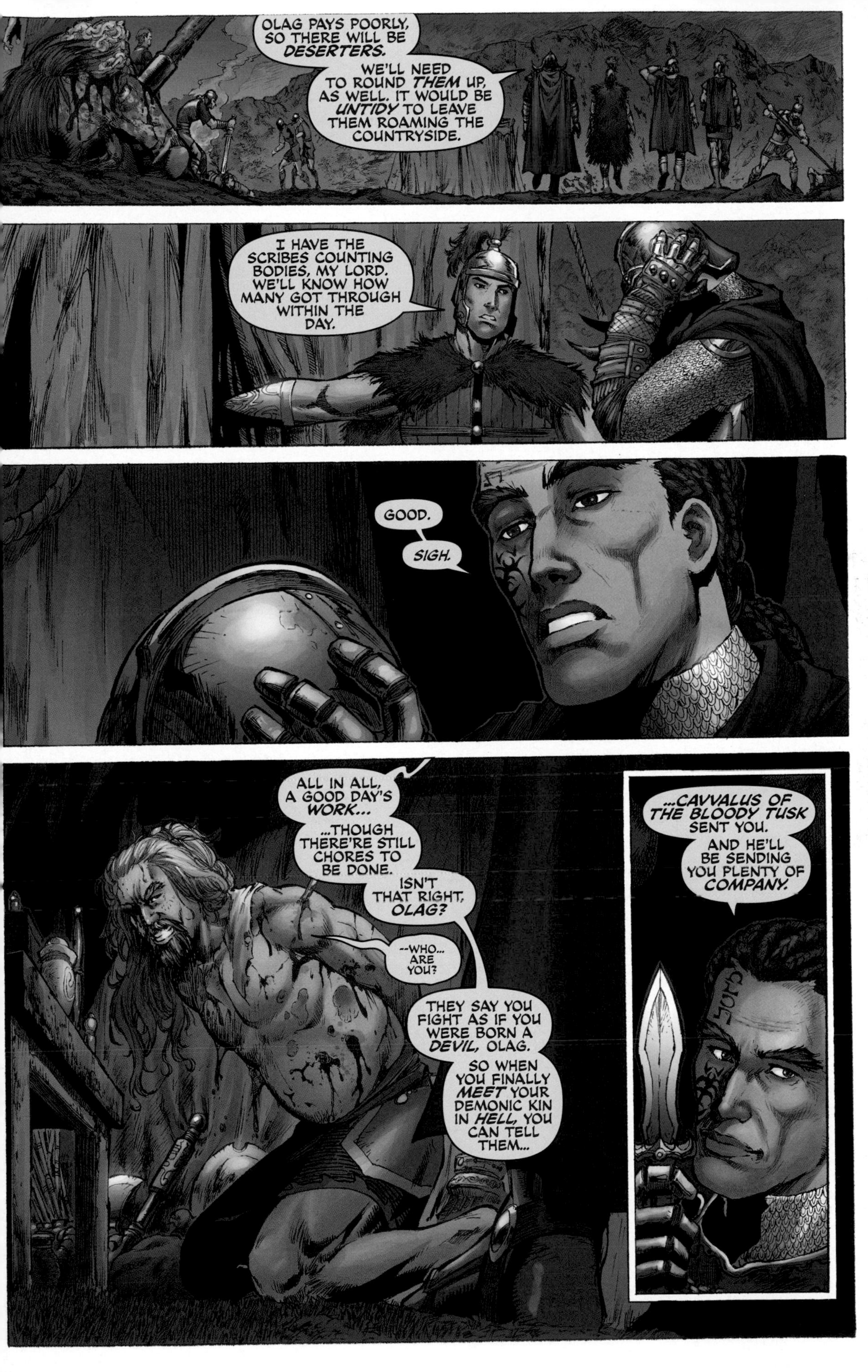

OLAG PAYS POORLY, SO THERE WILL BE *DESERTERS.*
WE'LL NEED TO ROUND *THEM* UP, AS WELL. IT WOULD BE *UNTIDY* TO LEAVE THEM ROAMING THE COUNTRYSIDE.
I HAVE THE SCRIBES COUNTING BODIES, MY LORD. WE'LL KNOW HOW MANY GOT THROUGH WITHIN THE DAY.
GOOD.
SIGH.
ALL IN ALL, A GOOD DAY'S *WORK...*
...THOUGH THERE'RE STILL CHORES TO BE DONE.
ISN'T THAT RIGHT, *OLAG?*
--WHO... ARE YOU?
THEY SAY YOU FIGHT AS IF YOU WERE BORN A *DEVIL,* OLAG.
SO WHEN YOU FINALLY *MEET* YOUR DEMONIC KIN IN *HELL,* YOU CAN TELL THEM...
...CAVVALUS OF THE BLOODY TUSK SENT YOU.
AND HE'LL BE SENDING YOU PLENTY OF *COMPANY.*

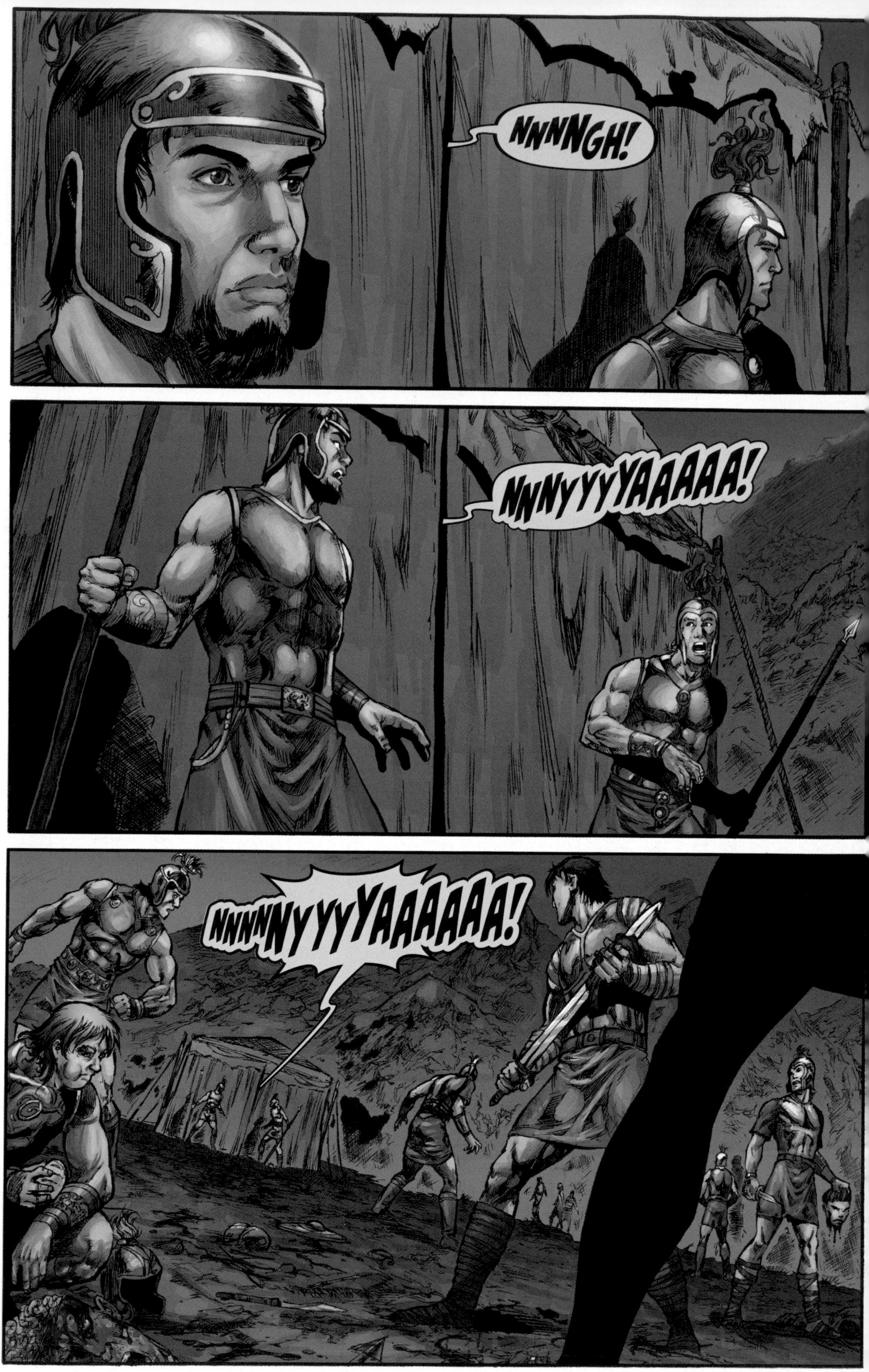
NNNNGH!
NNNyyyYAAAAA!
NNNNNyyyYAAAAAA!

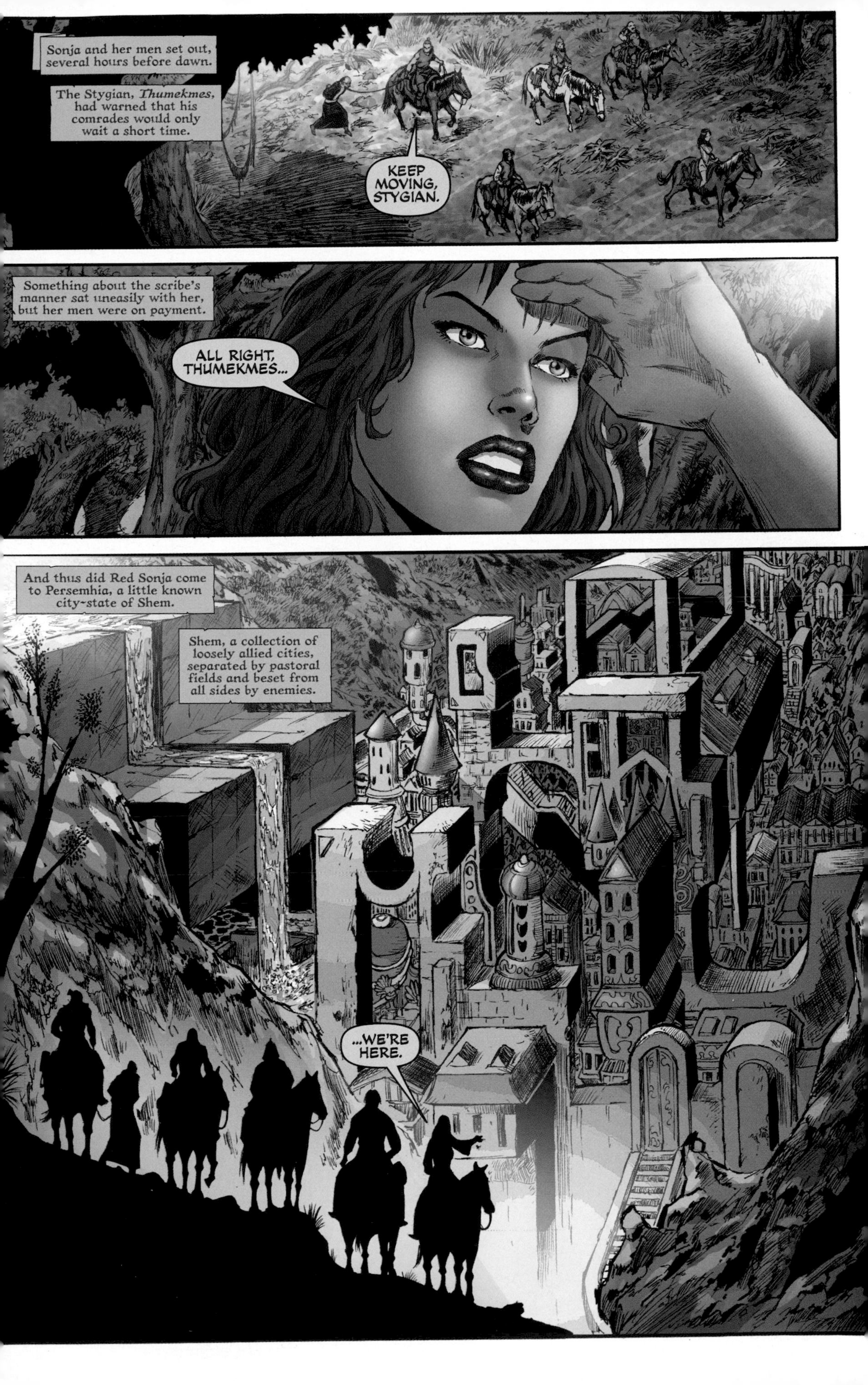
Sonja and her men set out, several hours before dawn.
The Stygian, *Thumekmes*, had warned that his comrades would only wait a short time.
KEEP MOVING, STYGIAN.
Something about the scribe's manner sat uneasily with her, but her men were on payment.
ALL RIGHT, THUMEKMES...
And thus did Red Sonja come to Persemhia, a little known city~state of Shem.
Shem, a collection of loosely allied cities, separated by pastoral fields and beset from all sides by enemies.
...WE'RE HERE.

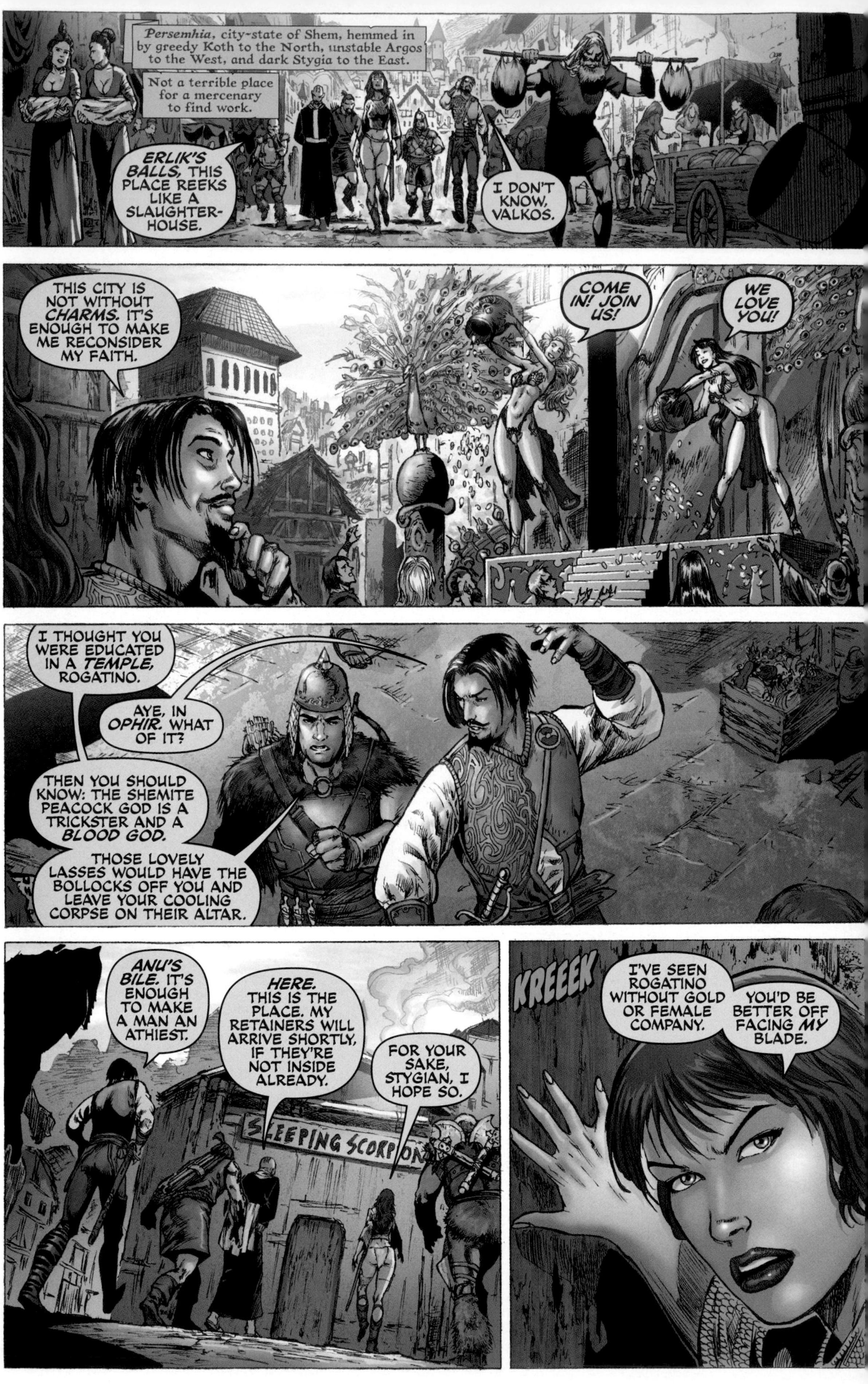
Persemhia, city-state of Shem, hemmed in by greedy Koth to the North, unstable Argos to the West, and dark Stygia to the East.
Not a terrible place for a mercenary to find work.
ERLIK'S BALLS, THIS PLACE REEKS LIKE A SLAUGHTER-HOUSE.
I DON'T KNOW, VALKOS.
THIS CITY IS NOT WITHOUT CHARMS. IT'S ENOUGH TO MAKE ME RECONSIDER MY FAITH.
COME IN! JOIN US!
WE LOVE YOU!
I THOUGHT YOU WERE EDUCATED IN A TEMPLE, ROGATINO.
AYE, IN OPHIR. WHAT OF IT?
THEN YOU SHOULD KNOW: THE SHEMITE PEACOCK GOD IS A TRICKSTER AND A BLOOD GOD.
THOSE LOVELY LASSES WOULD HAVE THE BOLLOCKS OFF YOU AND LEAVE YOUR COOLING CORPSE ON THEIR ALTAR.
ANU'S BILE. IT'S ENOUGH TO MAKE A MAN AN ATHIEST.
HERE. THIS IS THE PLACE. MY RETAINERS WILL ARRIVE SHORTLY, IF THEY'RE NOT INSIDE ALREADY.
FOR YOUR SAKE, STYGIAN, I HOPE SO.
SLEEPING SCORPION
KREEEK
I'VE SEEN ROGATINO WITHOUT GOLD OR FEMALE COMPANY.
YOU'D BE BETTER OFF FACING MY BLADE.

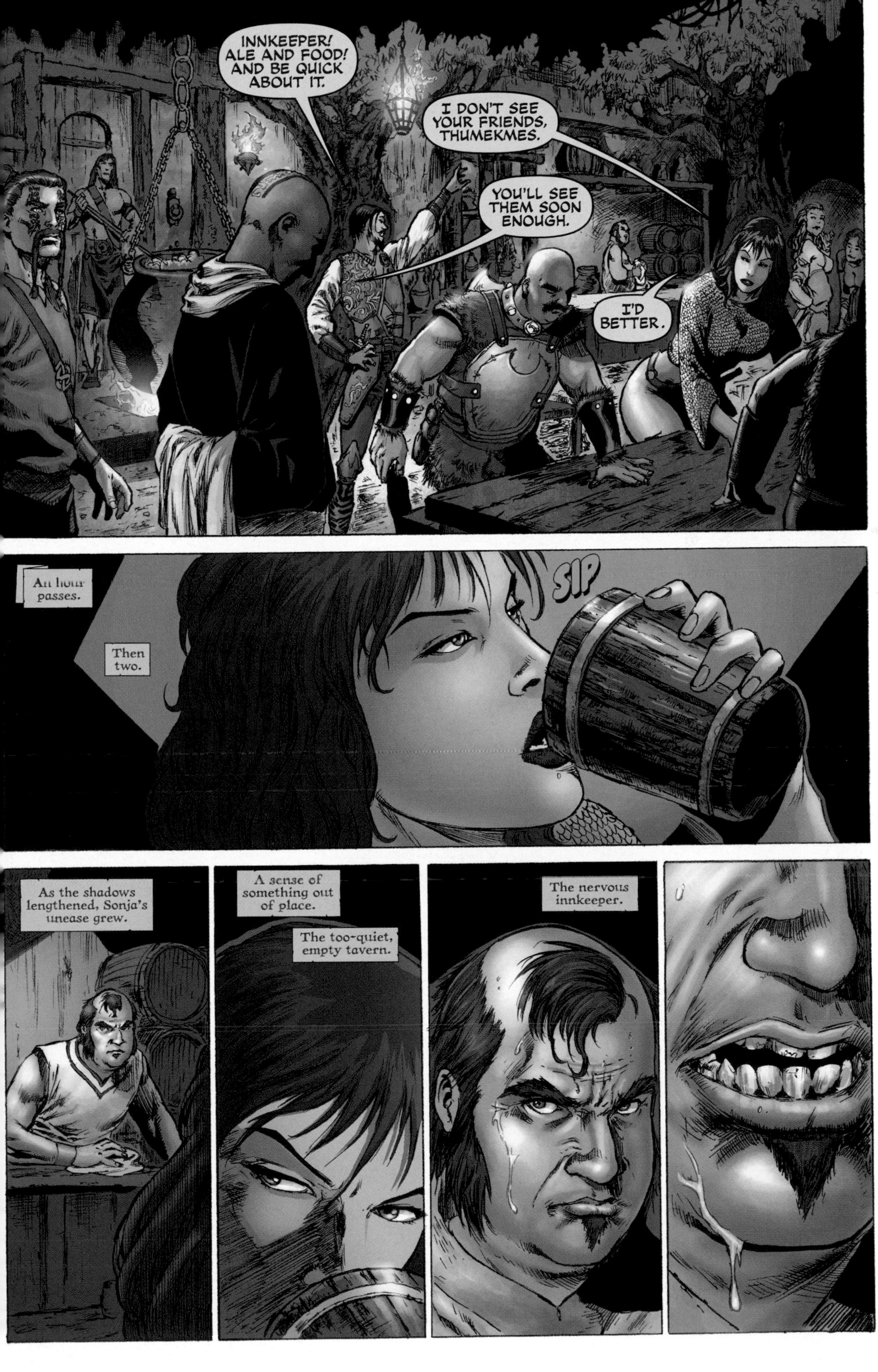
INNKEEPER! ALE AND FOOD! AND BE QUICK ABOUT IT.
I DON'T SEE YOUR FRIENDS, THUMEKMES.
YOU'LL SEE THEM SOON ENOUGH.
I'D BETTER.
An hour passes.
Then two.
SIP
As the shadows lengthened, Sonja's unease grew.
A sense of something out of place.
The too-quiet, empty tavern.
The nervous innkeeper.

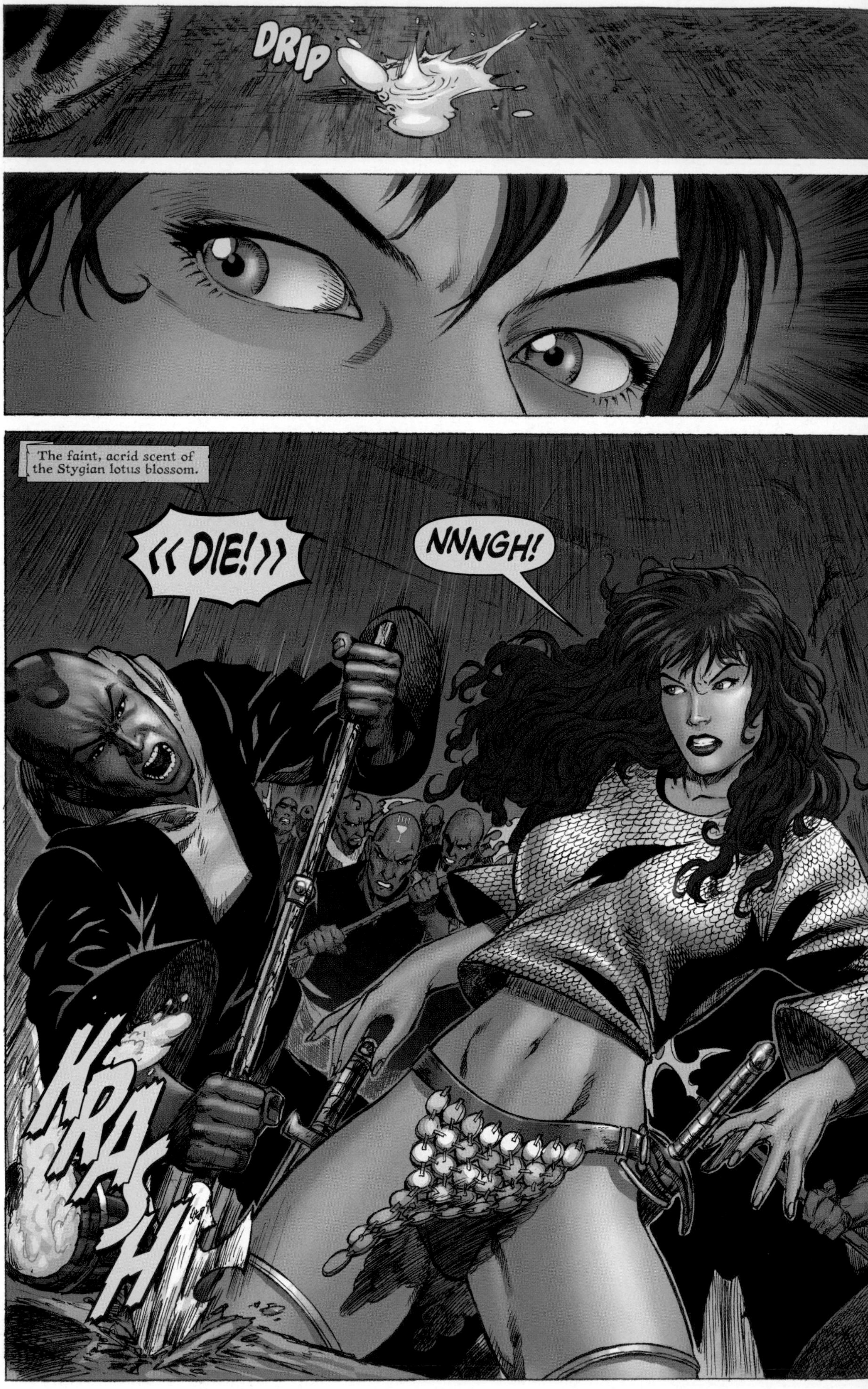
DRIP
The faint, acrid scent of the Stygian lotus blossom.
‹‹ DIE! ››
NNNGH!
KRASH!

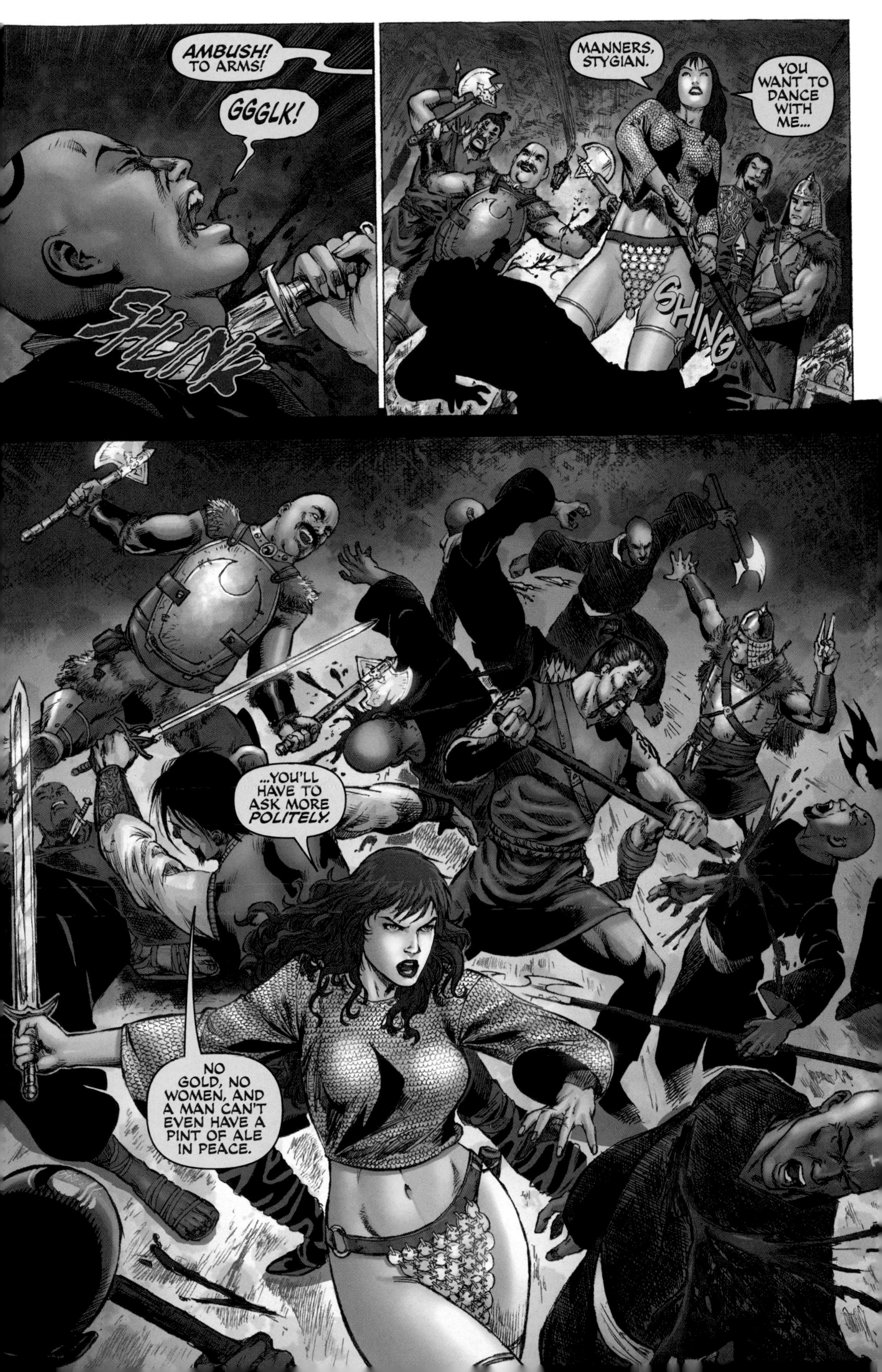

AMBUSH! TO ARMS!
GGGLK!
SHUNK
MANNERS, STYGIAN.
YOU WANT TO DANCE WITH ME...
SHING
...YOU'LL HAVE TO ASK MORE POLITELY.
NO GOLD, NO WOMEN, AND A MAN CAN'T EVEN HAVE A PINT OF ALE IN PEACE.

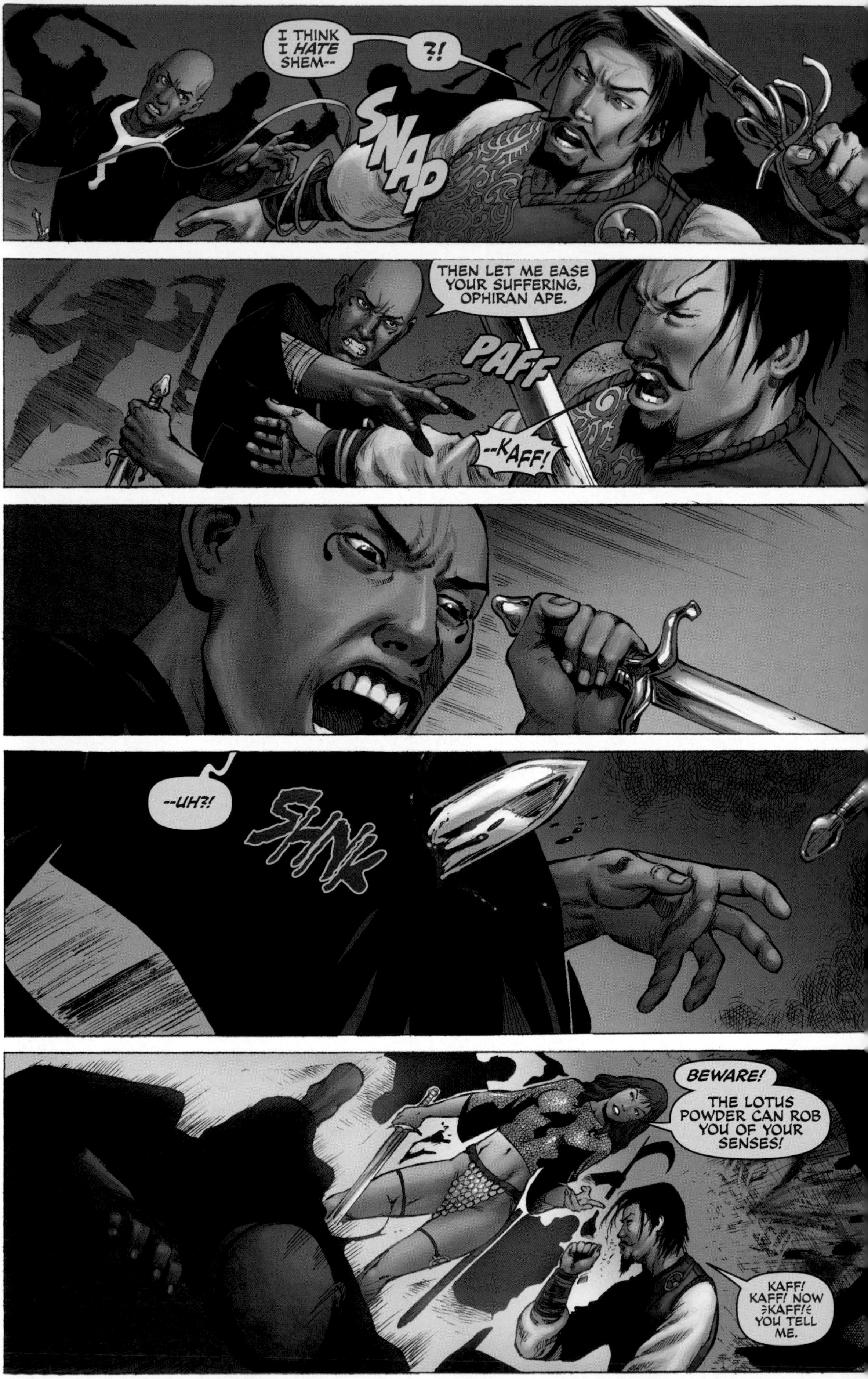
I THINK I *HATE* SHEM--
?!
SNAP
THEN LET ME EASE YOUR SUFFERING, OPHIRAN APE.
PAFF
--KAFF!
--UH?!
SHNK
BEWARE!
THE LOTUS POWDER CAN ROB YOU OF YOUR SENSES!
KAFF! KAFF! NOW *KAFF!* YOU TELL ME.

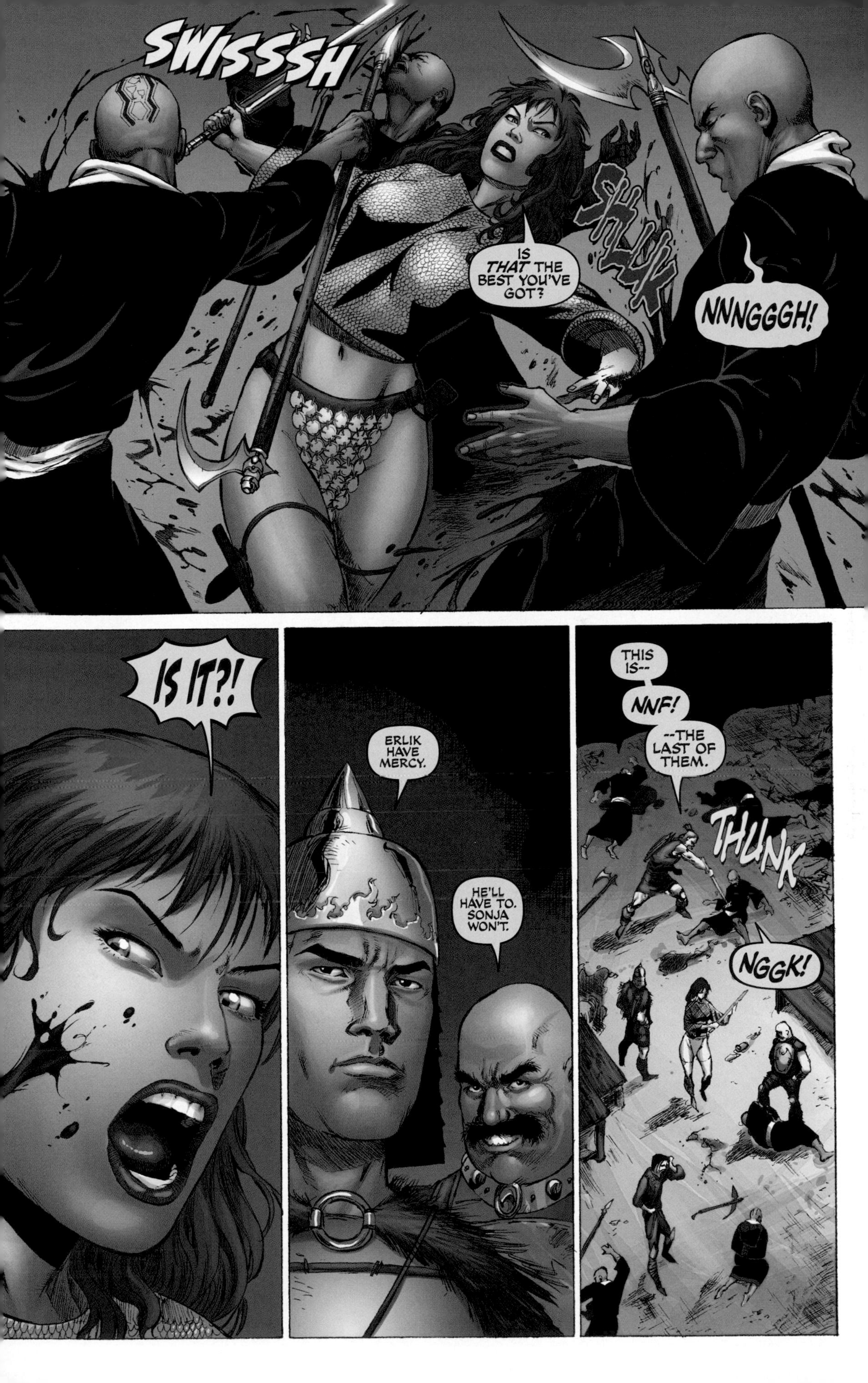
SWISSSH
IS THAT THE BEST YOU'VE GOT?
SHLUK
NNNGGGH!
IS IT?!
ERLIK HAVE MERCY.
HE'LL HAVE TO. SONJA WON'T.
THIS IS--
NNF!
--THE LAST OF THEM.
THUNK
NGGK!

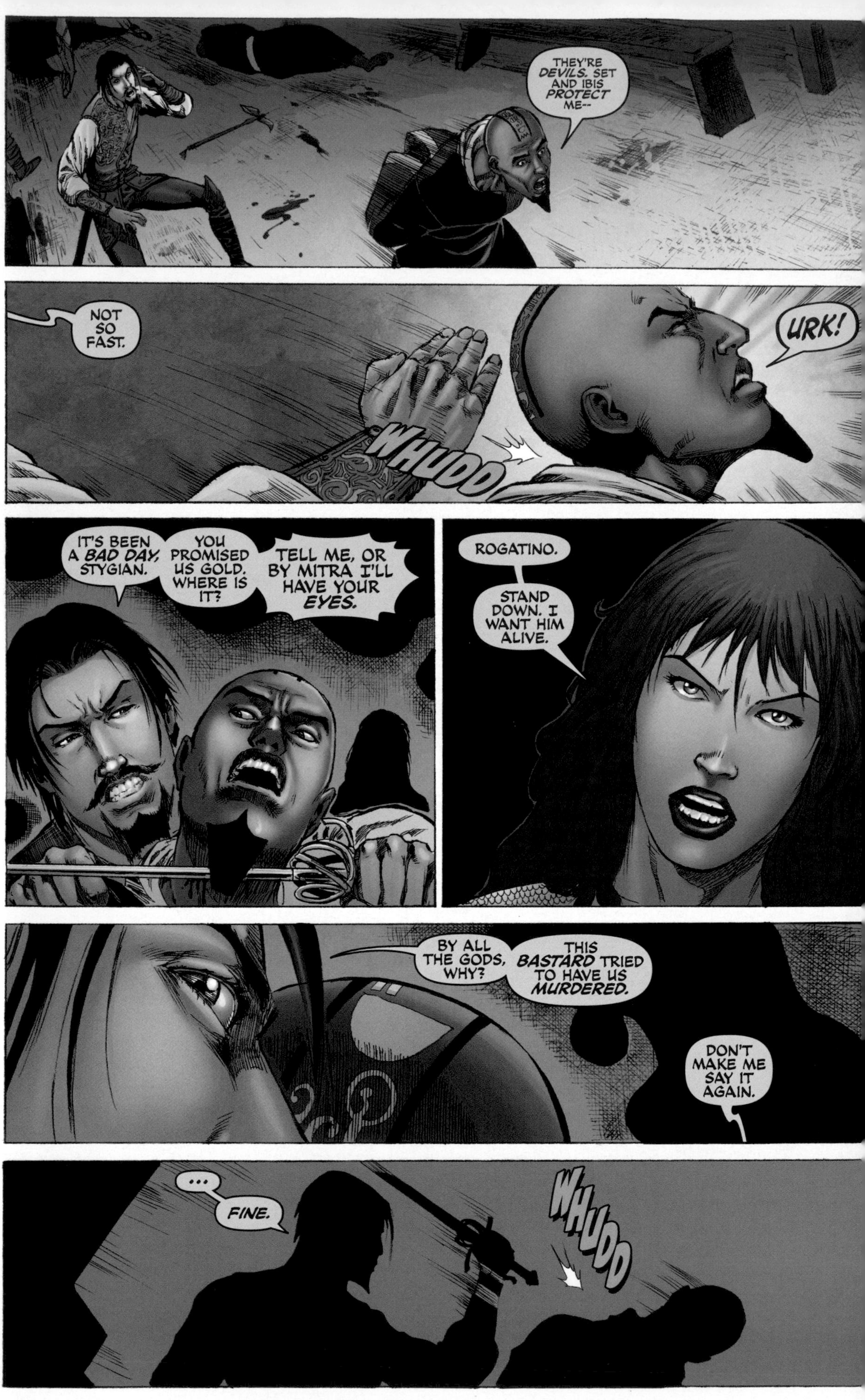
THEY'RE DEVILS. SET AND IBIS PROTECT ME--
NOT SO FAST.
URK!
WHUDD
IT'S BEEN A BAD DAY, STYGIAN.
YOU PROMISED US GOLD. WHERE IS IT?
TELL ME, OR BY MITRA I'LL HAVE YOUR EYES.
ROGATINO.
STAND DOWN. I WANT HIM ALIVE.
BY ALL THE GODS, WHY?
THIS BASTARD TRIED TO HAVE US MURDERED.
DON'T MAKE ME SAY IT AGAIN.
...
FINE.
WHUDD

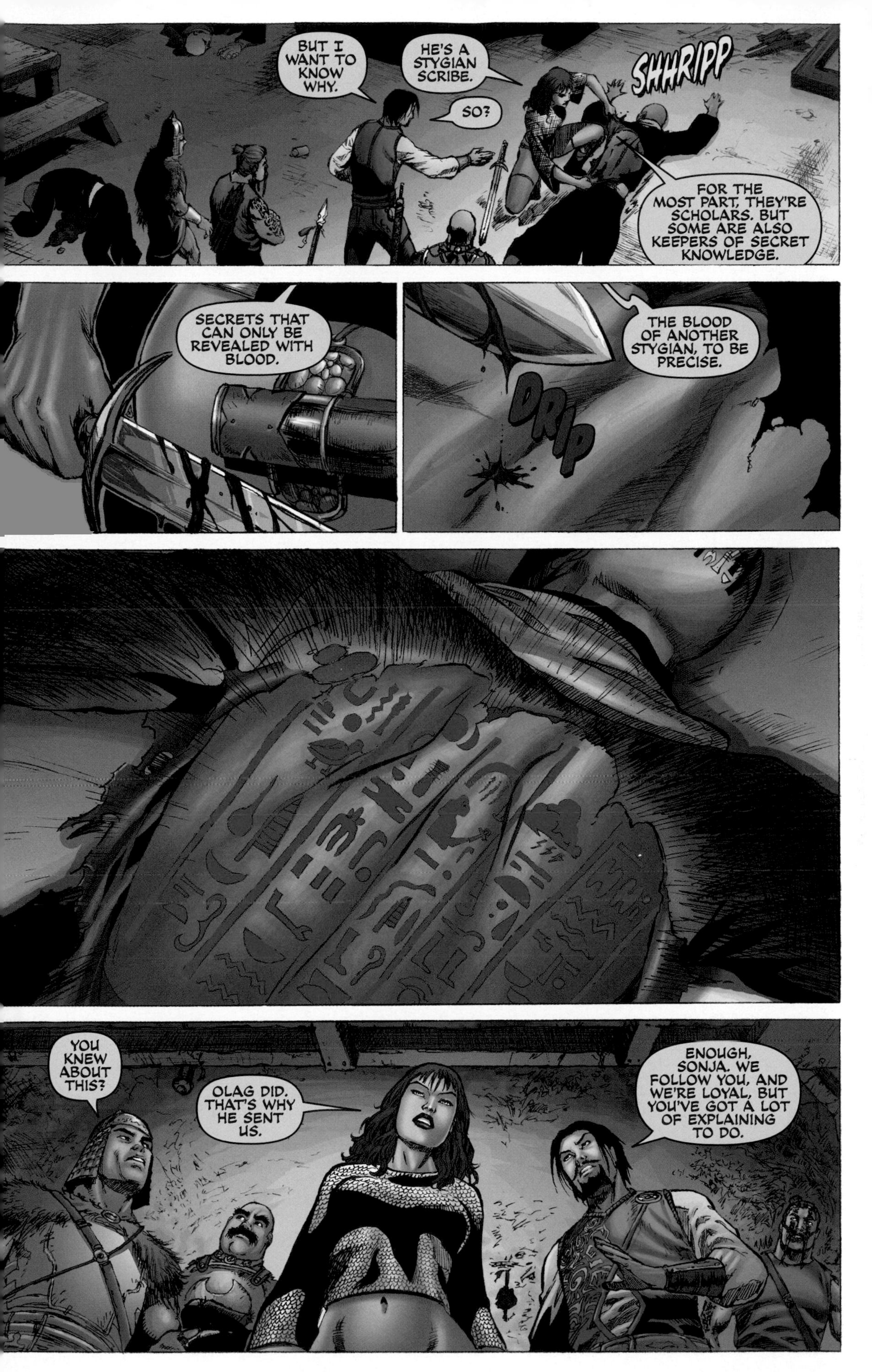

BUT I WANT TO KNOW WHY.
HE'S A STYGIAN SCRIBE.
SO?
SHHRIPP
FOR THE MOST PART, THEY'RE SCHOLARS. BUT SOME ARE ALSO KEEPERS OF SECRET KNOWLEDGE.
SECRETS THAT CAN ONLY BE REVEALED WITH BLOOD.
THE BLOOD OF ANOTHER STYGIAN, TO BE PRECISE.
DRIP
YOU KNEW ABOUT THIS?
OLAG DID. THAT'S WHY HE SENT US.
ENOUGH, SONJA. WE FOLLOW YOU, AND WE'RE LOYAL, BUT YOU'VE GOT A LOT OF EXPLAINING TO DO.

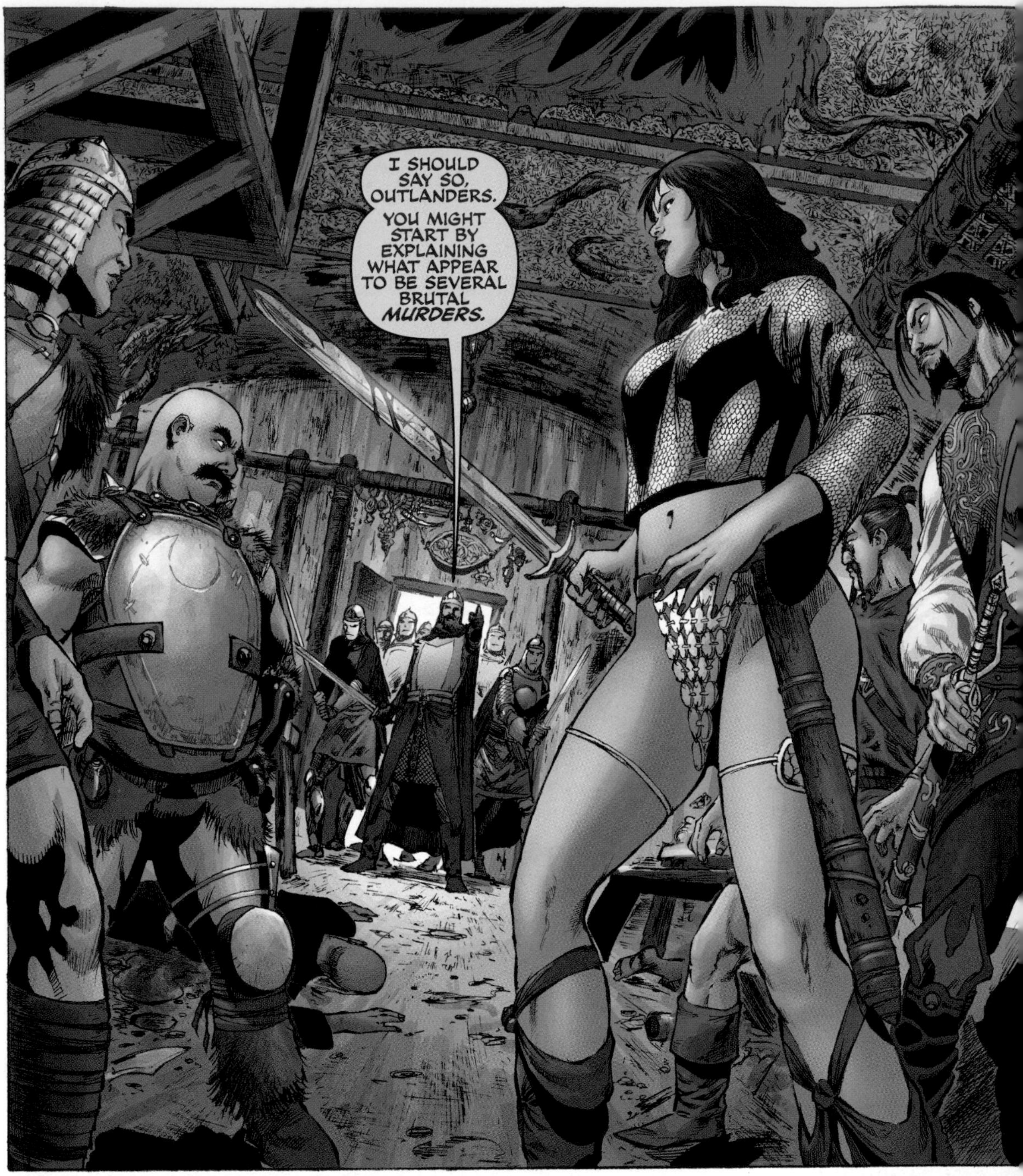
I SHOULD SAY SO, OUTLANDERS.
YOU MIGHT START BY EXPLAINING WHAT APPEAR TO BE SEVERAL BRUTAL MURDERS.

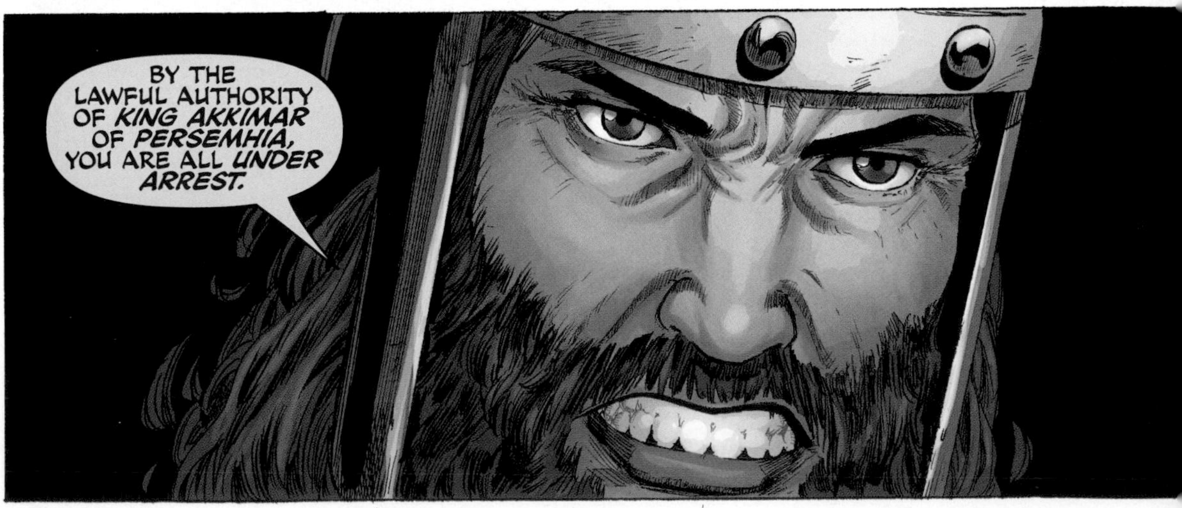
BY THE LAWFUL AUTHORITY OF KING AKKIMAR OF PERSEMHIA, YOU ARE ALL UNDER ARREST.

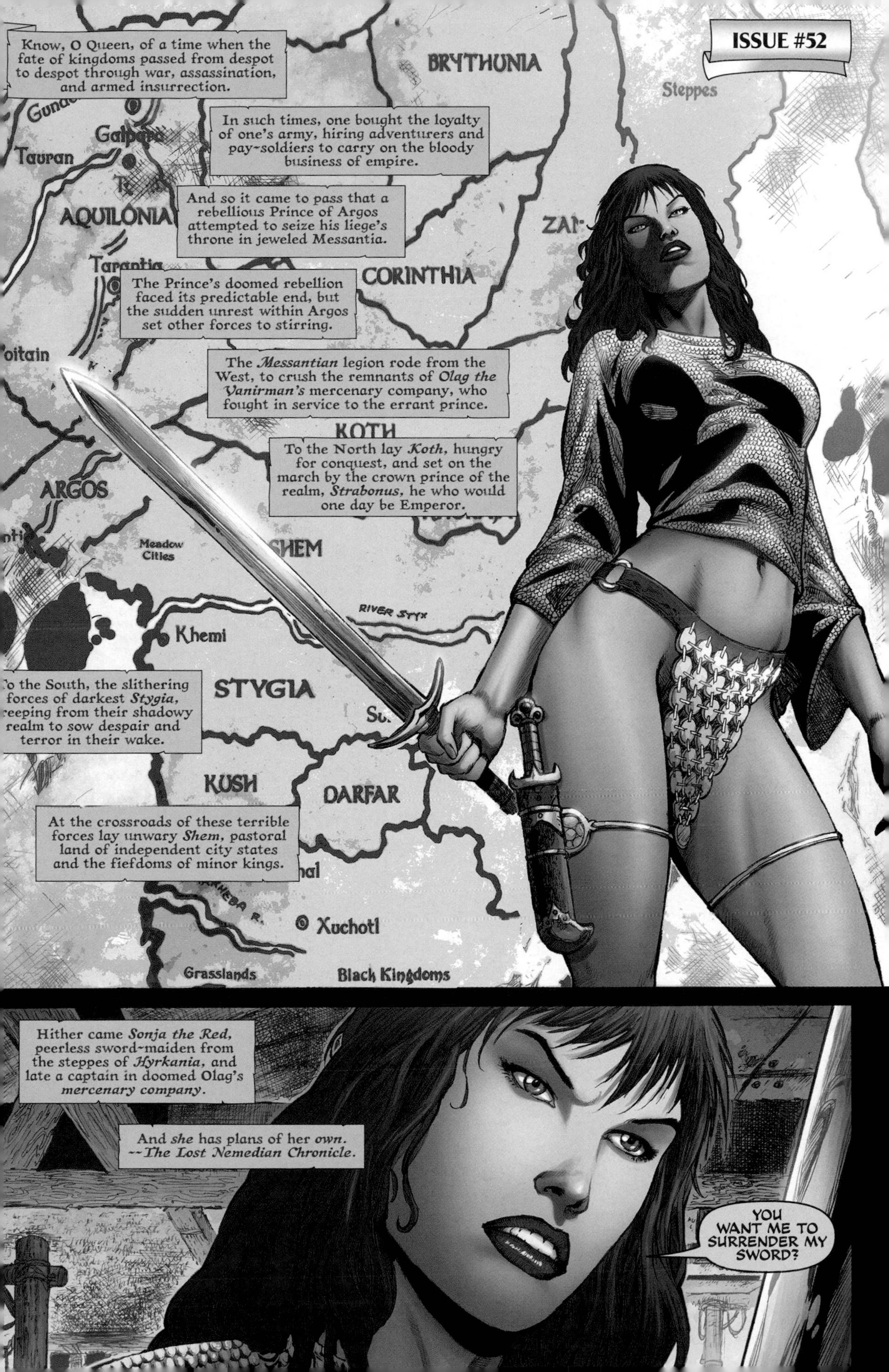
ISSUE #52
Know, O Queen, of a time when the fate of kingdoms passed from despot to despot through war, assassination, and armed insurrection.
In such times, one bought the loyalty of one's army, hiring adventurers and pay-soldiers to carry on the bloody business of empire.
And so it came to pass that a rebellious Prince of Argos attempted to seize his liege's throne in jeweled Messantia.
The Prince's doomed rebellion faced its predictable end, but the sudden unrest within Argos set other forces to stirring.
The *Messantian* legion rode from the West, to crush the remnants of *Olag the Vanirman's* mercenary company, who fought in service to the errant prince.
To the North lay *Koth*, hungry for conquest, and set on the march by the crown prince of the realm, *Strabonus*, he who would one day be Emperor.
o the South, the slithering forces of darkest *Stygia*, reeping from their shadowy realm to sow despair and terror in their wake.
At the crossroads of these terrible forces lay unwary *Shem*, pastoral land of independent city states and the fiefdoms of minor kings.
BRYTHUNIA
Steppes
Tauran
AQUILONIA
CORINTHIA
KOTH
ARGOS
Meadow Cities
RIVER STYX
Khemi
STYGIA
KUSH
DARFAR
Xuchotl
Grasslands
Black Kingdoms
Hither came *Sonja the Red*, peerless sword-maiden from the steppes of *Hyrkania*, and late a captain in doomed Olag's *mercenary company*.
And *she* has plans of her *own*.
--*The Lost Nemedian Chronicle*.
YOU WANT ME TO SURRENDER MY SWORD?

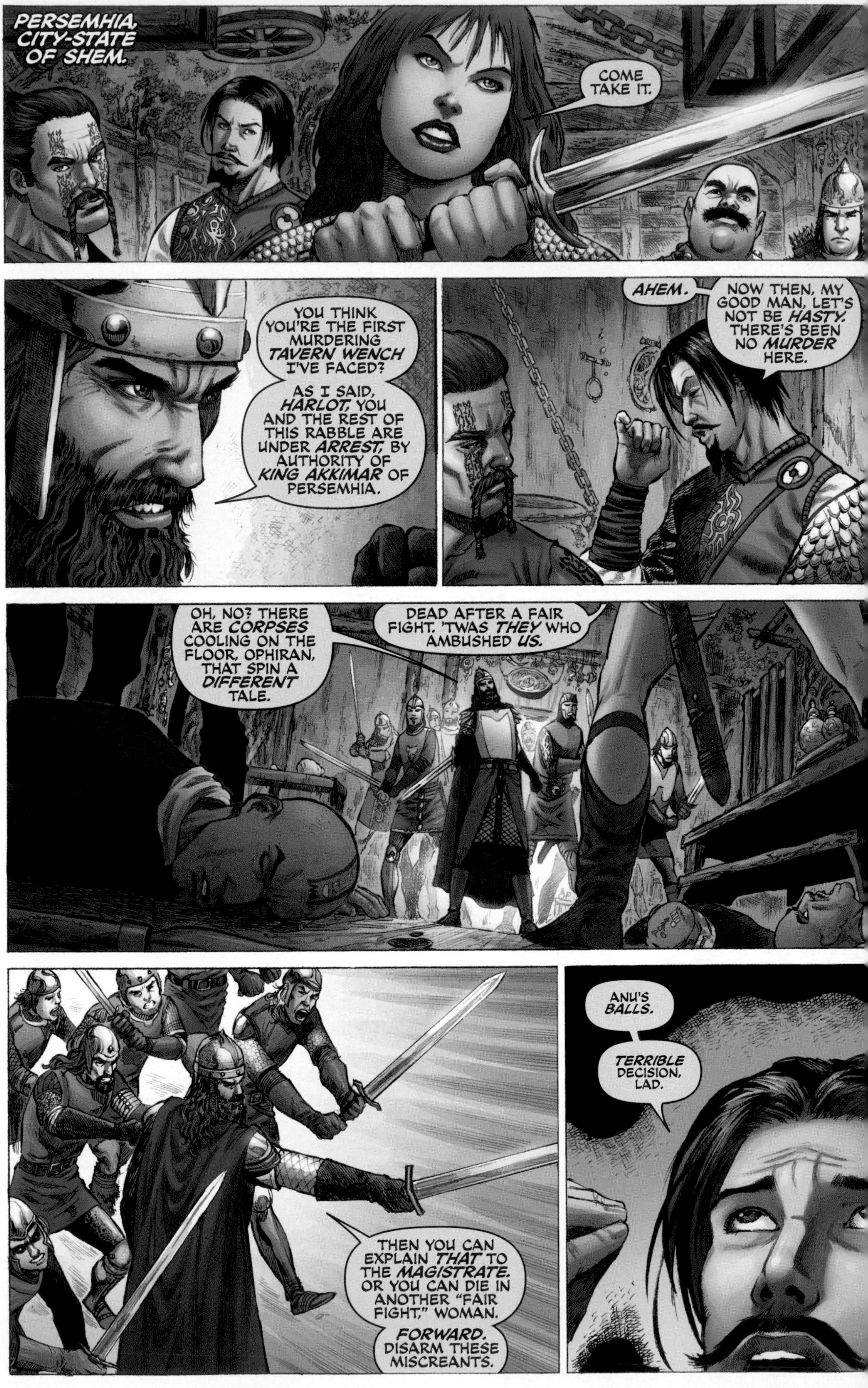
PERSEMHIA, CITY-STATE OF SHEM.
COME TAKE IT.
YOU THINK YOU'RE THE FIRST MURDERING TAVERN WENCH I'VE FACED?
AS I SAID, HARLOT, YOU AND THE REST OF THIS RABBLE ARE UNDER ARREST, BY AUTHORITY OF KING AKKIMAR OF PERSEMHIA.
AHEM.
NOW THEN, MY GOOD MAN, LET'S NOT BE HASTY. THERE'S BEEN NO MURDER HERE.
OH, NO? THERE ARE CORPSES COOLING ON THE FLOOR, OPHIRAN, THAT SPIN A DIFFERENT TALE.
DEAD AFTER A FAIR FIGHT. 'TWAS THEY WHO AMBUSHED US.
THEN YOU CAN EXPLAIN THAT TO THE MAGISTRATE. OR YOU CAN DIE IN ANOTHER "FAIR FIGHT," WOMAN.
FORWARD. DISARM THESE MISCREANTS.
ANU'S BALLS.
TERRIBLE DECISION, LAD.

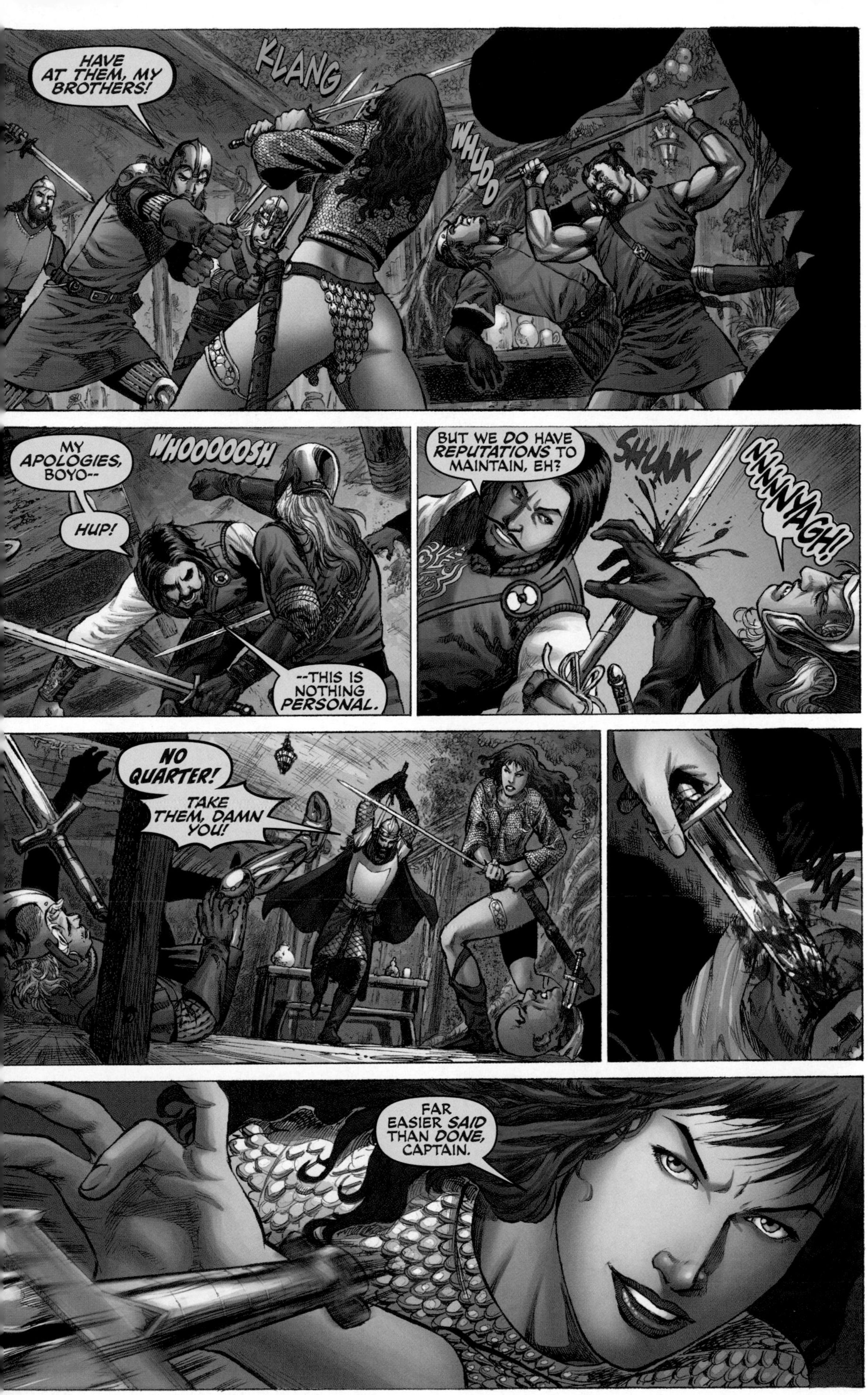
HAVE AT THEM, MY BROTHERS!
KLANG
WHUDD
MY APOLOGIES, BOYO--
WHOOOOOSH
HUP!
--THIS IS NOTHING PERSONAL.
BUT WE DO HAVE REPUTATIONS TO MAINTAIN, EH?
SHUNK
NNNNYAGH!
NO QUARTER!
TAKE THEM, DAMN YOU!
SHUNK
FAR EASIER SAID THAN DONE, CAPTAIN.

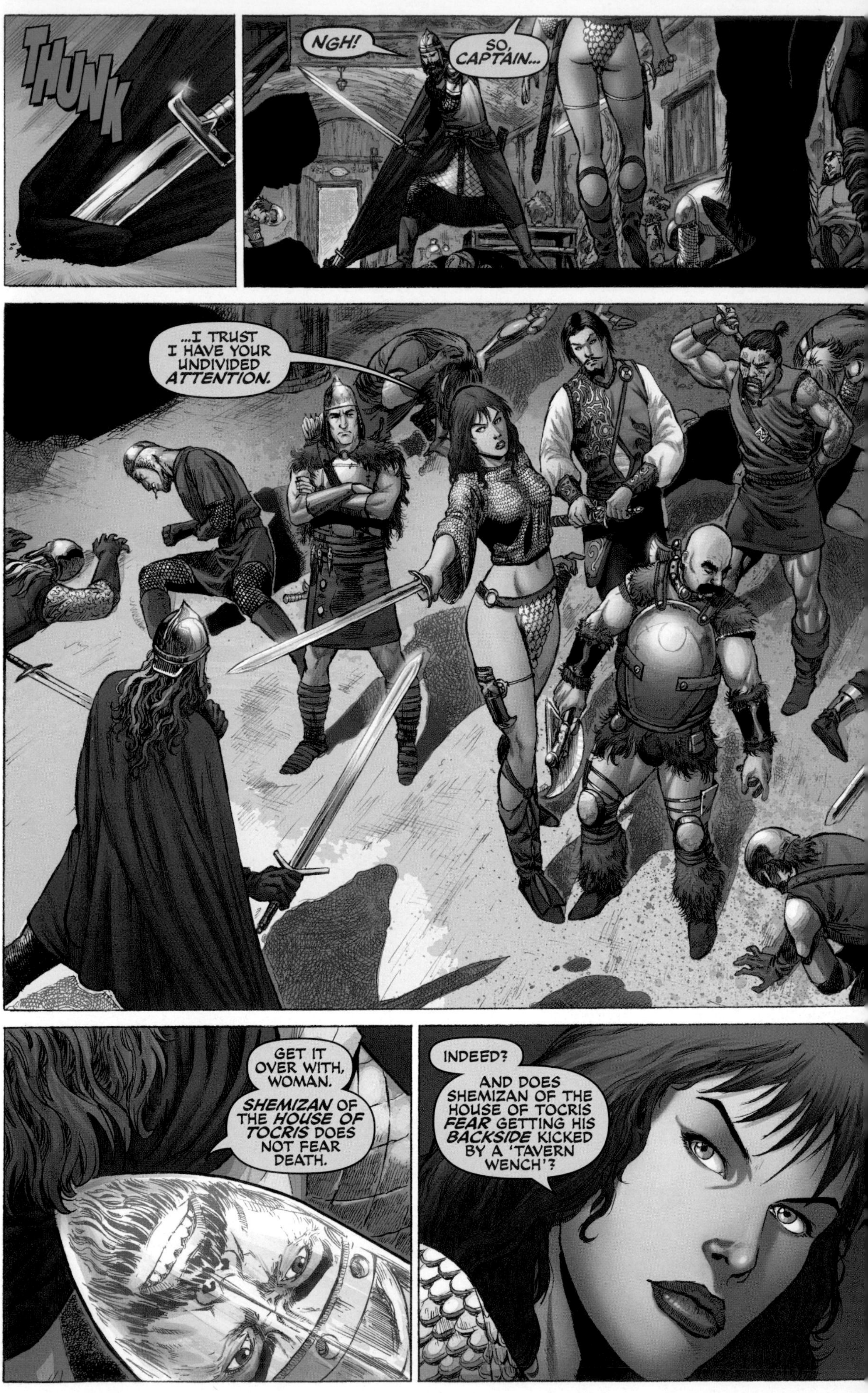
THUNK
NGH!
SO, CAPTAIN...
...I TRUST I HAVE YOUR UNDIVIDED ATTENTION.
GET IT OVER WITH, WOMAN. SHEMIZAN OF THE HOUSE OF TOCRIS DOES NOT FEAR DEATH.
INDEED?
AND DOES SHEMIZAN OF THE HOUSE OF TOCRIS FEAR GETTING HIS BACKSIDE KICKED BY A 'TAVERN WENCH'?

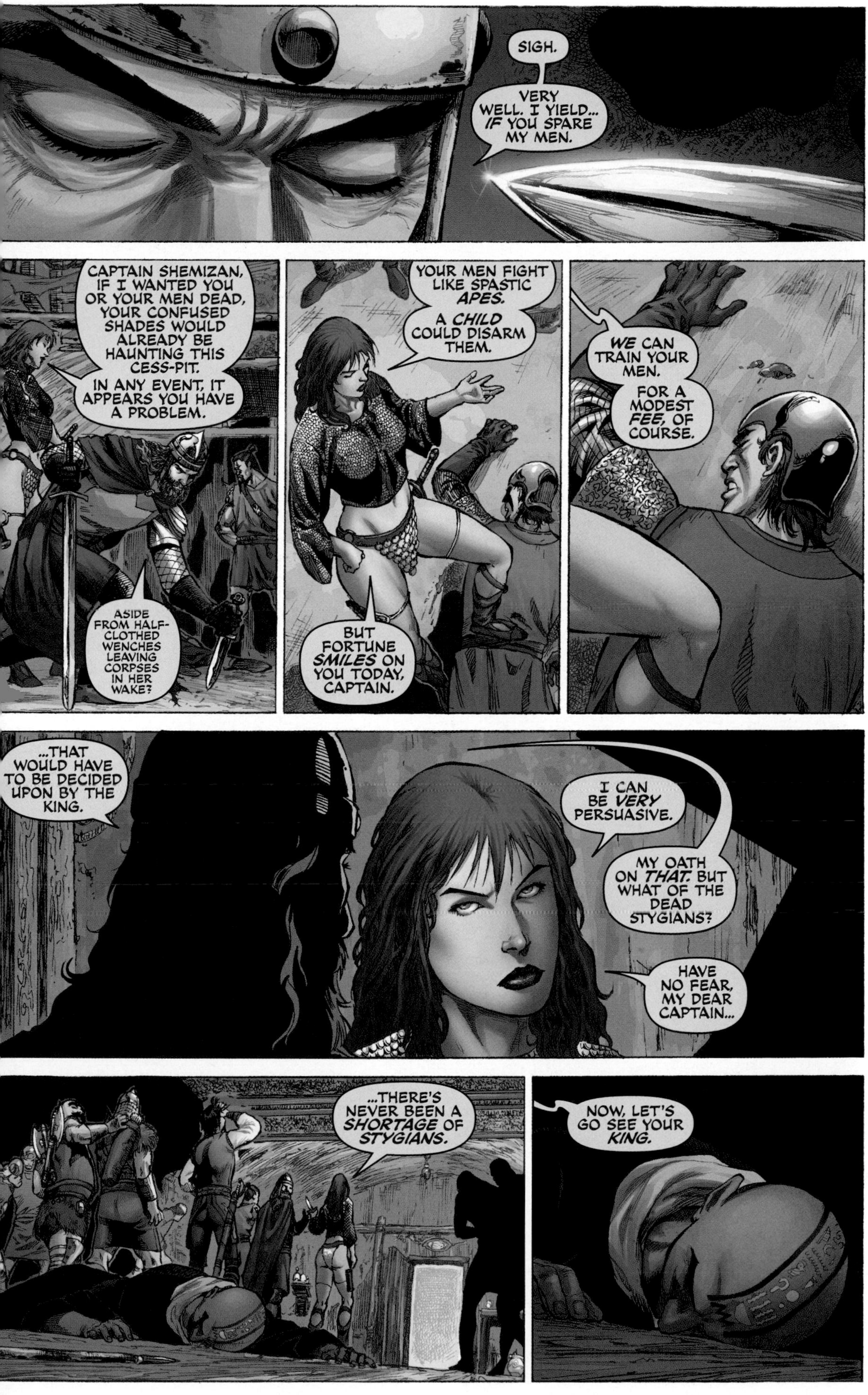
SIGH.
VERY WELL. I YIELD... *IF* YOU SPARE MY MEN.
CAPTAIN SHEMIZAN, IF I WANTED YOU OR YOUR MEN DEAD, YOUR CONFUSED SHADES WOULD ALREADY BE HAUNTING THIS CESS-PIT.
IN ANY EVENT, IT APPEARS YOU HAVE A PROBLEM.
ASIDE FROM HALF-CLOTHED WENCHES LEAVING CORPSES IN HER WAKE?
YOUR MEN FIGHT LIKE SPASTIC *APES.*
A *CHILD* COULD DISARM THEM.
BUT FORTUNE *SMILES* ON YOU TODAY, CAPTAIN.
WE CAN TRAIN YOUR MEN.
FOR A MODEST *FEE,* OF COURSE.
...THAT WOULD HAVE TO BE DECIDED UPON BY THE KING.
I CAN BE *VERY* PERSUASIVE.
MY OATH ON *THAT.* BUT WHAT OF THE DEAD STYGIANS?
HAVE NO FEAR, MY DEAR CAPTAIN...
...THERE'S NEVER BEEN A *SHORTAGE* OF *STYGIANS.*
NOW, LET'S GO SEE YOUR *KING.*

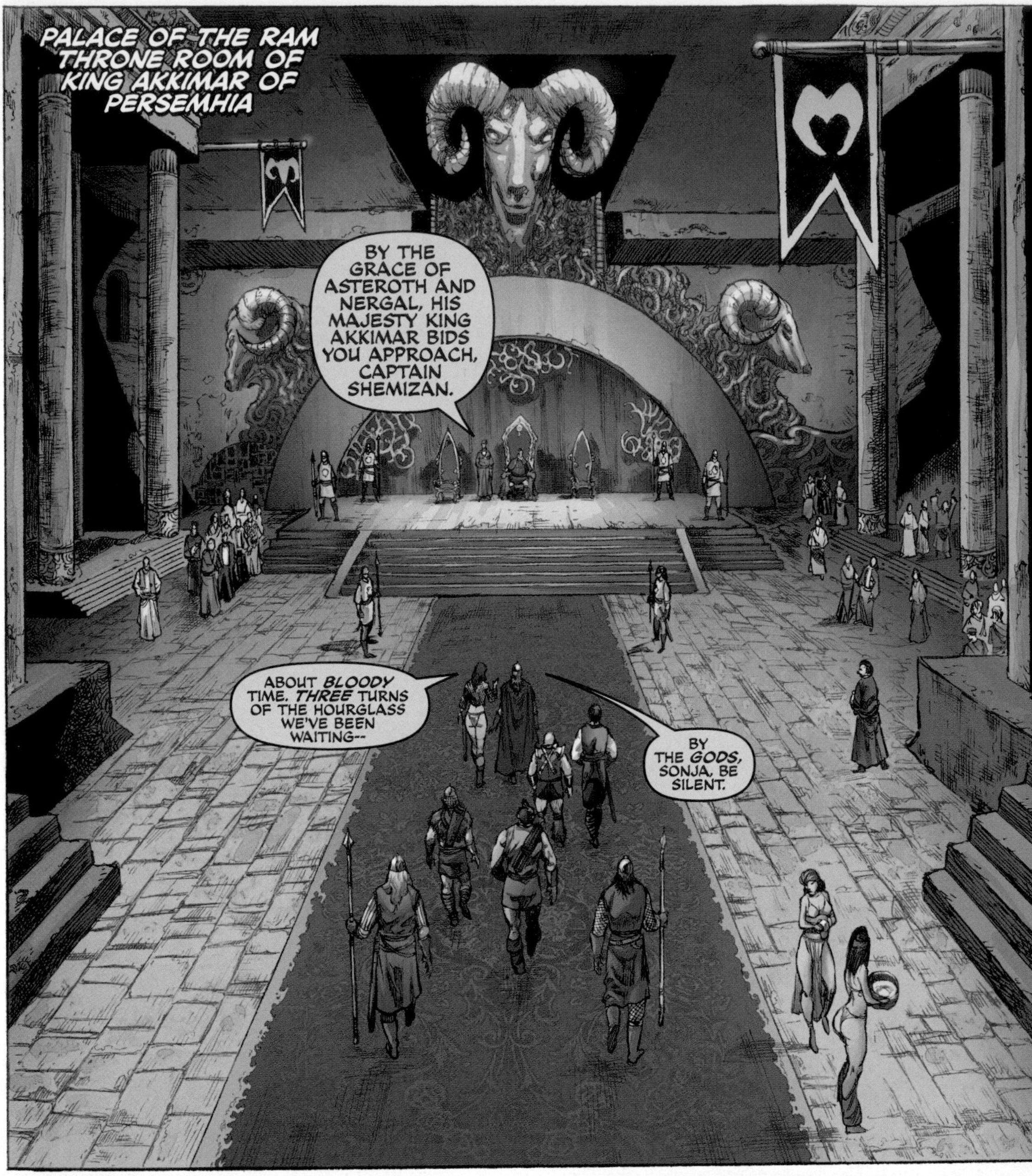
PALACE OF THE RAM THRONE ROOM OF KING AKKIMAR OF PERSEMHIA
BY THE GRACE OF ASTEROTH AND NERGAL, HIS MAJESTY KING AKKIMAR BIDS YOU APPROACH, CAPTAIN SHEMIZAN.
ABOUT BLOODY TIME. THREE TURNS OF THE HOURGLASS WE'VE BEEN WAITING--
BY THE GODS, SONJA, BE SILENT.

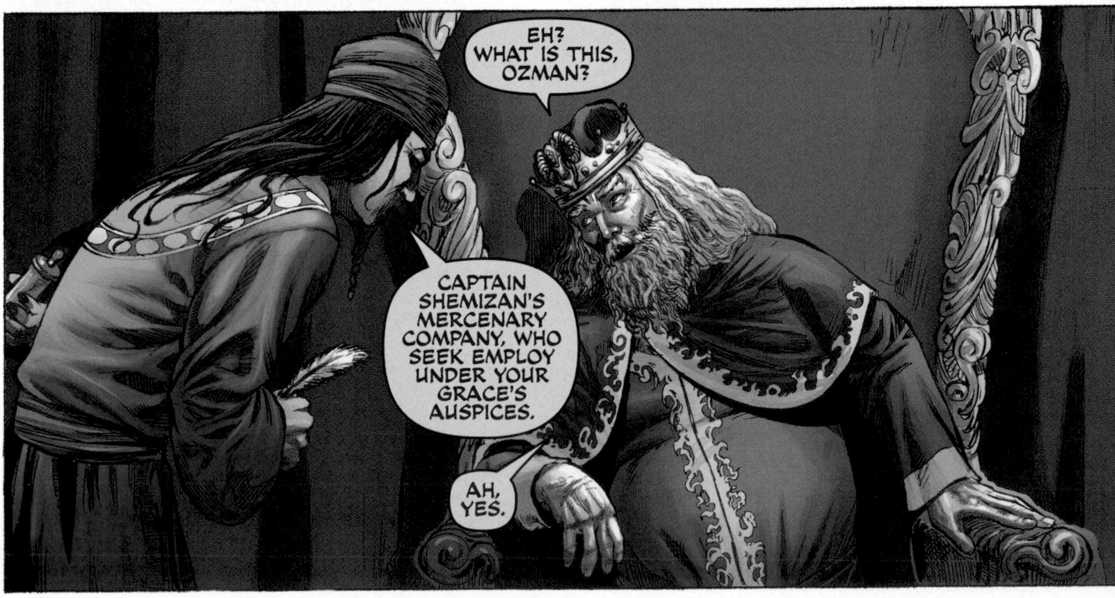
EH? WHAT IS THIS, OZMAN?
CAPTAIN SHEMIZAN'S MERCENARY COMPANY, WHO SEEK EMPLOY UNDER YOUR GRACE'S AUSPICES.
AH, YES.

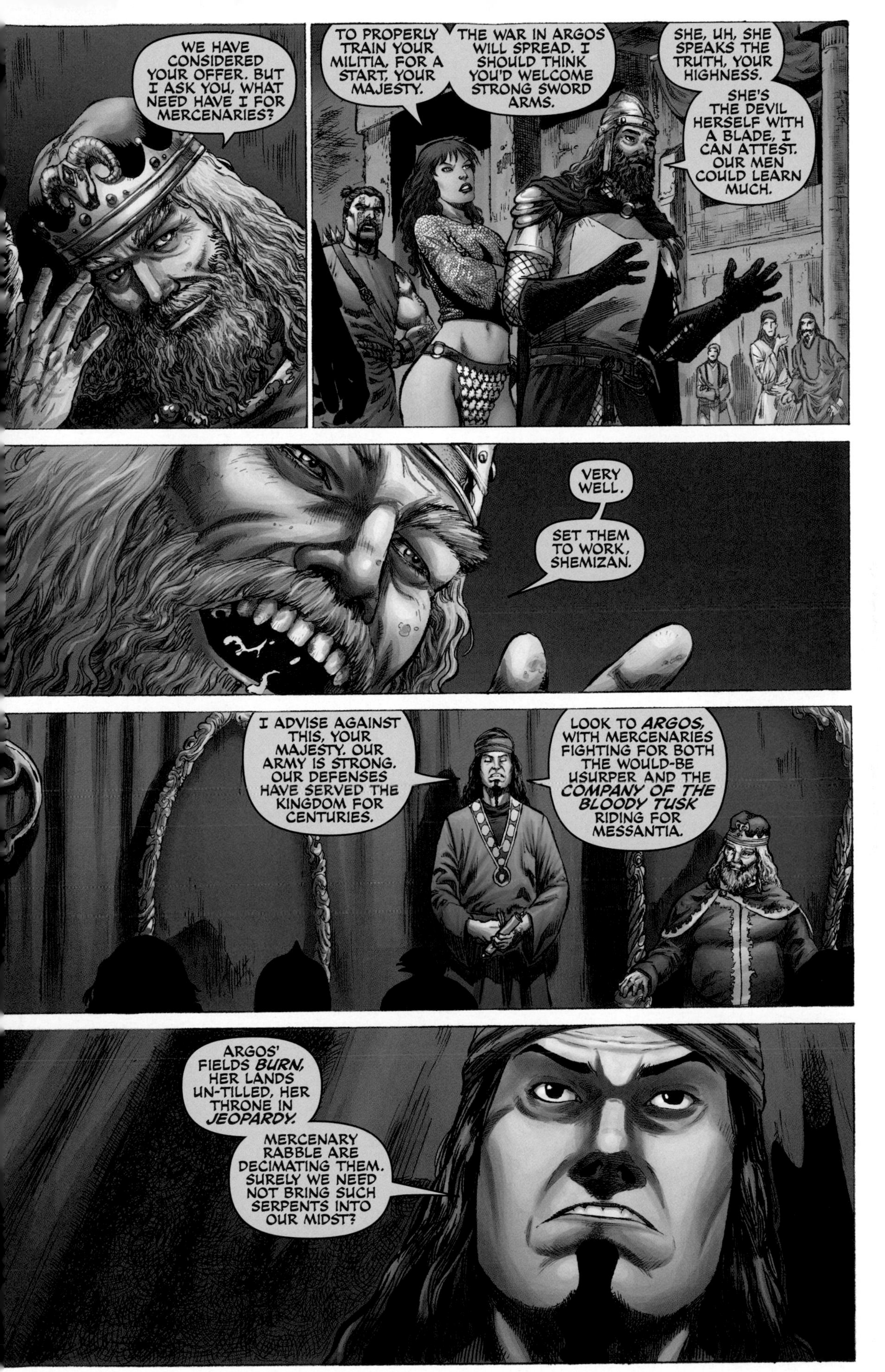

WE HAVE CONSIDERED YOUR OFFER. BUT I ASK YOU, WHAT NEED HAVE I FOR MERCENARIES?
TO PROPERLY TRAIN YOUR MILITIA, FOR A START, YOUR MAJESTY.
THE WAR IN ARGOS WILL SPREAD. I SHOULD THINK YOU'D WELCOME STRONG SWORD ARMS.
SHE, UH, SHE SPEAKS THE TRUTH, YOUR HIGHNESS.
SHE'S THE DEVIL HERSELF WITH A BLADE, I CAN ATTEST. OUR MEN COULD LEARN MUCH.
VERY WELL.
SET THEM TO WORK, SHEMIZAN.
I ADVISE AGAINST THIS, YOUR MAJESTY. OUR ARMY IS STRONG. OUR DEFENSES HAVE SERVED THE KINGDOM FOR CENTURIES.
LOOK TO ARGOS, WITH MERCENARIES FIGHTING FOR BOTH THE WOULD-BE USURPER AND THE COMPANY OF THE BLOODY TUSK RIDING FOR MESSANTIA.
ARGOS' FIELDS BURN, HER LANDS UN-TILLED, HER THRONE IN JEOPARDY.
MERCENARY RABBLE ARE DECIMATING THEM. SURELY WE NEED NOT BRING SUCH SERPENTS INTO OUR MIDST?

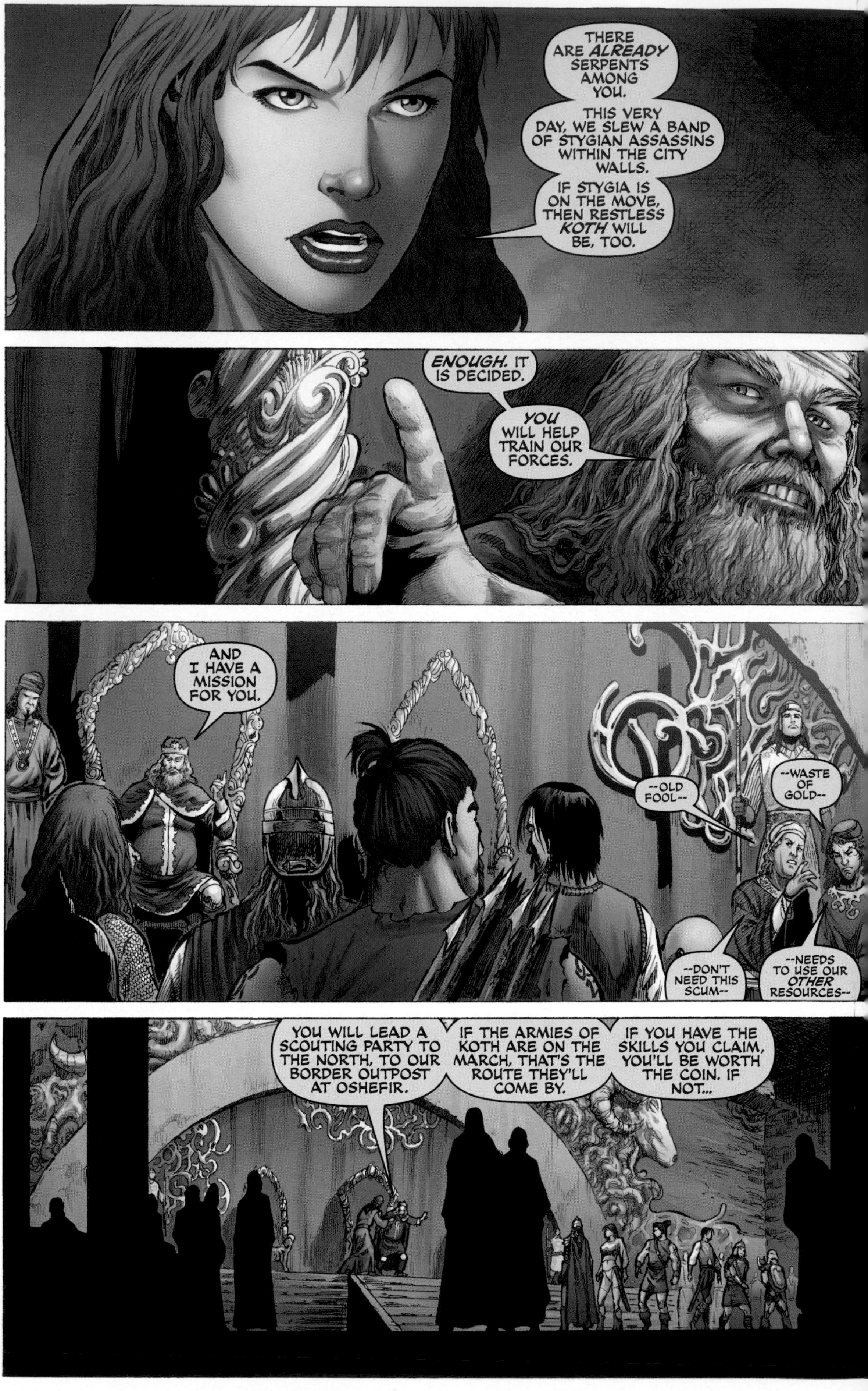
THERE ARE *ALREADY* SERPENTS AMONG YOU.
THIS VERY DAY, WE SLEW A BAND OF STYGIAN ASSASSINS WITHIN THE CITY WALLS.
IF STYGIA IS ON THE MOVE, THEN RESTLESS *KOTH* WILL BE, TOO.
ENOUGH. IT IS DECIDED.
YOU WILL HELP TRAIN OUR FORCES.
AND I HAVE A MISSION FOR YOU.
--OLD FOOL--
--WASTE OF GOLD--
--DON'T NEED THIS SCUM--
--NEEDS TO USE OUR *OTHER* RESOURCES--
YOU WILL LEAD A SCOUTING PARTY TO THE NORTH, TO OUR BORDER OUTPOST AT OSHEFIR.
IF THE ARMIES OF KOTH ARE ON THE MARCH, THAT'S THE ROUTE THEY'LL COME BY.
IF YOU HAVE THE SKILLS YOU CLAIM, YOU'LL BE WORTH THE COIN. IF NOT...

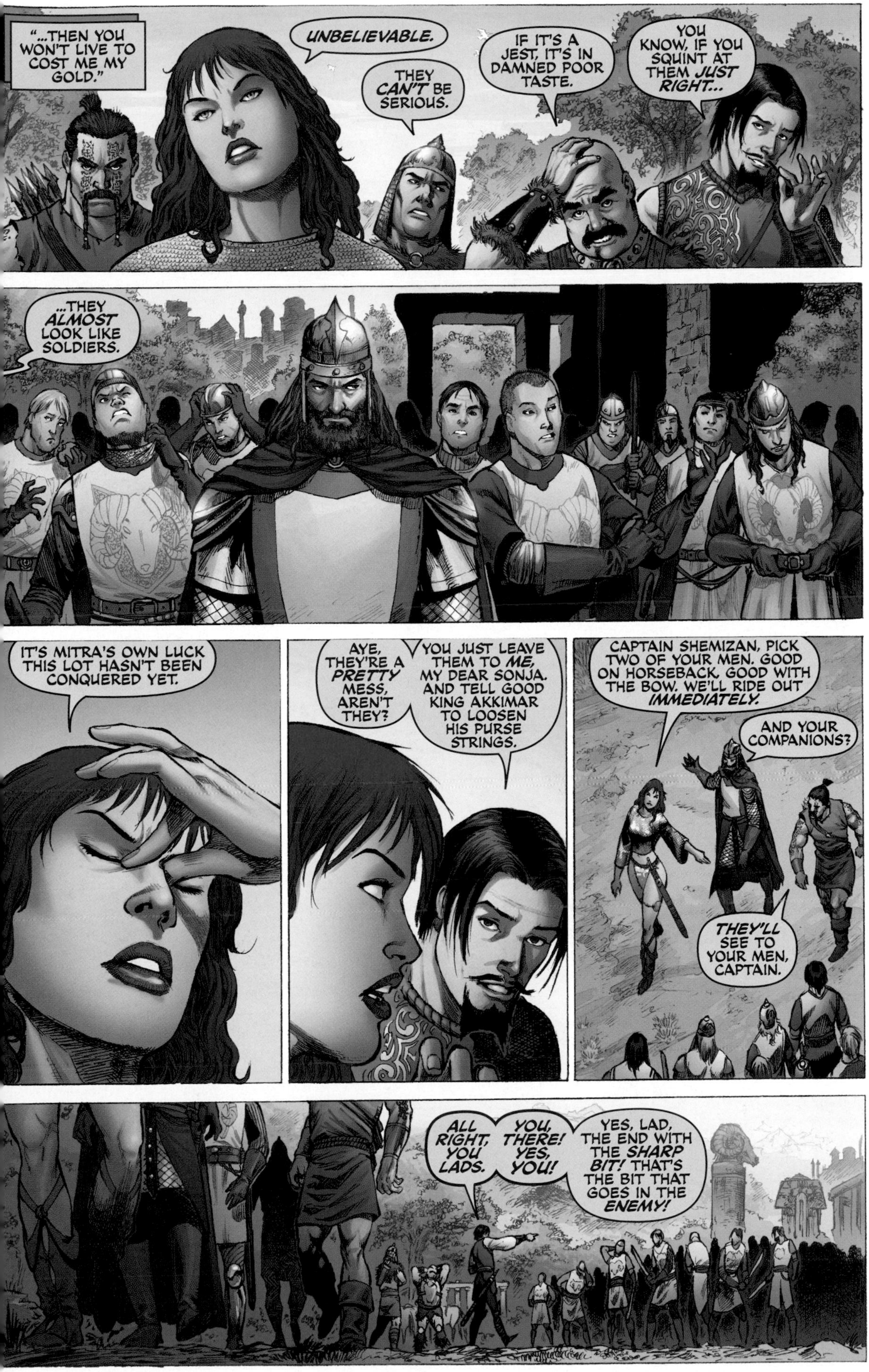
"...THEN YOU WON'T LIVE TO COST ME MY GOLD."
UNBELIEVABLE.
THEY CAN'T BE SERIOUS.
IF IT'S A JEST, IT'S IN DAMNED POOR TASTE.
YOU KNOW, IF YOU SQUINT AT THEM JUST RIGHT...
...THEY ALMOST LOOK LIKE SOLDIERS.
IT'S MITRA'S OWN LUCK THIS LOT HASN'T BEEN CONQUERED YET.
AYE, THEY'RE A PRETTY MESS, AREN'T THEY?
YOU JUST LEAVE THEM TO ME, MY DEAR SONJA. AND TELL GOOD KING AKKIMAR TO LOOSEN HIS PURSE STRINGS.
CAPTAIN SHEMIZAN, PICK TWO OF YOUR MEN. GOOD ON HORSEBACK, GOOD WITH THE BOW. WE'LL RIDE OUT IMMEDIATELY.
AND YOUR COMPANIONS?
THEY'LL SEE TO YOUR MEN, CAPTAIN.
ALL RIGHT, YOU LADS.
YOU, THERE! YES, YOU!
YES, LAD, THE END WITH THE SHARP BIT! THAT'S THE BIT THAT GOES IN THE ENEMY!

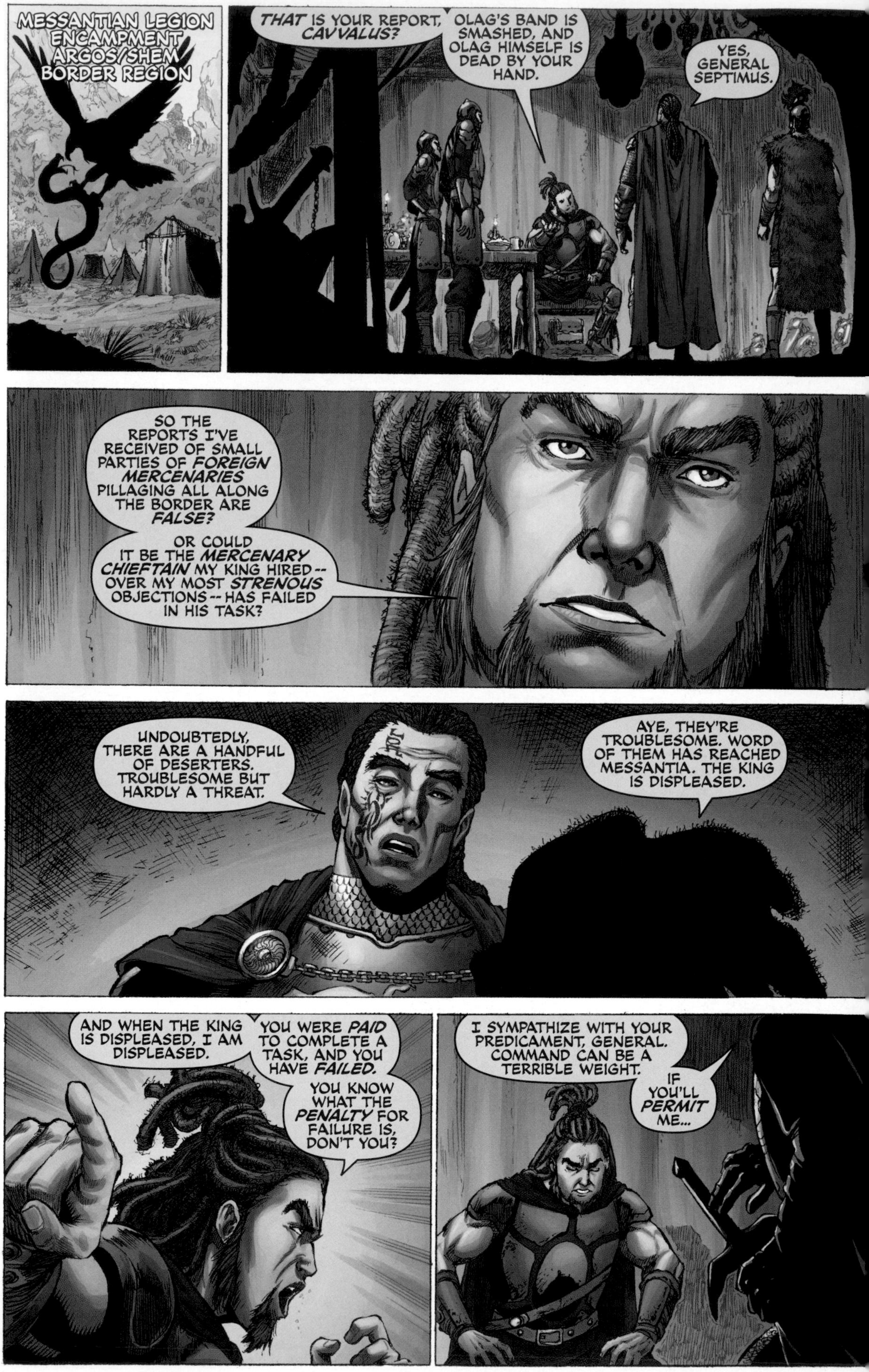
MESSANTIAN LEGION ENCAMPMENT ARGOS/SHEM BORDER REGION
THAT IS YOUR REPORT, CAVVALUS?
OLAG'S BAND IS SMASHED, AND OLAG HIMSELF IS DEAD BY YOUR HAND.
YES, GENERAL SEPTIMUS.
SO THE REPORTS I'VE RECEIVED OF SMALL PARTIES OF FOREIGN MERCENARIES PILLAGING ALL ALONG THE BORDER ARE FALSE?
OR COULD IT BE THE MERCENARY CHIEFTAIN MY KING HIRED-- OVER MY MOST STRENOUS OBJECTIONS-- HAS FAILED IN HIS TASK?
UNDOUBTEDLY, THERE ARE A HANDFUL OF DESERTERS. TROUBLESOME BUT HARDLY A THREAT.
AYE, THEY'RE TROUBLESOME. WORD OF THEM HAS REACHED MESSANTIA. THE KING IS DISPLEASED.
AND WHEN THE KING IS DISPLEASED, I AM DISPLEASED.
YOU WERE PAID TO COMPLETE A TASK, AND YOU HAVE FAILED.
YOU KNOW WHAT THE PENALTY FOR FAILURE IS, DON'T YOU?
I SYMPATHIZE WITH YOUR PREDICAMENT, GENERAL. COMMAND CAN BE A TERRIBLE WEIGHT.
IF YOU'LL PERMIT ME...

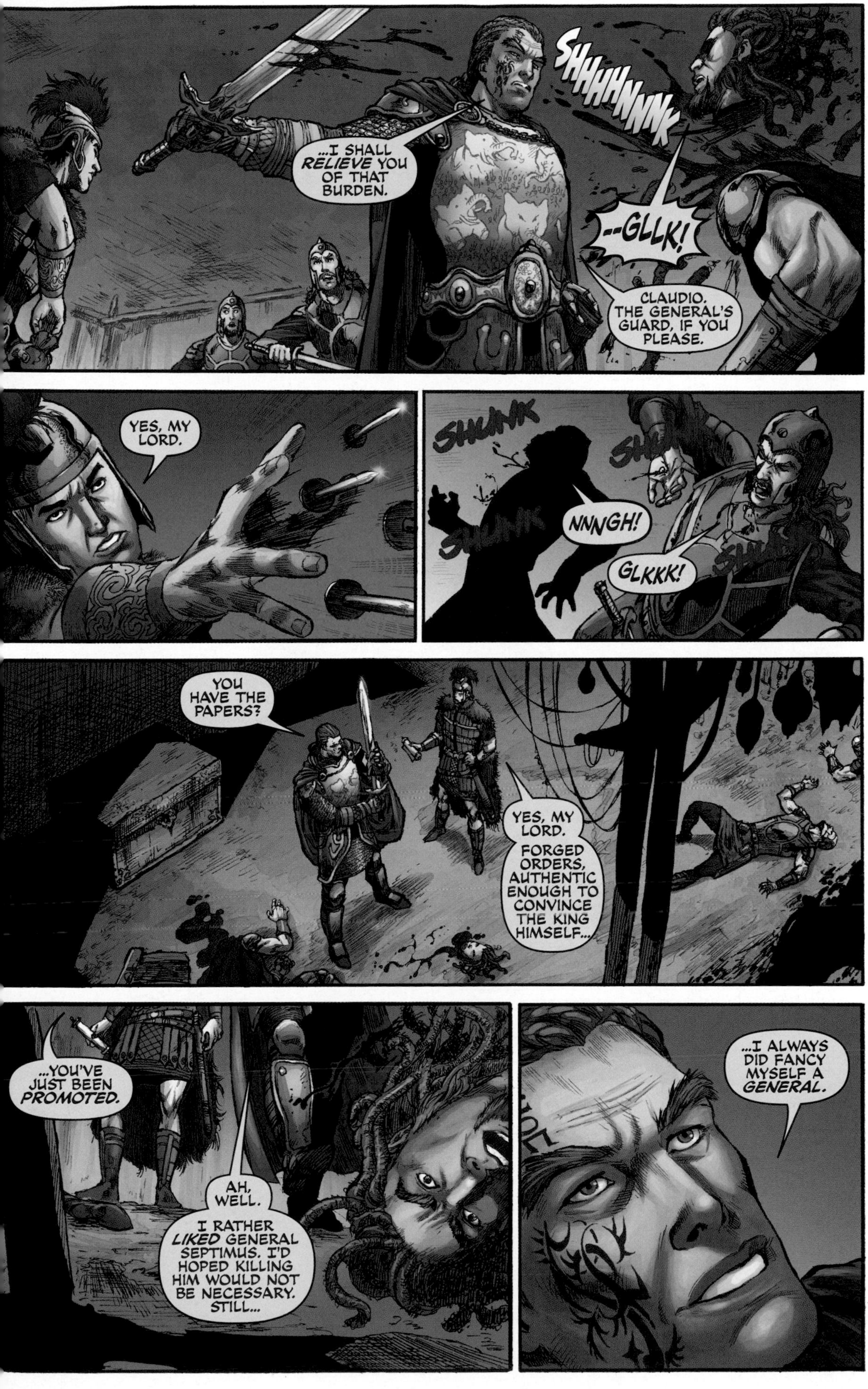
SHHHHNNNK
...I SHALL *RELIEVE* YOU OF THAT BURDEN.
--GLLK!
CLAUDIO. THE GENERAL'S GUARD, IF YOU PLEASE.
YES, MY LORD.
SHUNK
SHUNK
NNNGH!
GLKKK!
YOU HAVE THE PAPERS?
YES, MY LORD.
FORGED ORDERS, AUTHENTIC ENOUGH TO CONVINCE THE KING HIMSELF...
AH, WELL.
I RATHER *LIKED* GENERAL SEPTIMUS. I'D HOPED KILLING HIM WOULD NOT BE NECESSARY. STILL...
...YOU'VE JUST BEEN *PROMOTED*.
...I ALWAYS DID FANCY MYSELF A *GENERAL*.

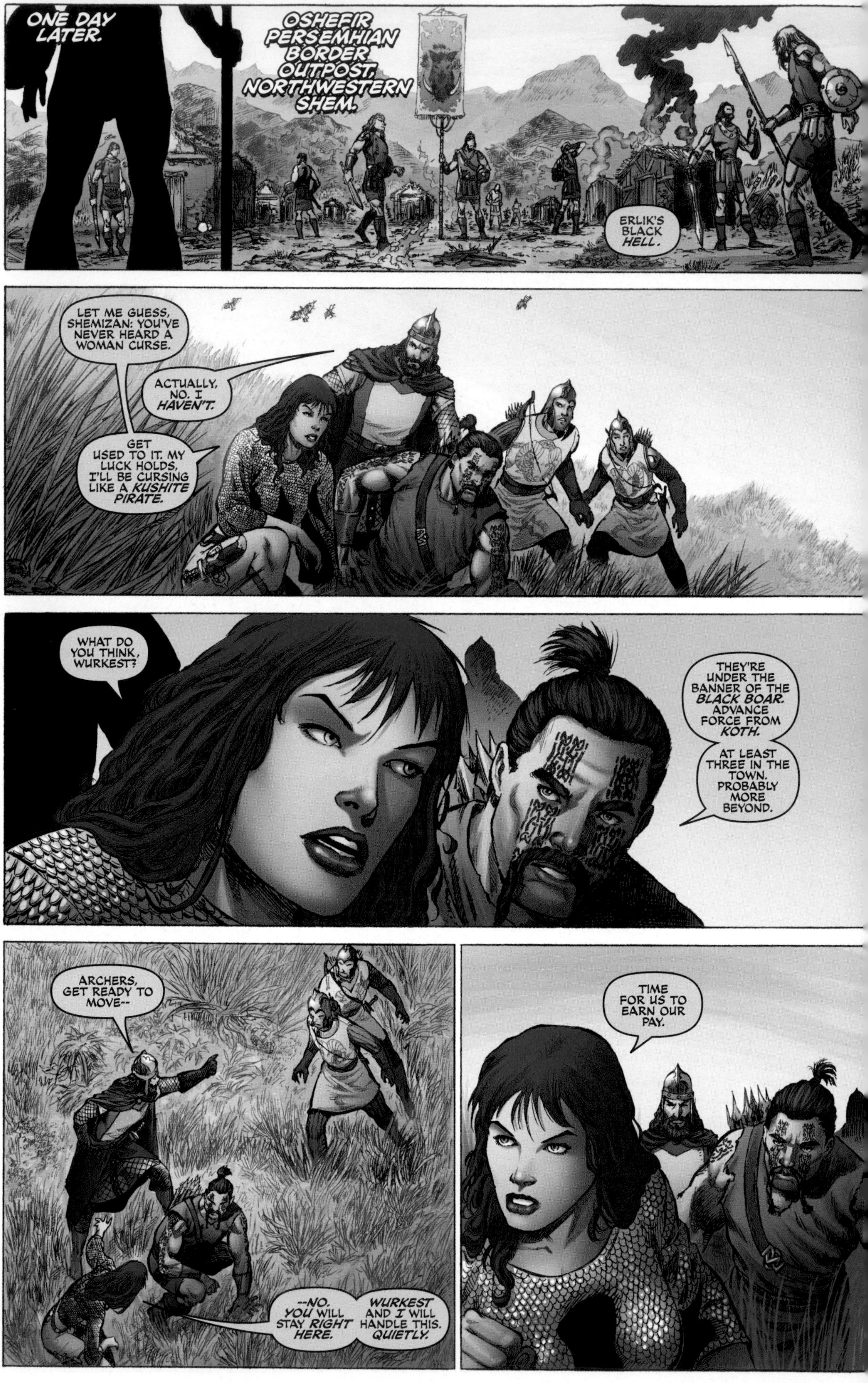
ONE DAY LATER.
OSHEFIR PERSEMHIAN BORDER OUTPOST, NORTHWESTERN SHEM.
ERLIK'S BLACK HELL.
LET ME GUESS, SHEMIZAN: YOU'VE NEVER HEARD A WOMAN CURSE.
ACTUALLY, NO. I HAVEN'T.
GET USED TO IT. MY LUCK HOLDS, I'LL BE CURSING LIKE A KUSHITE PIRATE.
WHAT DO YOU THINK, WURKEST?
THEY'RE UNDER THE BANNER OF THE BLACK BOAR. ADVANCE FORCE FROM KOTH.
AT LEAST THREE IN THE TOWN. PROBABLY MORE BEYOND.
ARCHERS, GET READY TO MOVE--
--NO. YOU WILL STAY RIGHT HERE.
WURKEST AND I WILL HANDLE THIS. QUIETLY.
TIME FOR US TO EARN OUR PAY.

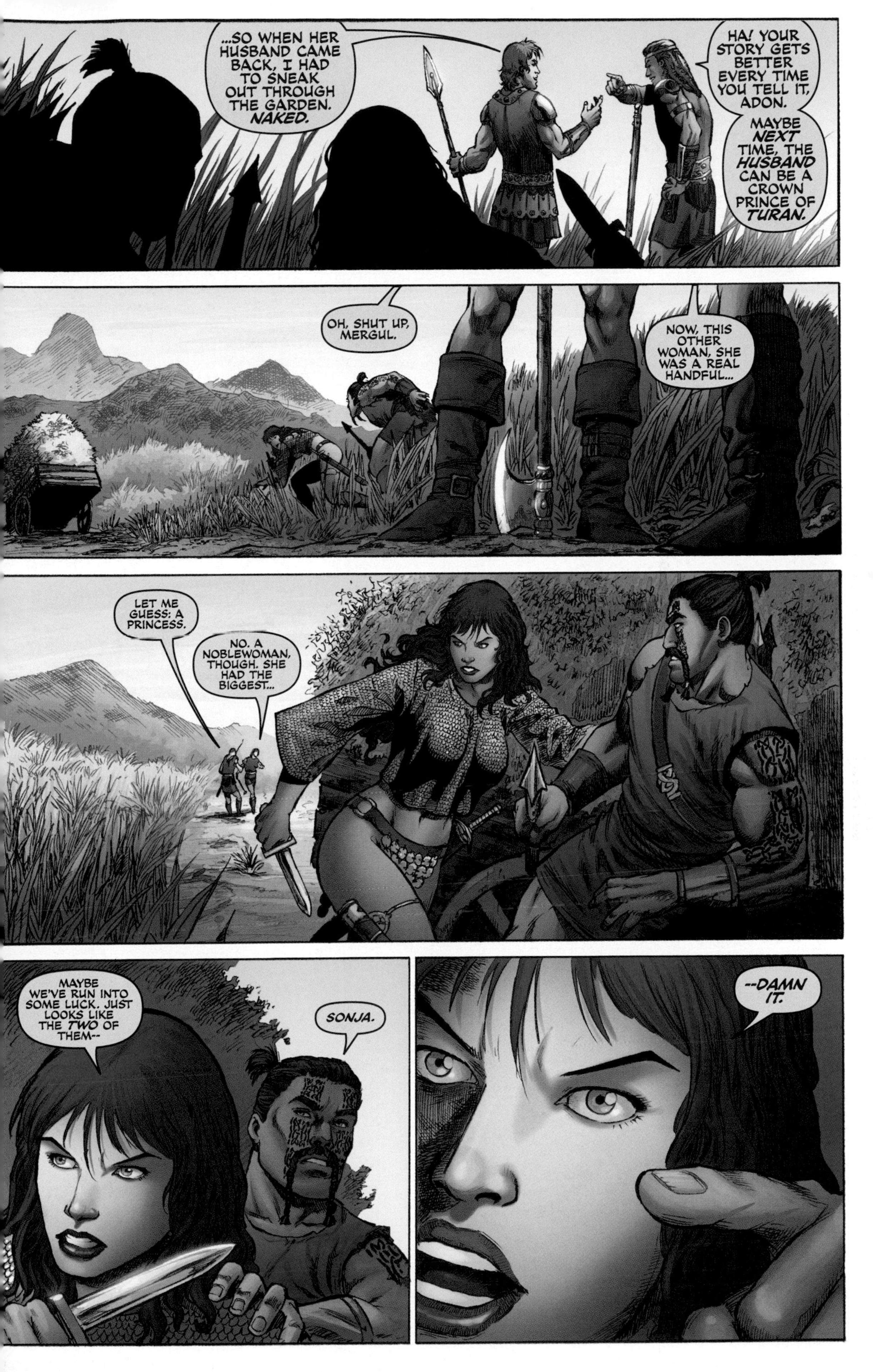
...SO WHEN HER HUSBAND CAME BACK, I HAD TO SNEAK OUT THROUGH THE GARDEN. NAKED.
HA! YOUR STORY GETS BETTER EVERY TIME YOU TELL IT, ADON.
MAYBE NEXT TIME, THE HUSBAND CAN BE A CROWN PRINCE OF TURAN.
OH, SHUT UP, MERGUL.
NOW, THIS OTHER WOMAN, SHE WAS A REAL HANDFUL...
LET ME GUESS: A PRINCESS.
NO. A NOBLEWOMAN, THOUGH. SHE HAD THE BIGGEST...
MAYBE WE'VE RUN INTO SOME LUCK. JUST LOOKS LIKE THE TWO OF THEM--
SONJA.
--DAMN IT.

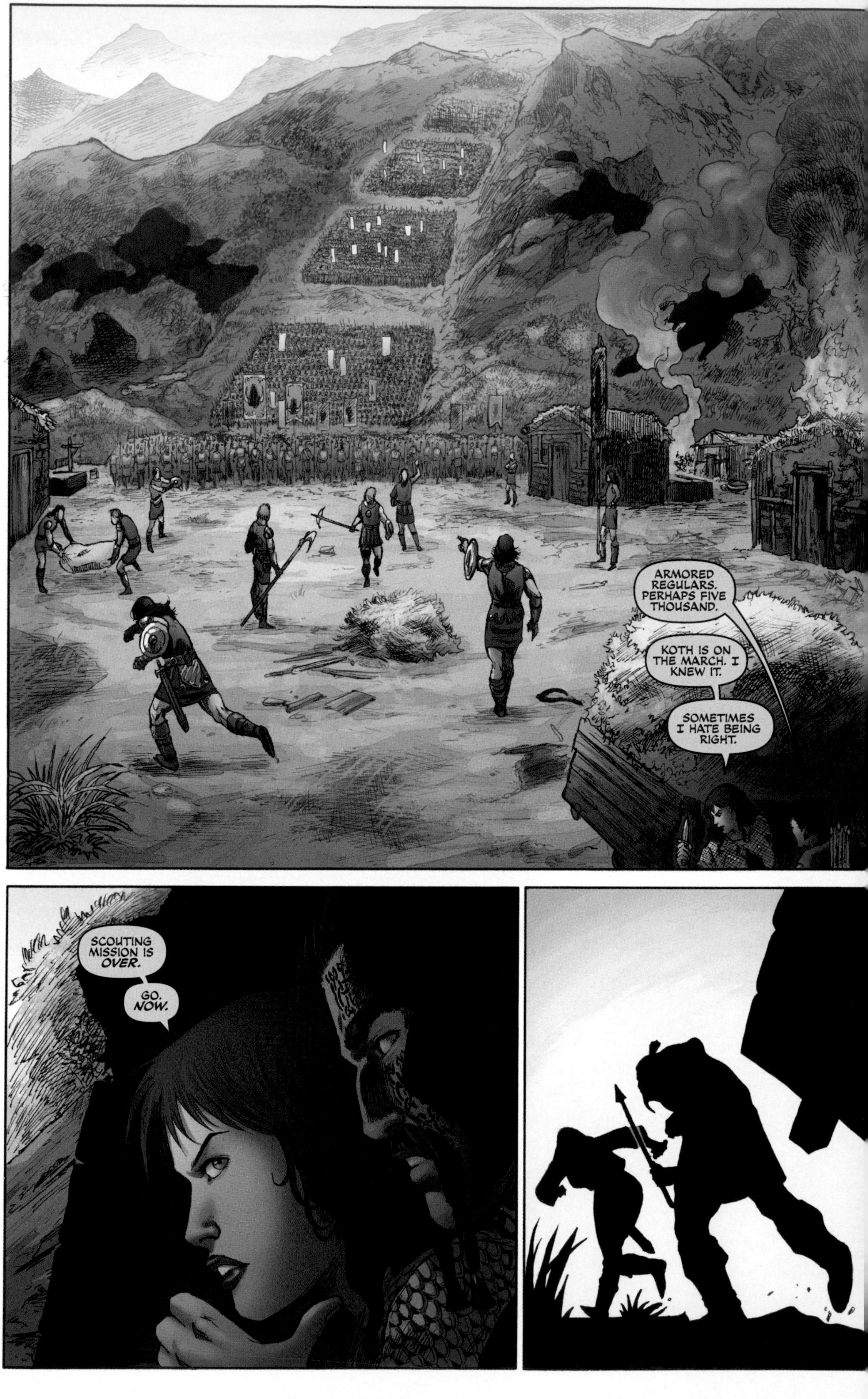
ARMORED REGULARS. PERHAPS FIVE THOUSAND.
KOTH IS ON THE MARCH. I KNEW IT.
SOMETIMES I HATE BEING RIGHT.
SCOUTING MISSION IS *OVER.*
GO. *NOW.*

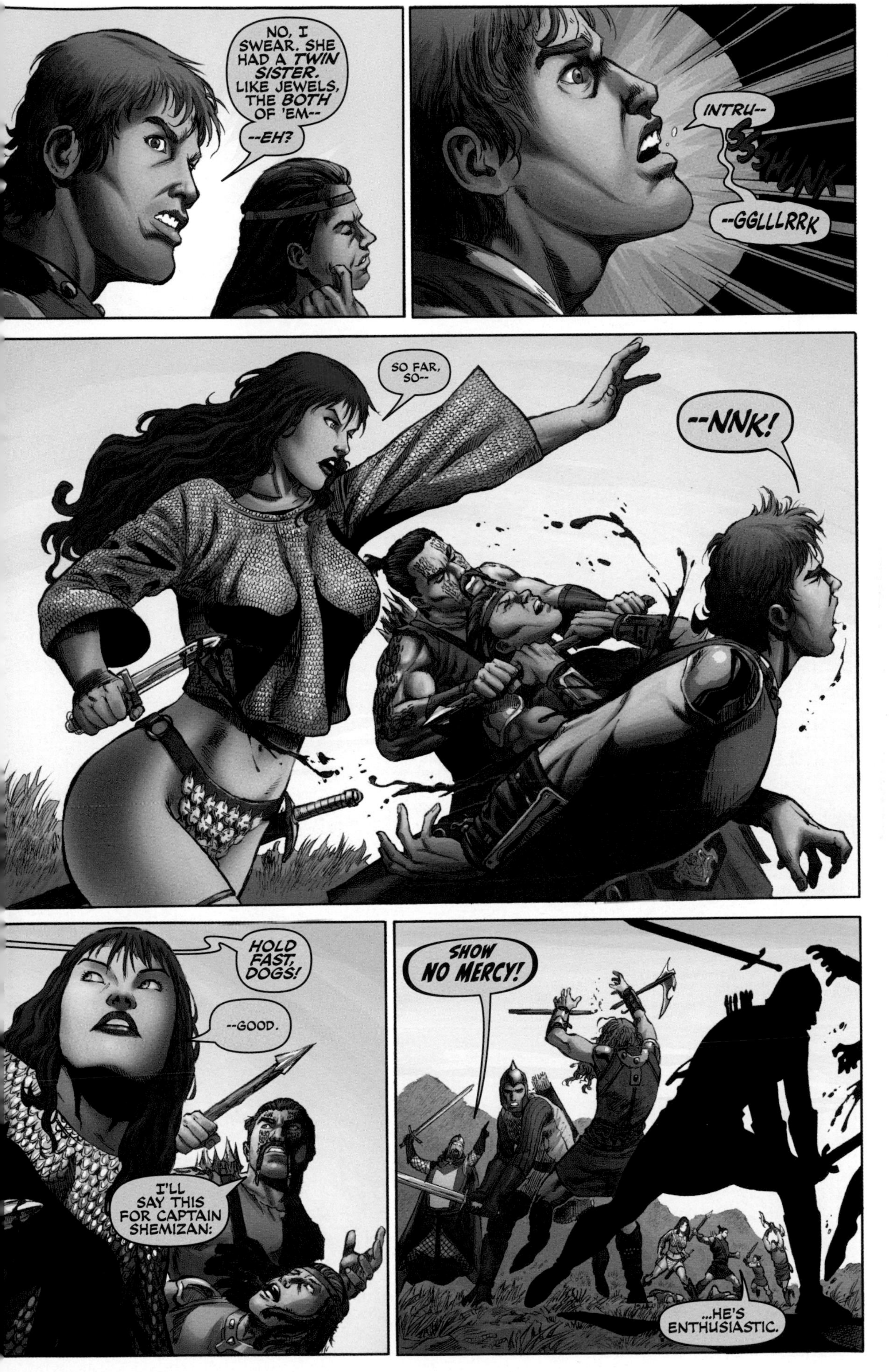
NO, I SWEAR. SHE HAD A TWIN SISTER. LIKE JEWELS, THE BOTH OF 'EM--
--EH?
INTRU--
SSSHUNK
--GGLLLRRK
SO FAR, SO--
--NNK!
HOLD FAST, DOGS!
--GOOD.
I'LL SAY THIS FOR CAPTAIN SHEMIZAN:
SHOW NO MERCY!
...HE'S ENTHUSIASTIC.

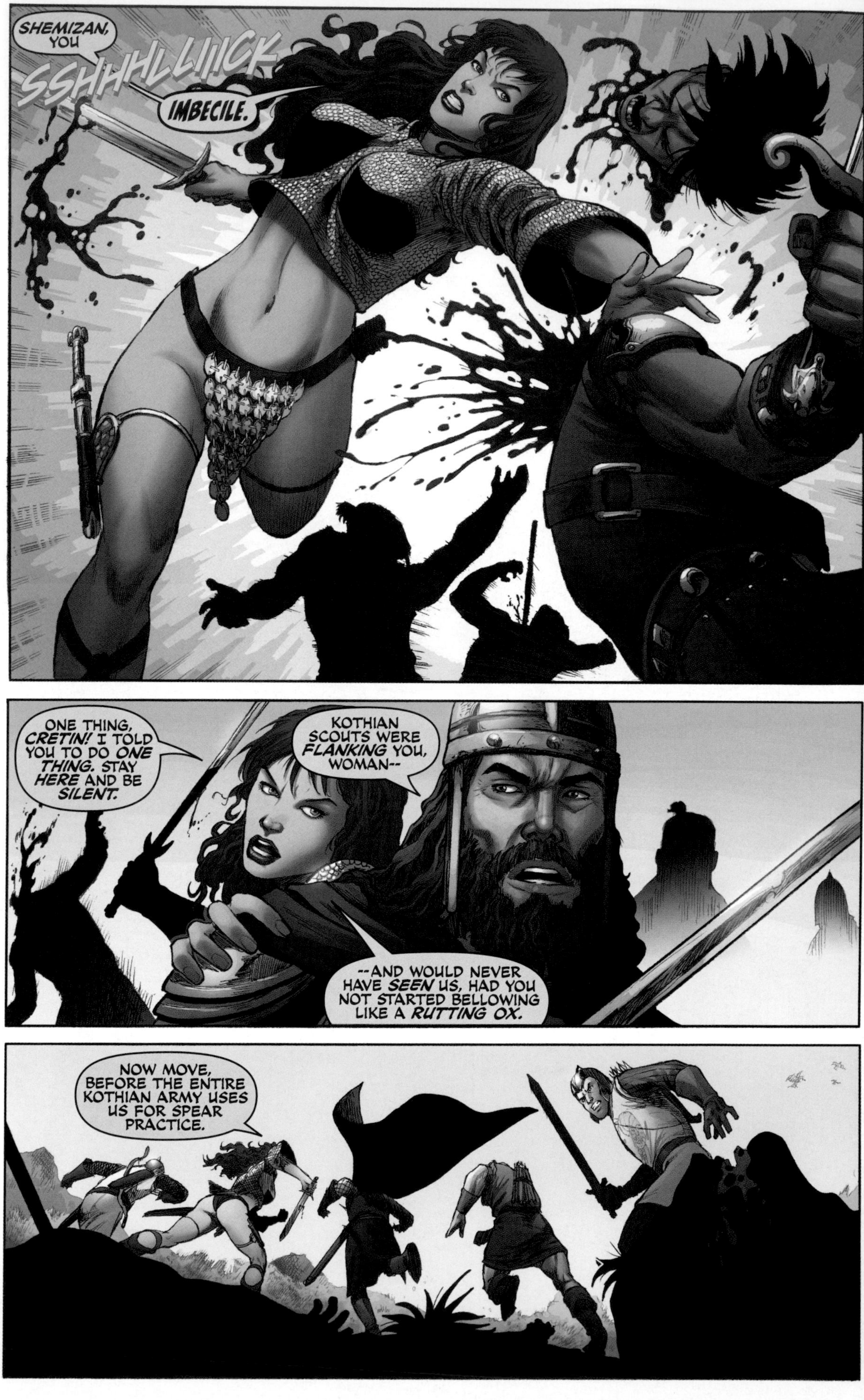
SHEMIZAN, YOU
SSHHHLLIIICK
IMBECILE.
ONE THING, CRETIN! I TOLD YOU TO DO ONE THING. STAY HERE AND BE SILENT.
KOTHIAN SCOUTS WERE FLANKING YOU, WOMAN--
--AND WOULD NEVER HAVE SEEN US, HAD YOU NOT STARTED BELLOWING LIKE A RUTTING OX.
NOW MOVE, BEFORE THE ENTIRE KOTHIAN ARMY USES US FOR SPEAR PRACTICE.

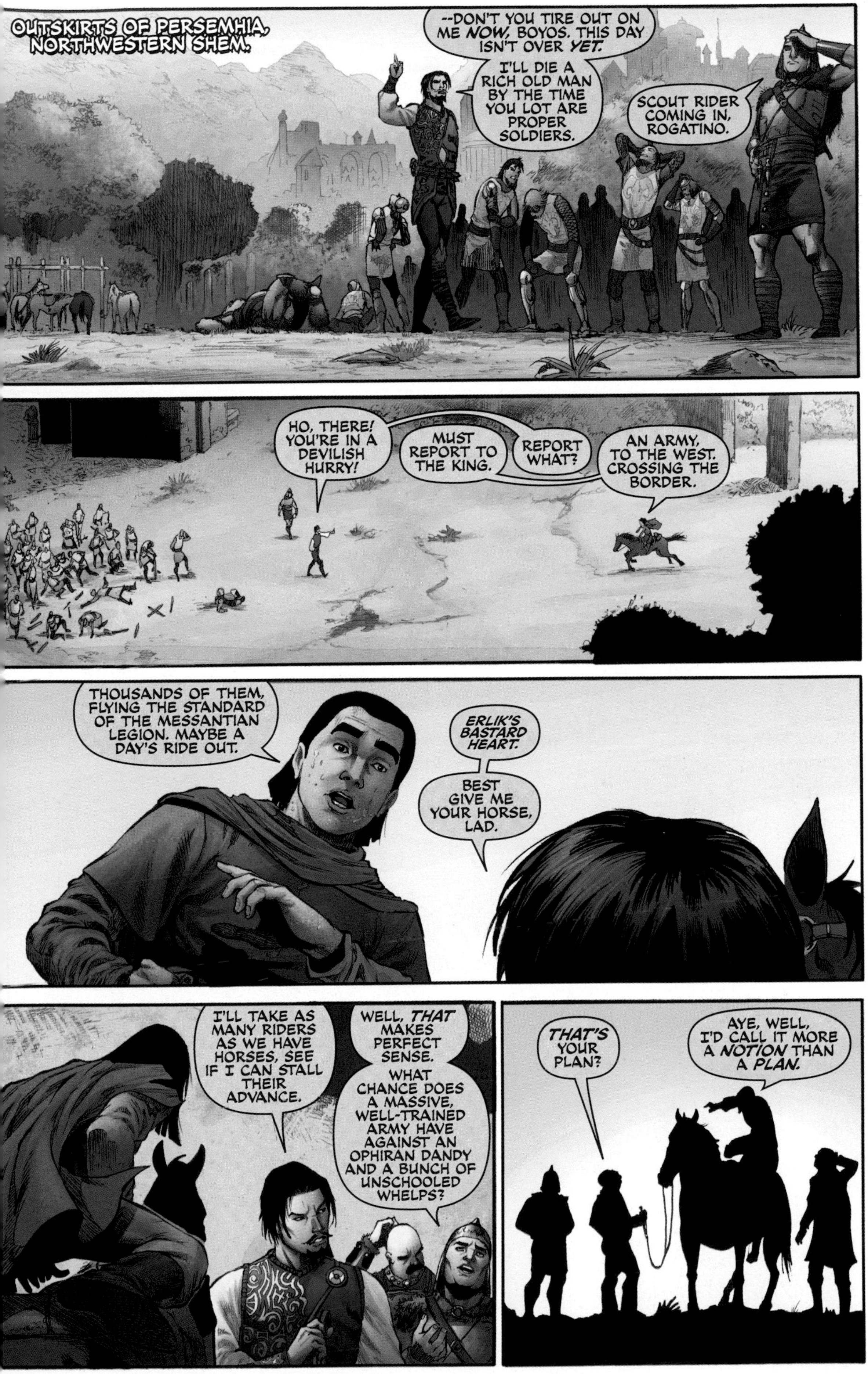
OUTSKIRTS OF PERSEMHIA, NORTHWESTERN SHEM.
--DON'T YOU TIRE OUT ON ME *NOW*, BOYOS. THIS DAY ISN'T OVER *YET*.
I'LL DIE A RICH OLD MAN BY THE TIME YOU LOT ARE PROPER SOLDIERS.
SCOUT RIDER COMING IN, ROGATINO.
HO, THERE! YOU'RE IN A DEVILISH HURRY!
MUST REPORT TO THE KING.
REPORT WHAT?
AN ARMY, TO THE WEST. CROSSING THE BORDER.
THOUSANDS OF THEM, FLYING THE STANDARD OF THE MESSANTIAN LEGION. MAYBE A DAY'S RIDE OUT.
ERLIK'S BASTARD HEART.
BEST GIVE ME YOUR HORSE, LAD.
I'LL TAKE AS MANY RIDERS AS WE HAVE HORSES, SEE IF I CAN STALL THEIR ADVANCE.
WELL, *THAT* MAKES PERFECT SENSE.
WHAT CHANCE DOES A MASSIVE, WELL-TRAINED ARMY HAVE AGAINST AN OPHIRAN DANDY AND A BUNCH OF UNSCHOOLED WHELPS?
THAT'S YOUR PLAN?
AYE, WELL, I'D CALL IT MORE A *NOTION* THAN A *PLAN*.

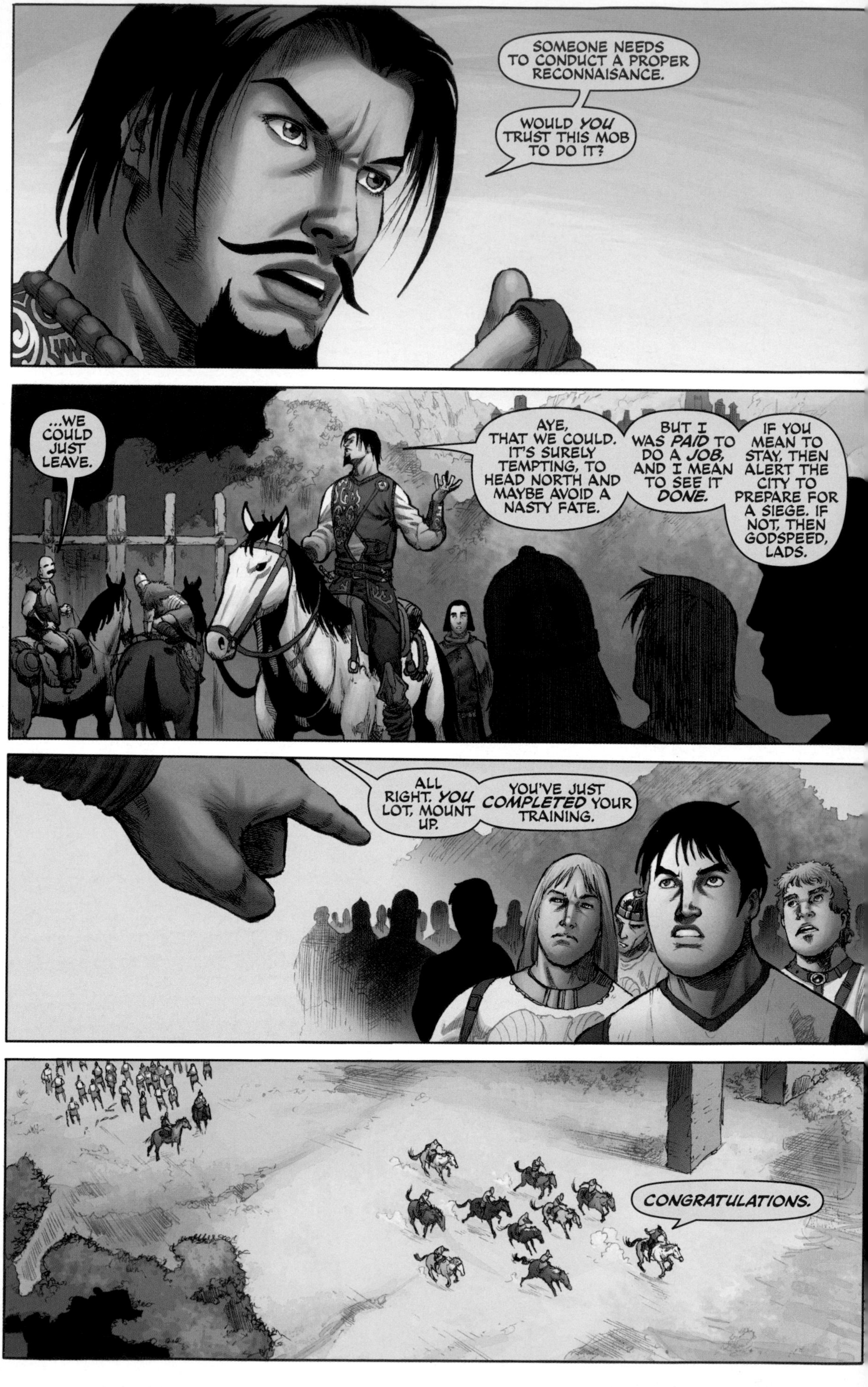
SOMEONE NEEDS TO CONDUCT A PROPER RECONNAISANCE.
WOULD *YOU* TRUST THIS MOB TO DO IT?
...WE COULD JUST LEAVE.
AYE, THAT WE COULD. IT'S SURELY TEMPTING, TO HEAD NORTH AND MAYBE AVOID A NASTY FATE.
BUT I WAS *PAID* TO DO A *JOB*, AND I MEAN TO SEE IT *DONE*.
IF YOU MEAN TO STAY, THEN ALERT THE CITY TO PREPARE FOR A SIEGE. IF NOT, THEN GODSPEED, LADS.
ALL RIGHT. *YOU* LOT, MOUNT UP.
YOU'VE JUST *COMPLETED* YOUR TRAINING.
CONGRATULATIONS.

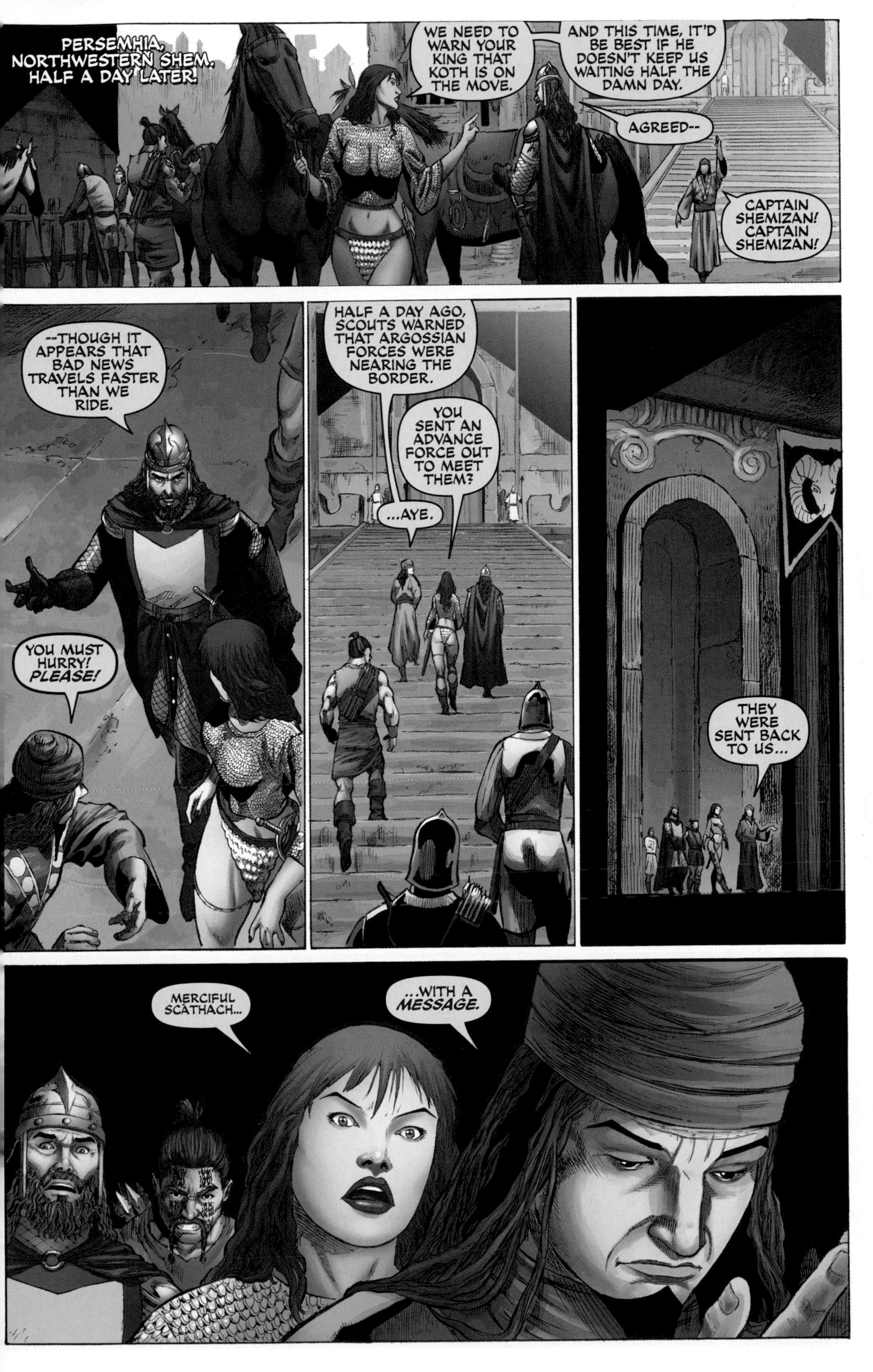

PERSEMHIA, NORTHWESTERN SHEM. HALF A DAY LATER.
WE NEED TO WARN YOUR KING THAT KOTH IS ON THE MOVE.
AND THIS TIME, IT'D BE BEST IF HE DOESN'T KEEP US WAITING HALF THE DAMN DAY.
AGREED--
CAPTAIN SHEMIZAN! CAPTAIN SHEMIZAN!
--THOUGH IT APPEARS THAT BAD NEWS TRAVELS FASTER THAN WE RIDE.
YOU MUST HURRY! PLEASE!
HALF A DAY AGO, SCOUTS WARNED THAT ARGOSSIAN FORCES WERE NEARING THE BORDER.
YOU SENT AN ADVANCE FORCE OUT TO MEET THEM?
...AYE.
THEY WERE SENT BACK TO US...
MERCIFUL SCÁTHACH...
...WITH A MESSAGE.

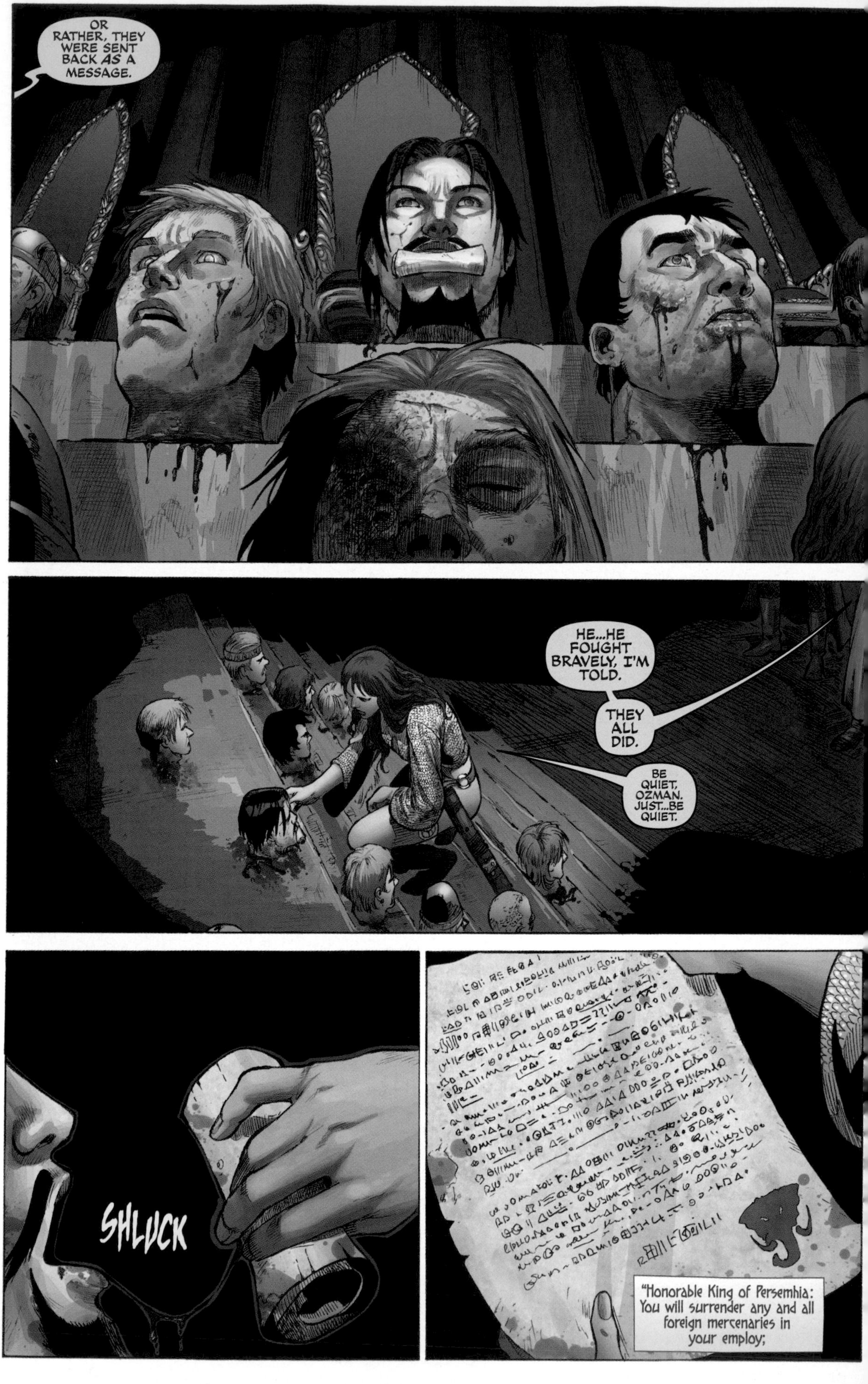
OR RATHER, THEY WERE SENT BACK AS A MESSAGE.
HE...HE FOUGHT BRAVELY, I'M TOLD.
THEY ALL DID.
BE QUIET, OZMAN. JUST...BE QUIET.
SHLUCK
"Honorable King of Persemhia: You will surrender any and all foreign mercenaries in your employ;

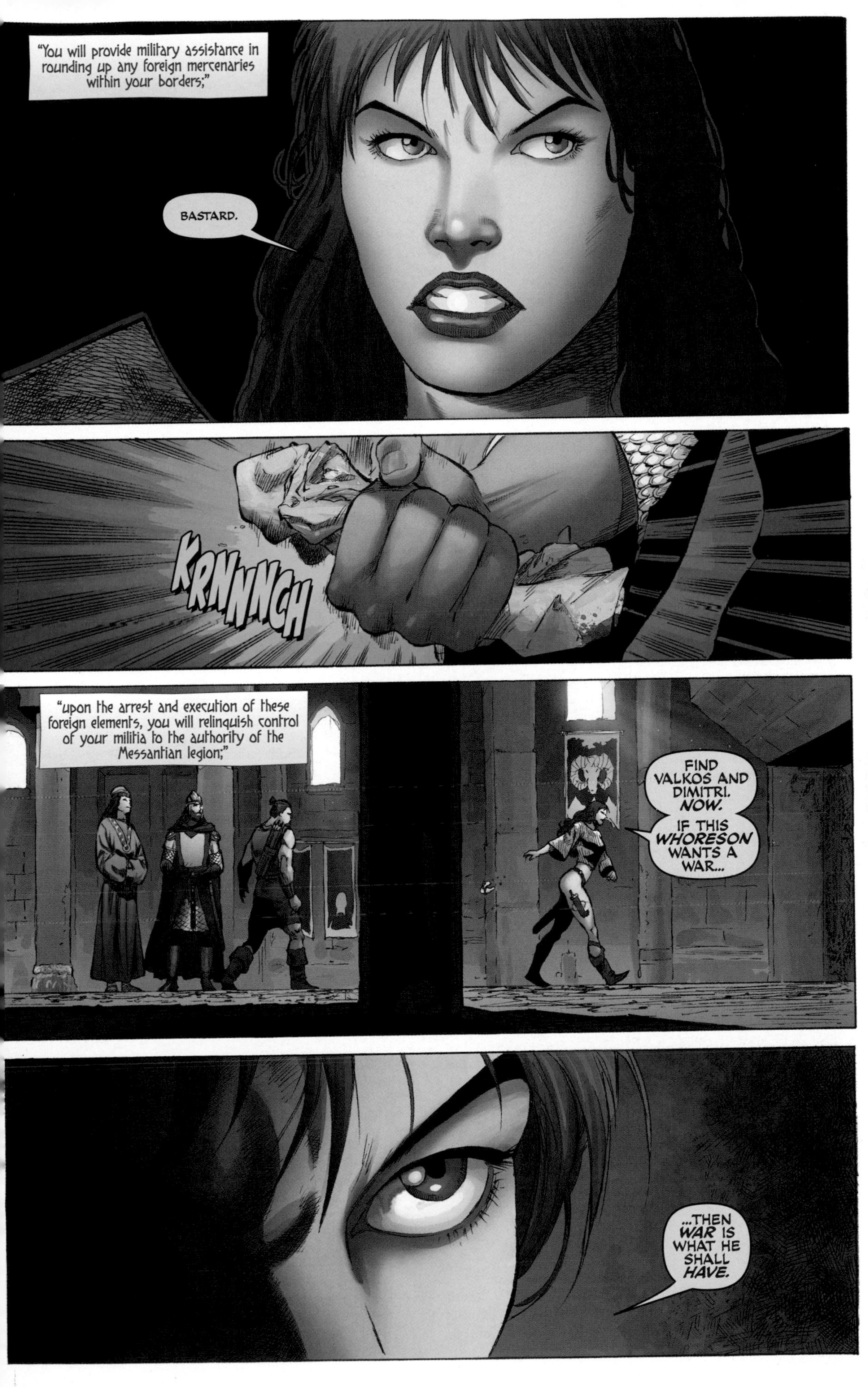

"You will provide military assistance in rounding up any foreign mercenaries within your borders;"
BASTARD.
KRNNNCH
"upon the arrest and execution of these foreign elements, you will relinquish control of your militia to the authority of the Messantian legion;"
FIND VALKOS AND DIMITRI. NOW.
IF THIS WHORESON WANTS A WAR...
...THEN WAR IS WHAT HE SHALL HAVE.

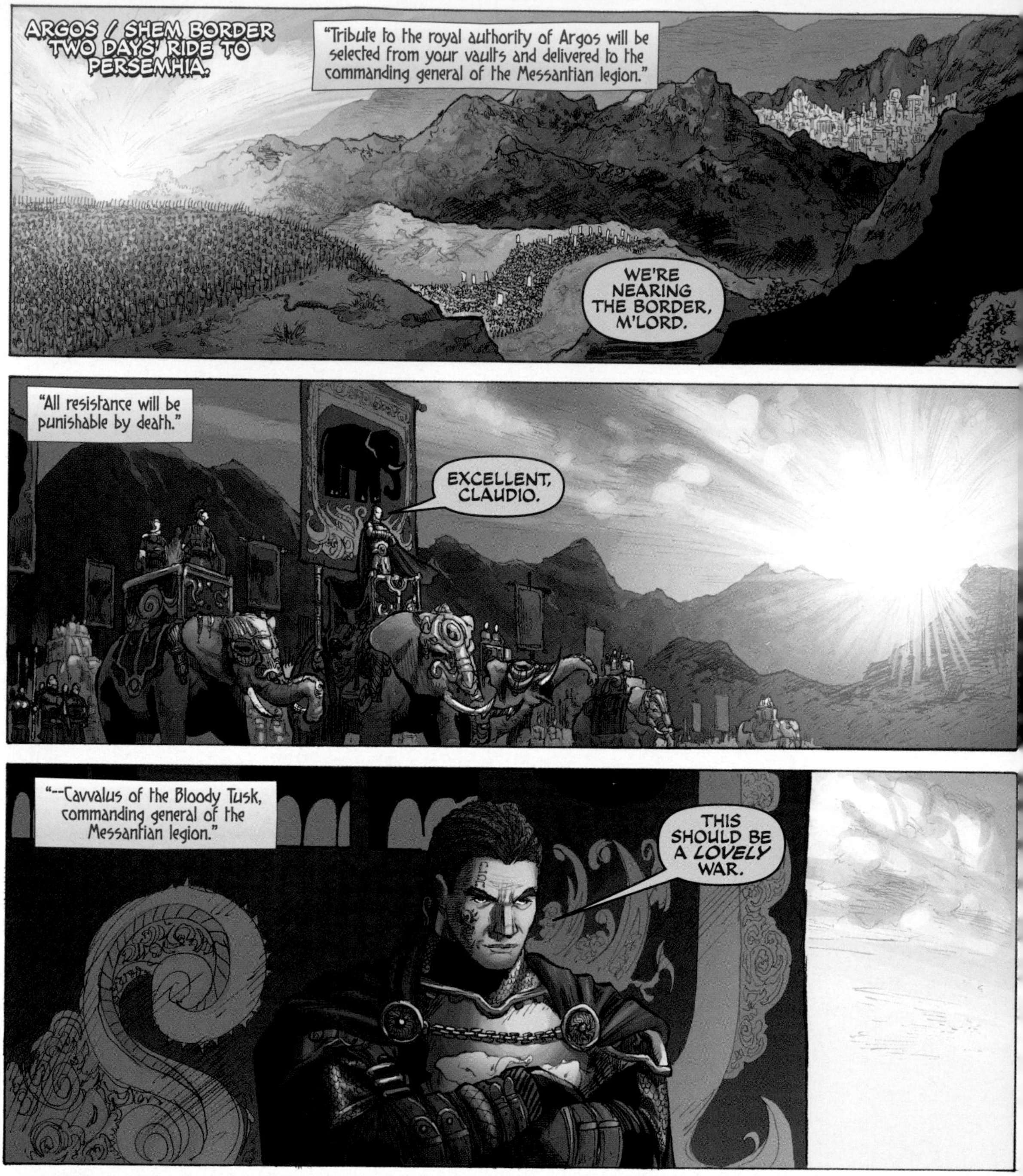
ARGOS / SHEM BORDER TWO DAYS' RIDE TO PERSEMHIA.
"Tribute to the royal authority of Argos will be selected from your vaults and delivered to the commanding general of the Messantian legion."
WE'RE NEARING THE BORDER, M'LORD.
"All resistance will be punishable by death."
EXCELLENT, CLAUDIO.
"--Cavvalus of the Bloody Tusk, commanding general of the Messantian legion."
THIS SHOULD BE A *LOVELY* WAR.

GRIM TIDINGS

WAR SEASON, PART 2

Written by: Eric S. Trautmann
Pencils by: Walter Geovanni
Colors by: Adriano Lucas
Letters by: Troy Peteri
Edited by: Joe Rybandt

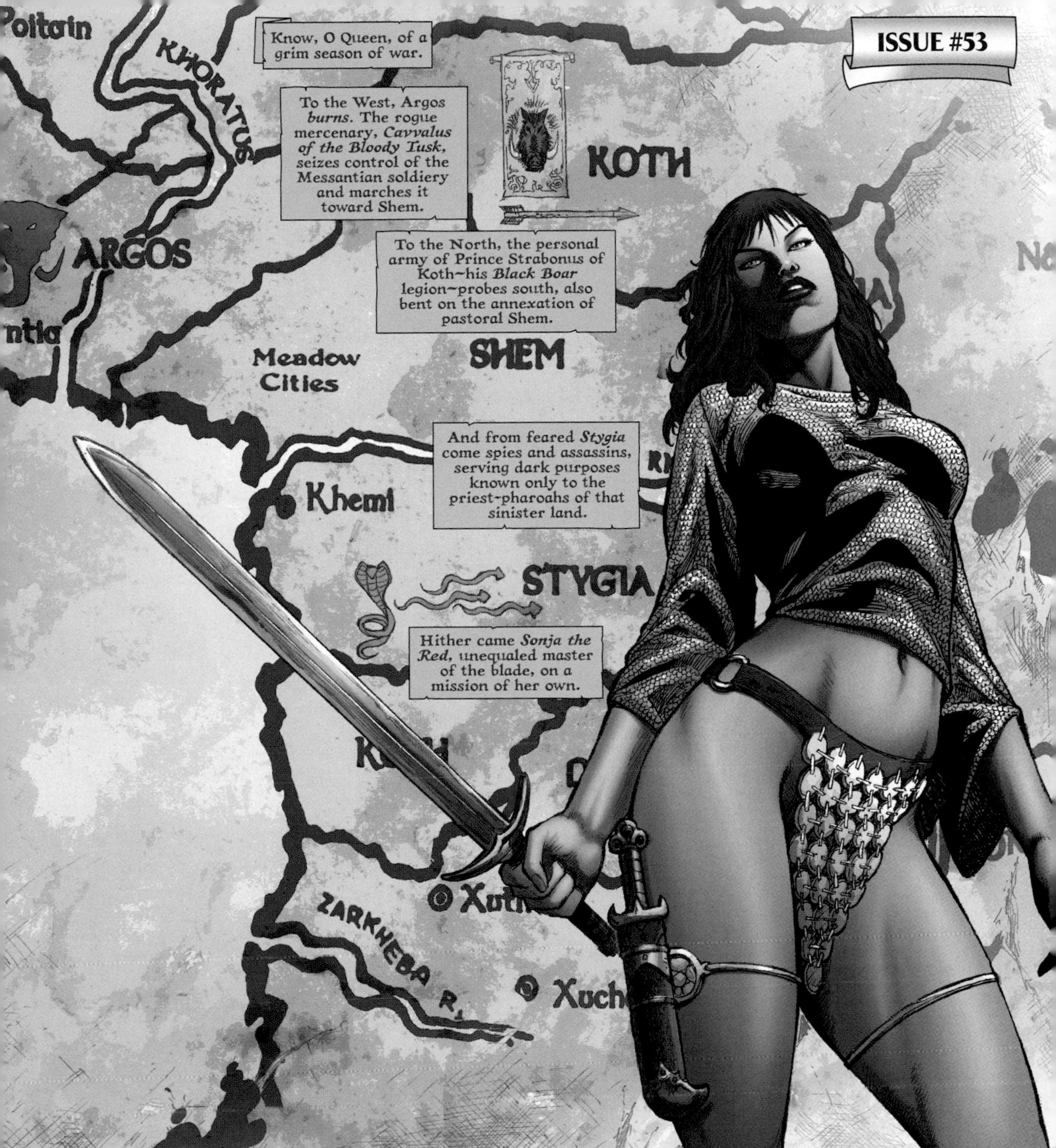
ISSUE #53
Know, O Queen, of a grim season of war.
To the West, Argos *burns*. The rogue mercenary, *Cavvalus of the Bloody Tusk*, seizes control of the Messantian soldiery and marches it toward Shem.
To the North, the personal army of Prince Strabonus of Koth~his *Black Boar* legion~probes south, also bent on the annexation of pastoral Shem.
And from feared *Stygia* come spies and assassins, serving dark purposes known only to the priest-pharoahs of that sinister land.
Hither came *Sonja the Red*, unequaled master of the blade, on a mission of her own.
Poitain
KHORATUS
ARGOS
KOTH
SHEM
Meadow Cities
Khemi
STYGIA
ZARKHEBA R.

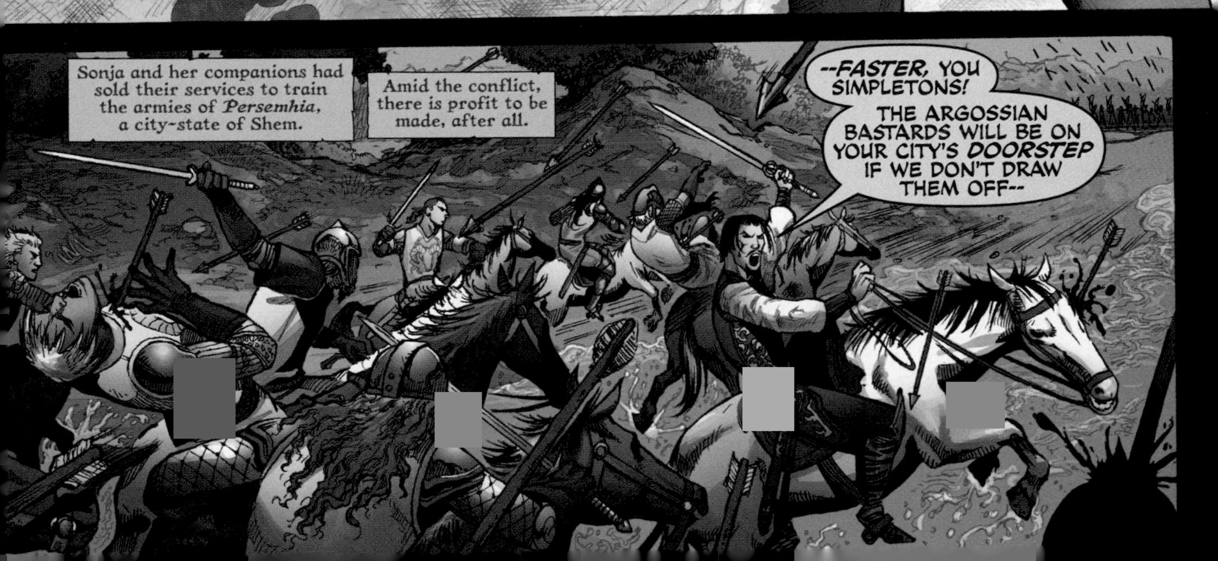
Sonja and her companions had sold their services to train the armies of *Persemhia*, a city-state of Shem.
Amid the conflict, there is profit to be made, after all.
--*FASTER*, YOU SIMPLETONS!
THE ARGOSSIAN BASTARDS WILL BE ON YOUR CITY'S *DOORSTEP* IF WE DON'T DRAW THEM OFF--

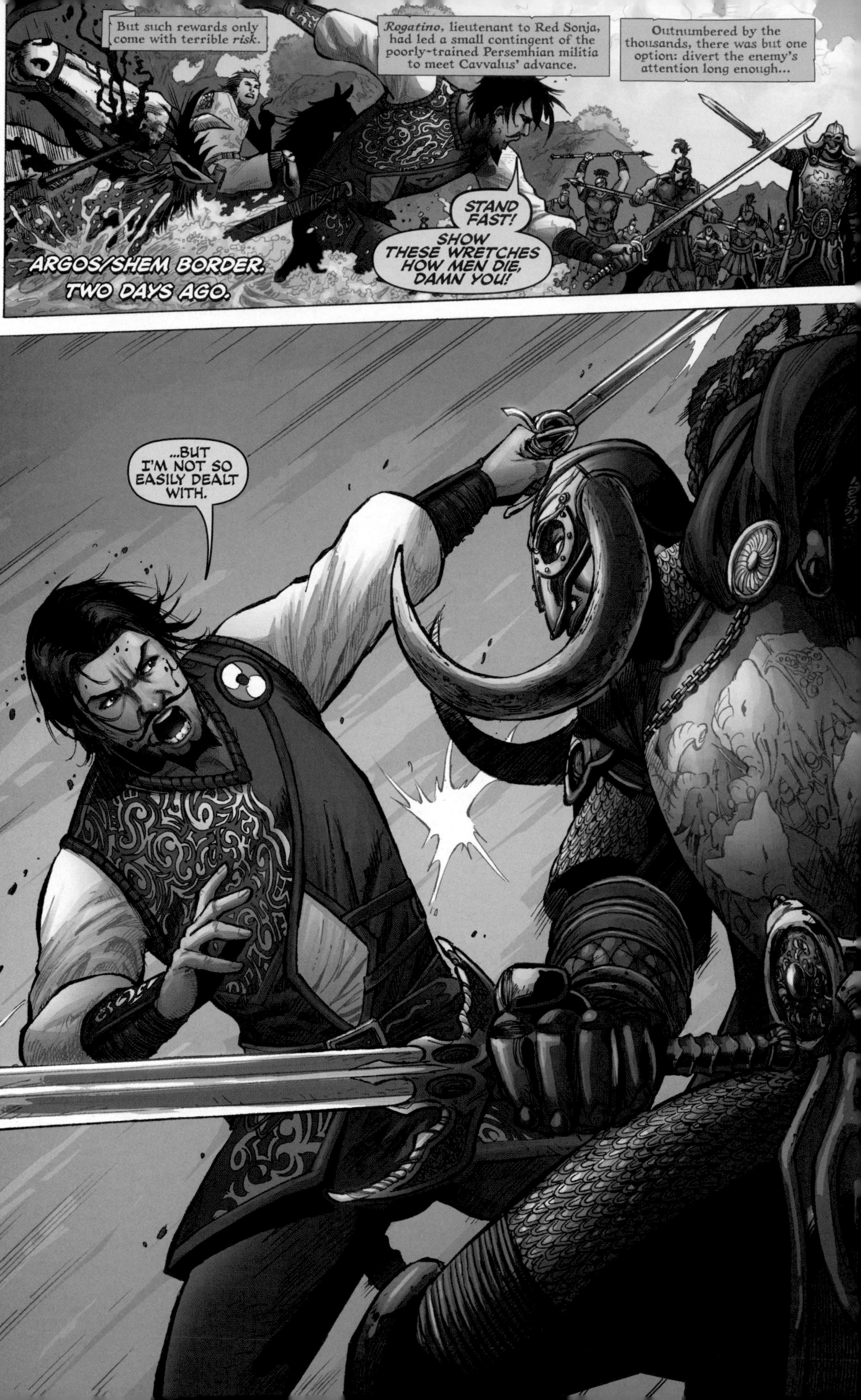
But such rewards only come with terrible *risk*.
Rogatino, lieutenant to Red Sonja, had led a small contingent of the poorly-trained Persemhian militia to meet Cavvalus' advance.
Outnumbered by the thousands, there was but one option: divert the enemy's attention long enough...
STAND FAST! SHOW THESE WRETCHES HOW MEN DIE, DAMN YOU!
ARGOS/SHEM BORDER. TWO DAYS AGO.
...BUT I'M NOT SO EASILY DEALT WITH.

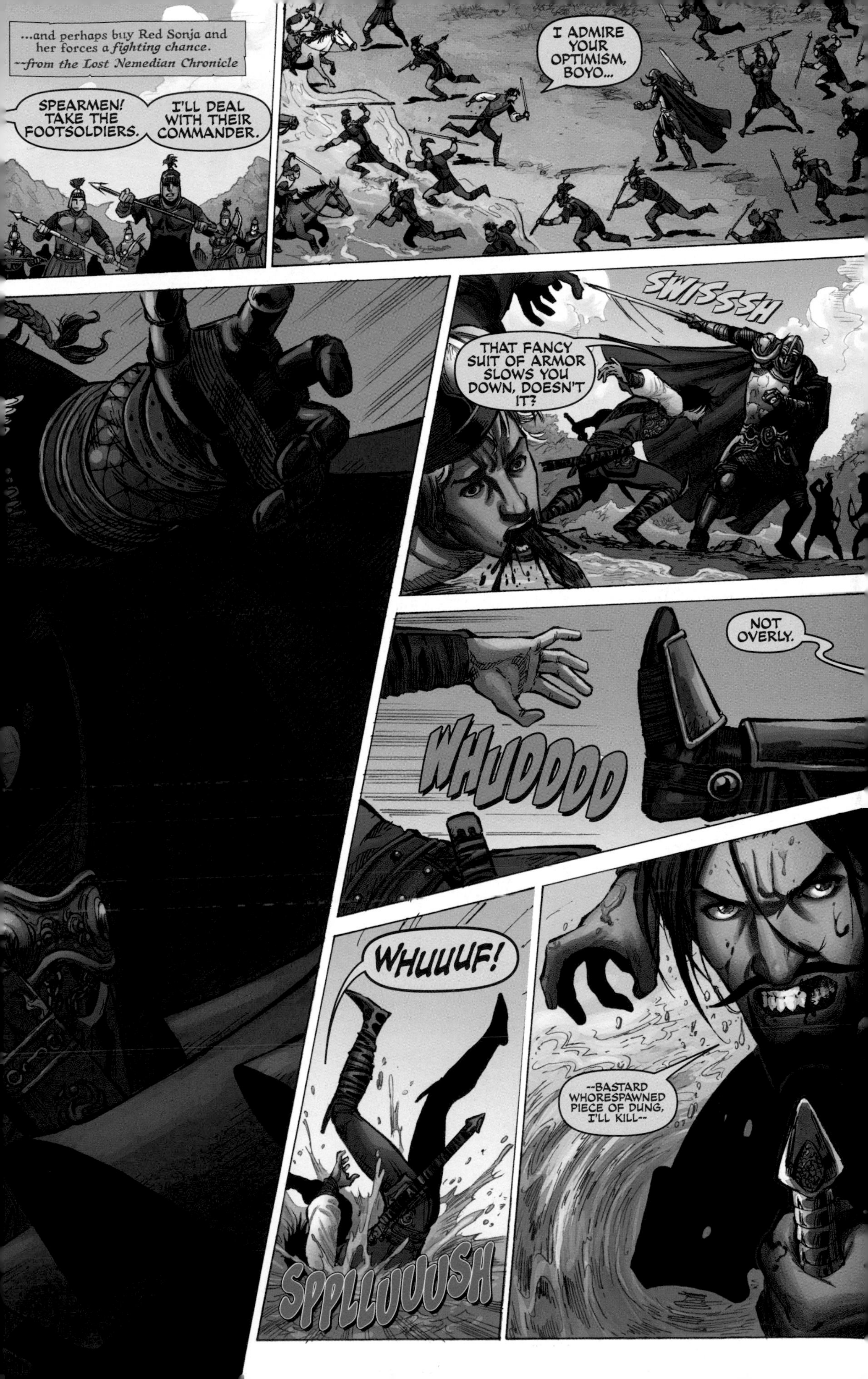
...and perhaps buy Red Sonja and her forces a *fighting chance*.
--from the Lost Nemedian Chronicle
SPEARMEN! TAKE THE FOOTSOLDIERS.
I'LL DEAL WITH THEIR COMMANDER.
I ADMIRE YOUR OPTIMISM, BOYO...
SWISSSH
THAT FANCY SUIT OF ARMOR SLOWS YOU DOWN, DOESN'T IT?
NOT OVERLY.
WHUDDDD
WHUUUF!
SPPLLUUUUSH
--BASTARD WHORESPAWNED PIECE OF DUNG, I'LL KILL--

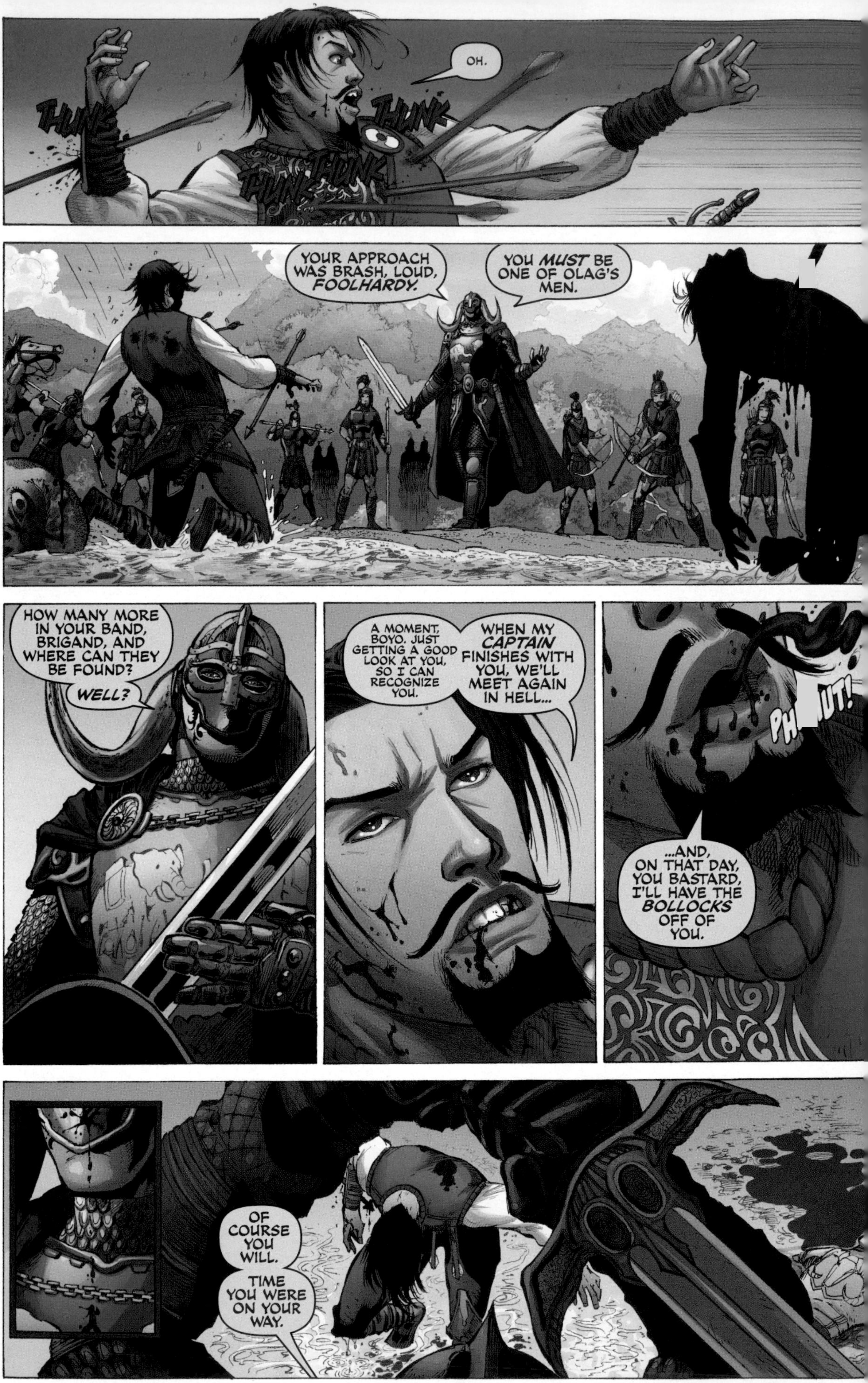
THUNK
OH.
THUNK
THUNK
THUNK
YOUR APPROACH WAS BRASH, LOUD, *FOOLHARDY.*
YOU *MUST* BE ONE OF OLAG'S MEN.
HOW MANY MORE IN YOUR BAND, BRIGAND, AND WHERE CAN THEY BE FOUND?
WELL?
A MOMENT, BOYO. JUST GETTING A GOOD LOOK AT YOU, SO I CAN RECOGNIZE YOU.
WHEN MY *CAPTAIN* FINISHES WITH YOU, WE'LL MEET AGAIN IN HELL...
...AND, ON THAT DAY, YOU BASTARD, I'LL HAVE THE *BOLLOCKS* OFF OF YOU.
OF COURSE YOU WILL.
TIME YOU WERE ON YOUR WAY.

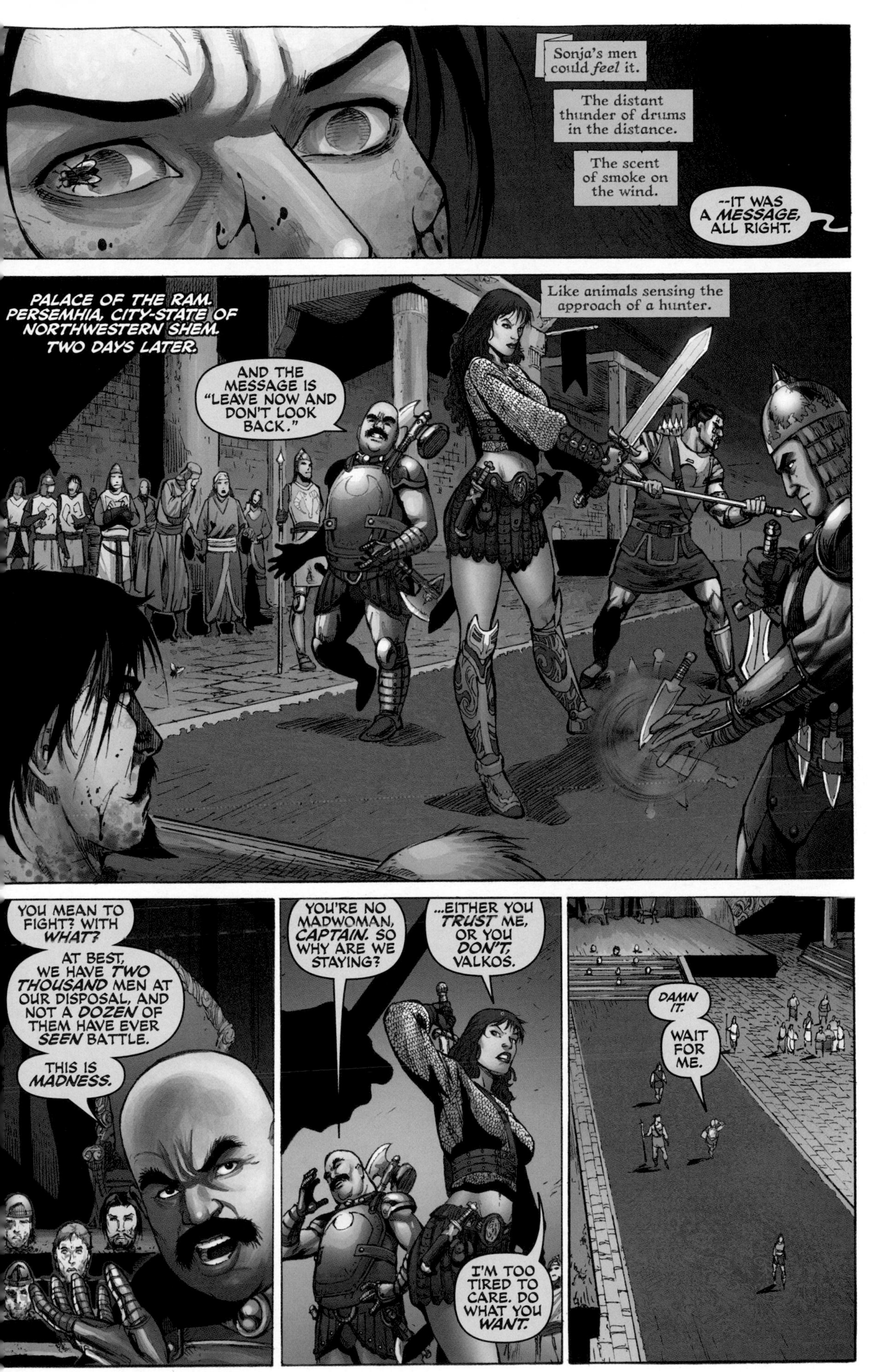
Sonja's men could *feel* it.
The distant thunder of drums in the distance.
The scent of smoke on the wind.
--IT WAS A *MESSAGE,* ALL RIGHT.
PALACE OF THE RAM. PERSEMHIA, CITY-STATE OF NORTHWESTERN SHEM. TWO DAYS LATER.
Like animals sensing the approach of a hunter.
AND THE MESSAGE IS "LEAVE NOW AND DON'T LOOK BACK."
YOU MEAN TO FIGHT? WITH *WHAT?*
AT BEST, WE HAVE *TWO THOUSAND* MEN AT OUR DISPOSAL, AND NOT A *DOZEN* OF THEM HAVE EVER *SEEN* BATTLE.
THIS IS *MADNESS.*
YOU'RE NO MADWOMAN, *CAPTAIN.* SO WHY ARE WE STAYING?
...EITHER YOU *TRUST* ME, OR YOU *DON'T,* VALKOS.
I'M TOO TIRED TO CARE. DO WHAT YOU *WANT.*
DAMN IT.
WAIT FOR ME.

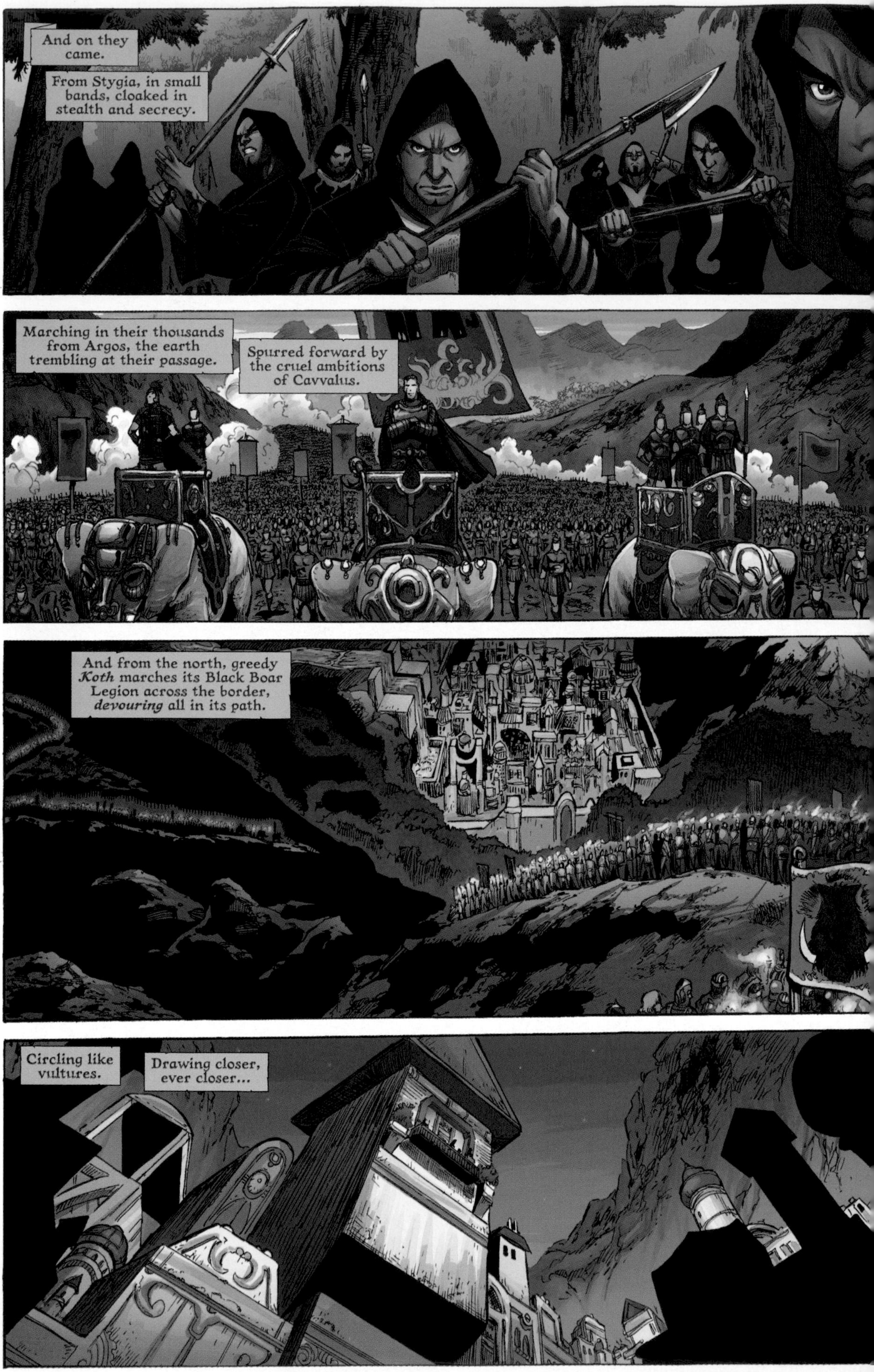
And on they came.
From Stygia, in small bands, cloaked in stealth and secrecy.
Marching in their thousands from Argos, the earth trembling at their passage.
Spurred forward by the cruel ambitions of Cavvalus.
And from the north, greedy *Koth* marches its Black Boar Legion across the border, *devouring* all in its path.
Circling like vultures.
Drawing closer, ever closer...

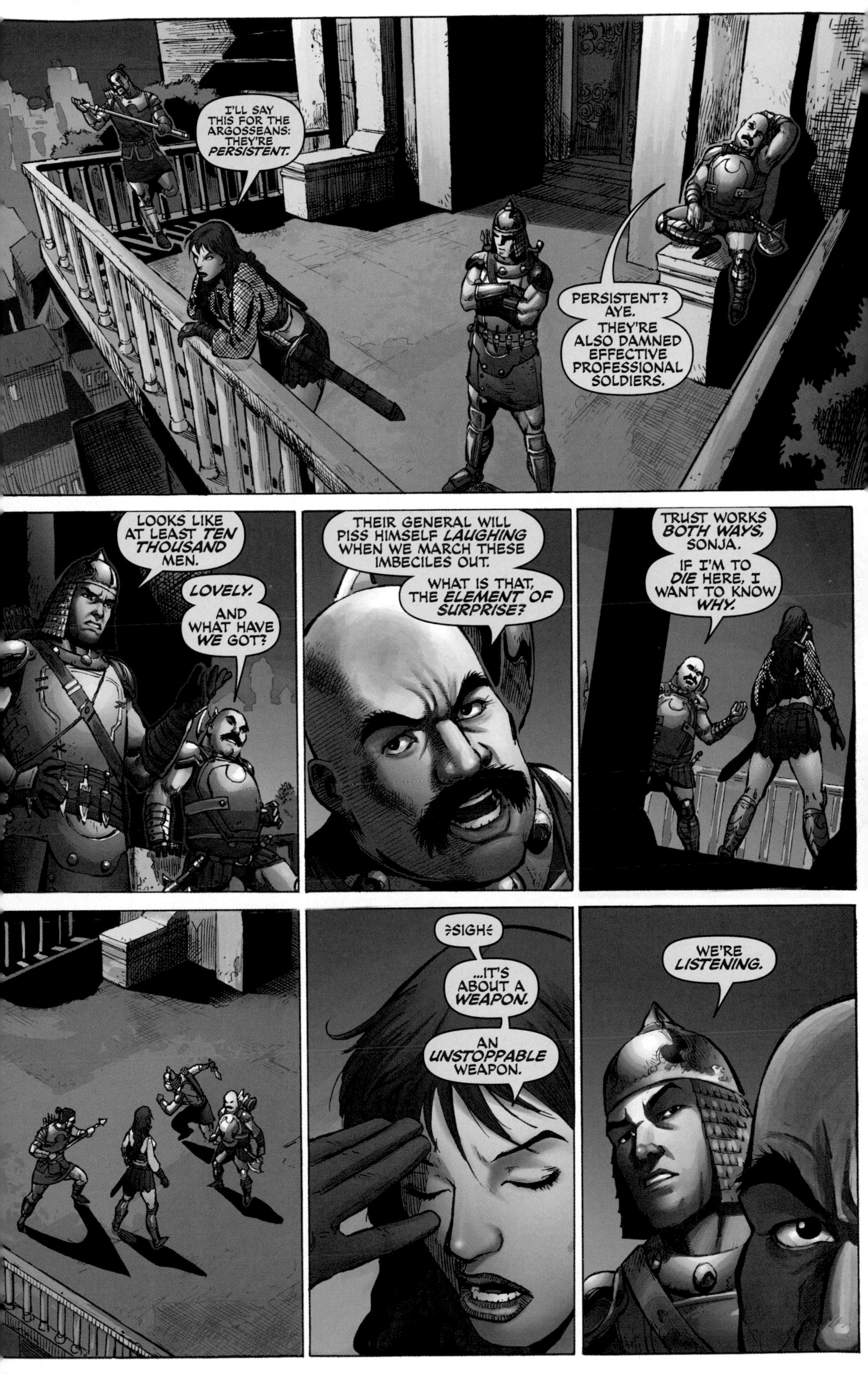
I'LL SAY THIS FOR THE ARGOSSEANS: THEY'RE *PERSISTENT.*
PERSISTENT? AYE. THEY'RE ALSO DAMNED EFFECTIVE PROFESSIONAL SOLDIERS.
LOOKS LIKE AT LEAST *TEN THOUSAND* MEN.
LOVELY.
AND WHAT HAVE *WE* GOT?
THEIR GENERAL WILL PISS HIMSELF *LAUGHING* WHEN WE MARCH THESE IMBECILES OUT.
WHAT IS THAT, THE *ELEMENT OF SURPRISE?*
TRUST WORKS *BOTH WAYS,* SONJA.
IF I'M TO *DIE* HERE, I WANT TO KNOW *WHY.*
SIGH
...IT'S ABOUT A *WEAPON.*
AN *UNSTOPPABLE* WEAPON.
WE'RE *LISTENING.*

OLAG SENT US OUT HERE TO STOP A MESSAGE RUNNER.

OLAG THOUGHT THE RUNNER WAS *ARGOSSEAN*, SUMMONING AID FROM THEIR BORDER ARMY.

BUT INSTEAD, WE CAUGHT A *STYGIAN*--

THUMEKMES, A SCRIBE.

CARRYING THE MESSAGE ON HIS *FLESH*.

I DON'T READ MUCH OF THEIR LANGUAGE, BUT I COPIED AS MUCH OF IT DOWN AS I COULD.

WHICH CONFIRMED A STORY I'D HEARD...

...FROM *OLAG*.

HE WAS IN HIS CUPS, BOASTING ABOUT HOW-- AFTER HE'D HELPED TOPPLE ARGOS' THRONE -- HE WOULD RIDE INTO SHEM.

HE'D HEARD A TALE FROM A TURANIAN MERCHANT, A FABLE OF A GOD-BLESSED WEAPON, ONE THAT MAKES AN ARMY, NO MATTER HOW SMALL, *INVINCIBLE*.

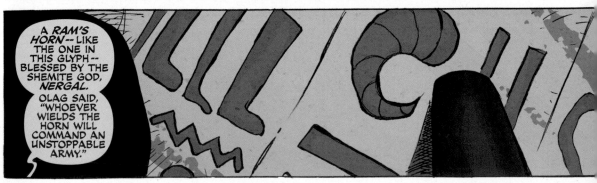

A *RAM'S HORN*-- LIKE THE ONE IN THIS GLYPH-- BLESSED BY THE SHEMITE GOD, *NERGAL*.

OLAG SAID, "WHOEVER WIELDS THE HORN WILL COMMAND AN UNSTOPPABLE ARMY."

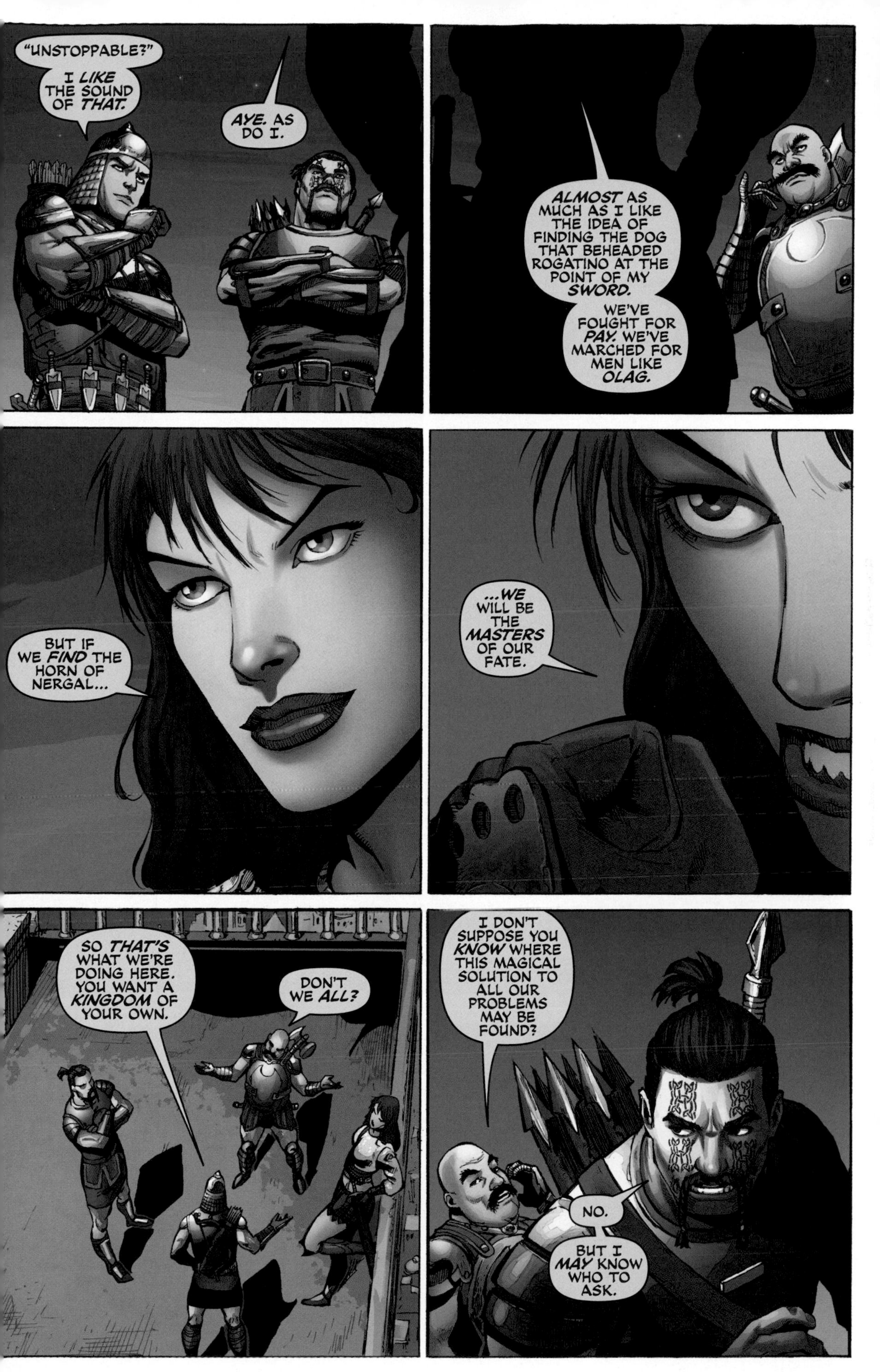
"UNSTOPPABLE?"
I LIKE THE SOUND OF THAT.
AYE. AS DO I.
ALMOST AS MUCH AS I LIKE THE IDEA OF FINDING THE DOG THAT BEHEADED ROGATINO AT THE POINT OF MY SWORD.
WE'VE FOUGHT FOR PAY. WE'VE MARCHED FOR MEN LIKE OLAG.
BUT IF WE FIND THE HORN OF NERGAL...
...WE WILL BE THE MASTERS OF OUR FATE.
SO THAT'S WHAT WE'RE DOING HERE. YOU WANT A KINGDOM OF YOUR OWN.
DON'T WE ALL?
I DON'T SUPPOSE YOU KNOW WHERE THIS MAGICAL SOLUTION TO ALL OUR PROBLEMS MAY BE FOUND?
NO.
BUT I MAY KNOW WHO TO ASK.

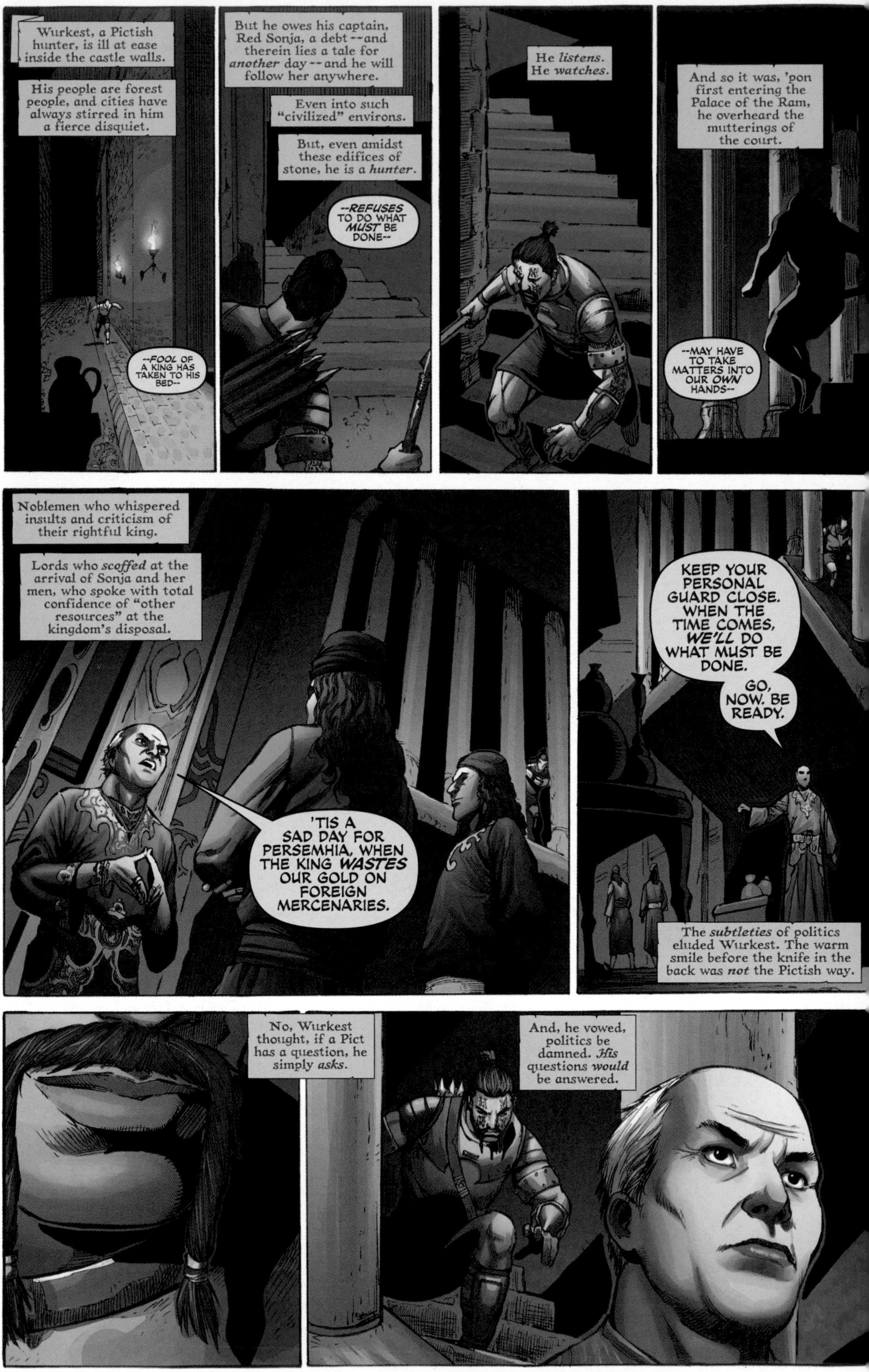

Wurkest, a Pictish hunter, is ill at ease inside the castle walls.
His people are forest people, and cities have always stirred in him a fierce disquiet.
--FOOL OF A KING HAS TAKEN TO HIS BED--
But he owes his captain, Red Sonja, a debt -- and therein lies a tale for *another* day -- and he will follow her anywhere.
Even into such "civilized" environs.
But, even amidst these edifices of stone, he is a *hunter*.
--*REFUSES* TO DO WHAT *MUST* BE DONE--
He *listens*. He *watches*.
And so it was, 'pon first entering the Palace of the Ram, he overheard the mutterings of the court.
--MAY HAVE TO TAKE MATTERS INTO OUR *OWN* HANDS--
Noblemen who whispered insults and criticism of their rightful king.
Lords who *scoffed* at the arrival of Sonja and her men, who spoke with total confidence of "other resources" at the kingdom's disposal.
'TIS A SAD DAY FOR PERSEMHIA, WHEN THE KING *WASTES* OUR GOLD ON FOREIGN MERCENARIES.
KEEP YOUR PERSONAL GUARD CLOSE. WHEN THE TIME COMES, *WE'LL* DO WHAT MUST BE DONE.
GO, NOW. BE READY.
The *subtleties* of politics eluded Wurkest. The warm smile before the knife in the back was *not* the Pictish way.
No, Wurkest thought, if a Pict has a question, he simply *asks*.
And, he vowed, politics be damned. *His* questions *would* be answered.

JUST PAST THE ARGOS/SHEM BORDER. HALF A DAY'S RIDE FROM PERSEMHIA.

--A MOMENT, MY LORD.

EMISSARIES FROM KOTH, UNDER A FLAG OF TRUCE, WISH TO PARLAY.

VERY WELL, CLAUDIO.

A *PITY*, ISN'T IT?

THAT THE GAME OF EMPIRE SHOULD BE BOGGED DOWN BY *BUREAUCRATS*.

ALAS, ONE SHOULD ALWAYS BE A *GRACIOUS HOST*.

HAIL, *GENERAL* CAVVALUS.

I BRING YOU THE *EXALTED* GREETINGS OF HIS HIGHNESS, *PRINCE STRABONUS* OF KOTH.

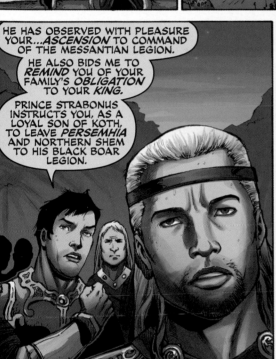

HE HAS OBSERVED WITH PLEASURE YOUR...*ASCENSION* TO COMMAND OF THE MESSANTIAN LEGION.

HE ALSO BIDS ME TO *REMIND* YOU OF YOUR FAMILY'S *OBLIGATION* TO YOUR *KING*.

PRINCE STRABONUS INSTRUCTS YOU, AS A LOYAL SON OF KOTH, TO LEAVE *PERSEMHIA* AND NORTHERN SHEM TO HIS BLACK BOAR LEGION.

A LOYAL SON OF KOTH.

DID YOU KNOW *STRABONUS* IS MY KIN, MESSENGER? THAT OUR FAMILES HAVE BEEN LINKED FOR CENTURIES.

MY FAMILY HELPED *FORGE* KOTH, IN FIRE AND STEEL.

UNTIL YOUR "EXALTED" PRINCE CONSPIRED TO FALSELY ACCUSE MY *FATHER* OF TREASON.

SO STRABONUS CAN GO TO *HELL*.

AND *I* WILL *TAKE* WHAT I PLEASE.

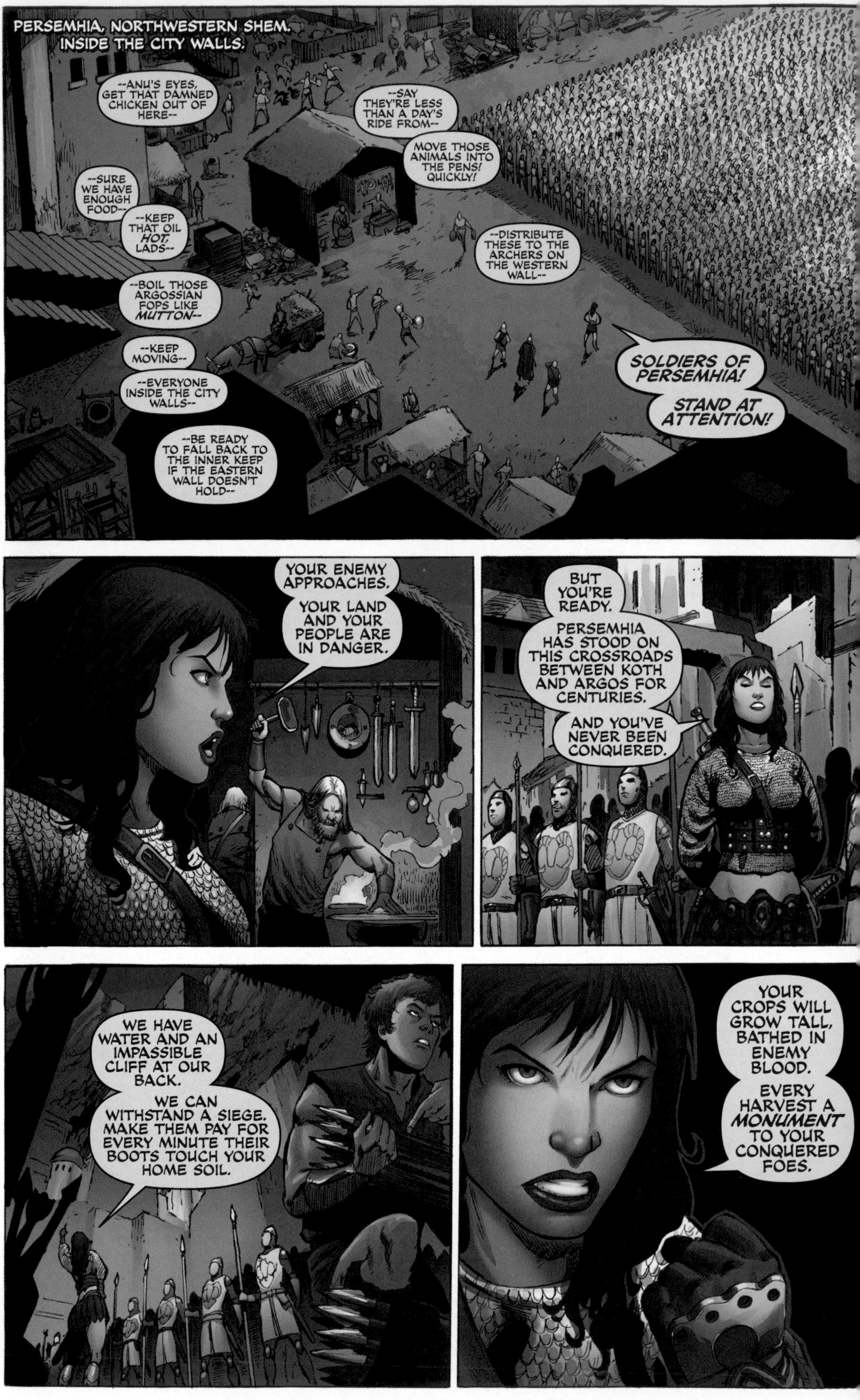
PERSEMHIA, NORTHWESTERN SHEM. INSIDE THE CITY WALLS.
--ANU'S EYES, GET THAT DAMNED CHICKEN OUT OF HERE--
--SAY THEY'RE LESS THAN A DAY'S RIDE FROM--
MOVE THOSE ANIMALS INTO THE PENS! QUICKLY!
--SURE WE HAVE ENOUGH FOOD--
--KEEP THAT OIL HOT, LADS--
--DISTRIBUTE THESE TO THE ARCHERS ON THE WESTERN WALL--
--BOIL THOSE ARGOSSIAN FOPS LIKE MUTTON--
--KEEP MOVING--
--EVERYONE INSIDE THE CITY WALLS--
--BE READY TO FALL BACK TO THE INNER KEEP IF THE EASTERN WALL DOESN'T HOLD--
SOLDIERS OF PERSEMHIA!
STAND AT ATTENTION!
YOUR ENEMY APPROACHES.
YOUR LAND AND YOUR PEOPLE ARE IN DANGER.
BUT YOU'RE READY.
PERSEMHIA HAS STOOD ON THIS CROSSROADS BETWEEN KOTH AND ARGOS FOR CENTURIES.
AND YOU'VE NEVER BEEN CONQUERED.
WE HAVE WATER AND AN IMPASSIBLE CLIFF AT OUR BACK.
WE CAN WITHSTAND A SIEGE. MAKE THEM PAY FOR EVERY MINUTE THEIR BOOTS TOUCH YOUR HOME SOIL.
YOUR CROPS WILL GROW TALL, BATHED IN ENEMY BLOOD.
EVERY HARVEST A MONUMENT TO YOUR CONQUERED FOES.

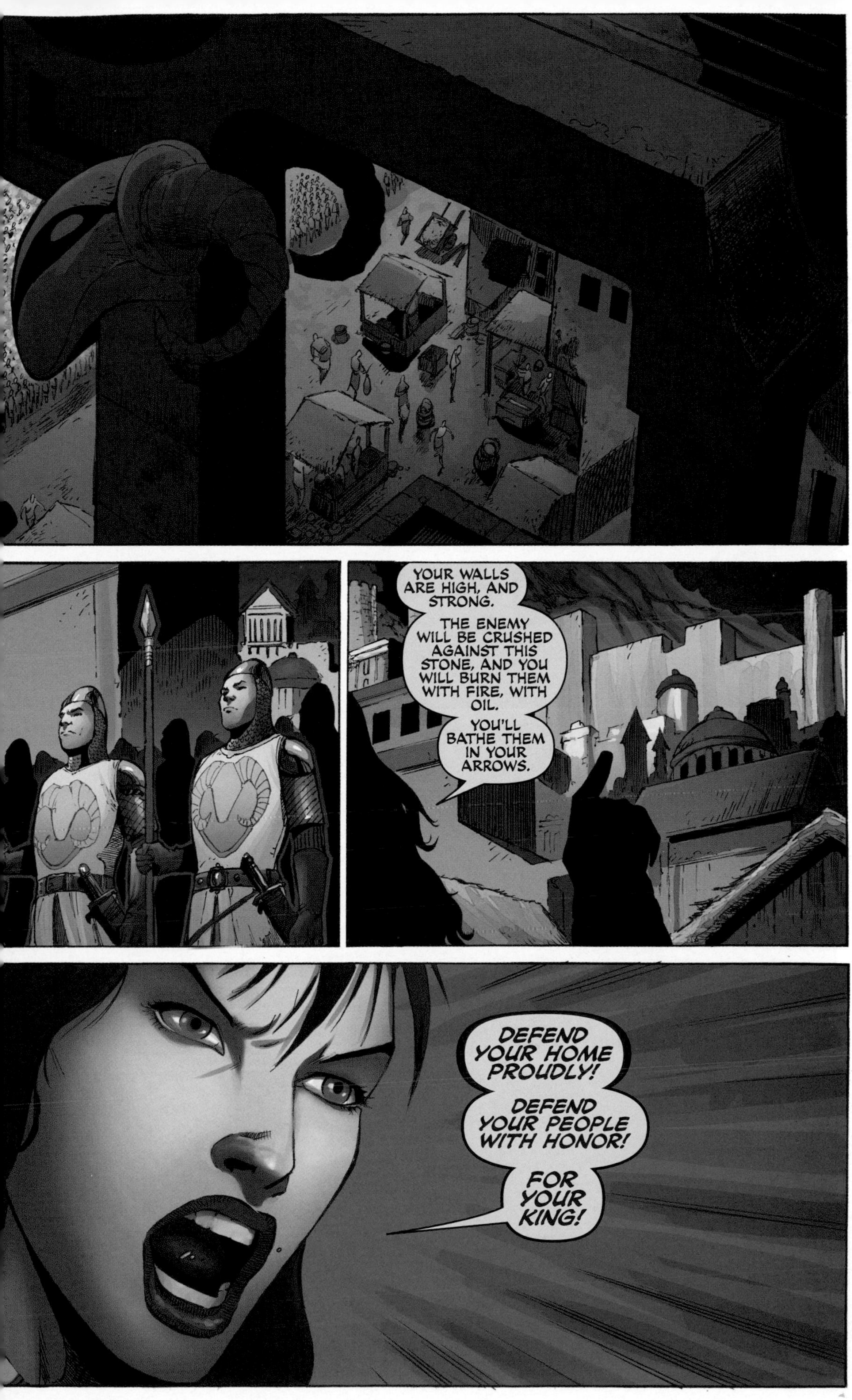
YOUR WALLS ARE HIGH, AND STRONG.
THE ENEMY WILL BE CRUSHED AGAINST THIS STONE, AND YOU WILL BURN THEM WITH FIRE, WITH OIL.
YOU'LL BATHE THEM IN YOUR ARROWS.
DEFEND YOUR HOME PROUDLY!
DEFEND YOUR PEOPLE WITH HONOR!
FOR YOUR KING!

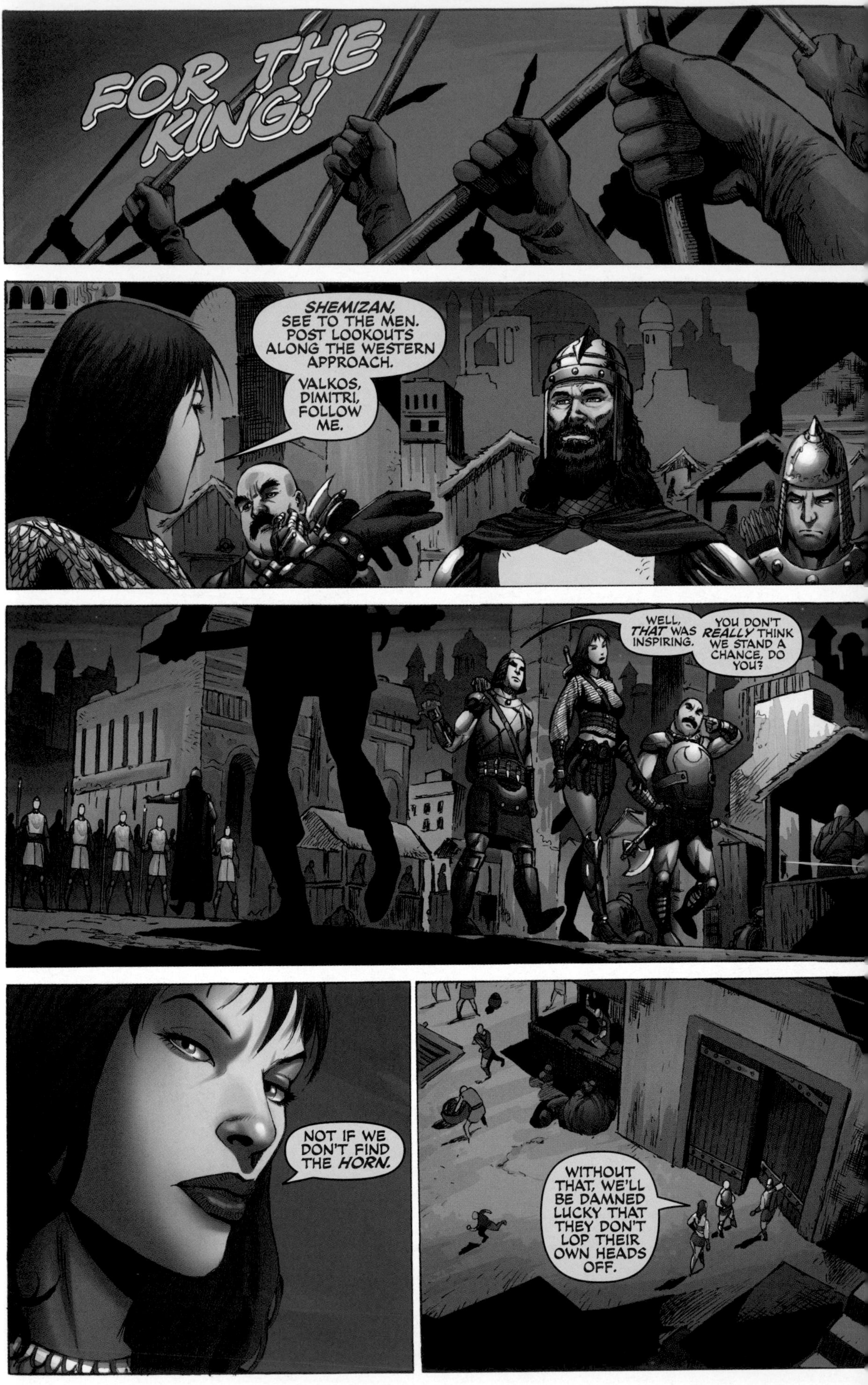
FOR THE KING!
SHEMIZAN, SEE TO THE MEN. POST LOOKOUTS ALONG THE WESTERN APPROACH.
VALKOS, DIMITRI, FOLLOW ME.
WELL, THAT WAS INSPIRING.
YOU DON'T REALLY THINK WE STAND A CHANCE, DO YOU?
NOT IF WE DON'T FIND THE HORN.
WITHOUT THAT, WE'LL BE DAMNED LUCKY THAT THEY DON'T LOP THEIR OWN HEADS OFF.

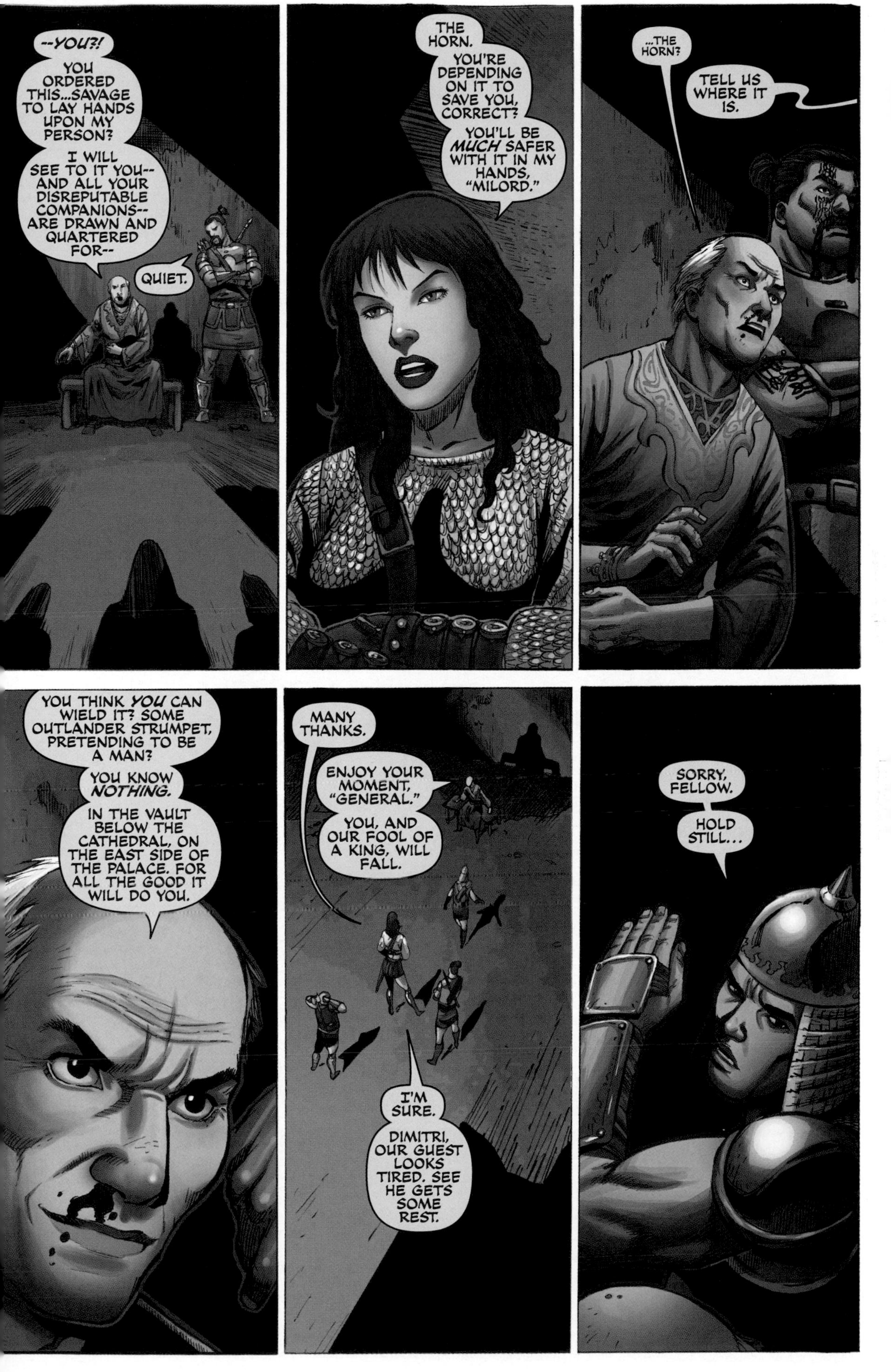
--YOU?!
YOU ORDERED THIS...SAVAGE TO LAY HANDS UPON MY PERSON?
I WILL SEE TO IT YOU--AND ALL YOUR DISREPUTABLE COMPANIONS--ARE DRAWN AND QUARTERED FOR--
QUIET.
THE HORN.
YOU'RE DEPENDING ON IT TO SAVE YOU, CORRECT?
YOU'LL BE MUCH SAFER WITH IT IN MY HANDS, "MILORD."
...THE HORN?
TELL US WHERE IT IS.
YOU THINK YOU CAN WIELD IT? SOME OUTLANDER STRUMPET, PRETENDING TO BE A MAN?
YOU KNOW NOTHING.
IN THE VAULT BELOW THE CATHEDRAL, ON THE EAST SIDE OF THE PALACE. FOR ALL THE GOOD IT WILL DO YOU.
MANY THANKS.
ENJOY YOUR MOMENT, "GENERAL."
YOU, AND OUR FOOL OF A KING, WILL FALL.
I'M SURE.
DIMITRI, OUR GUEST LOOKS TIRED. SEE HE GETS SOME REST.
SORRY, FELLOW.
HOLD STILL...

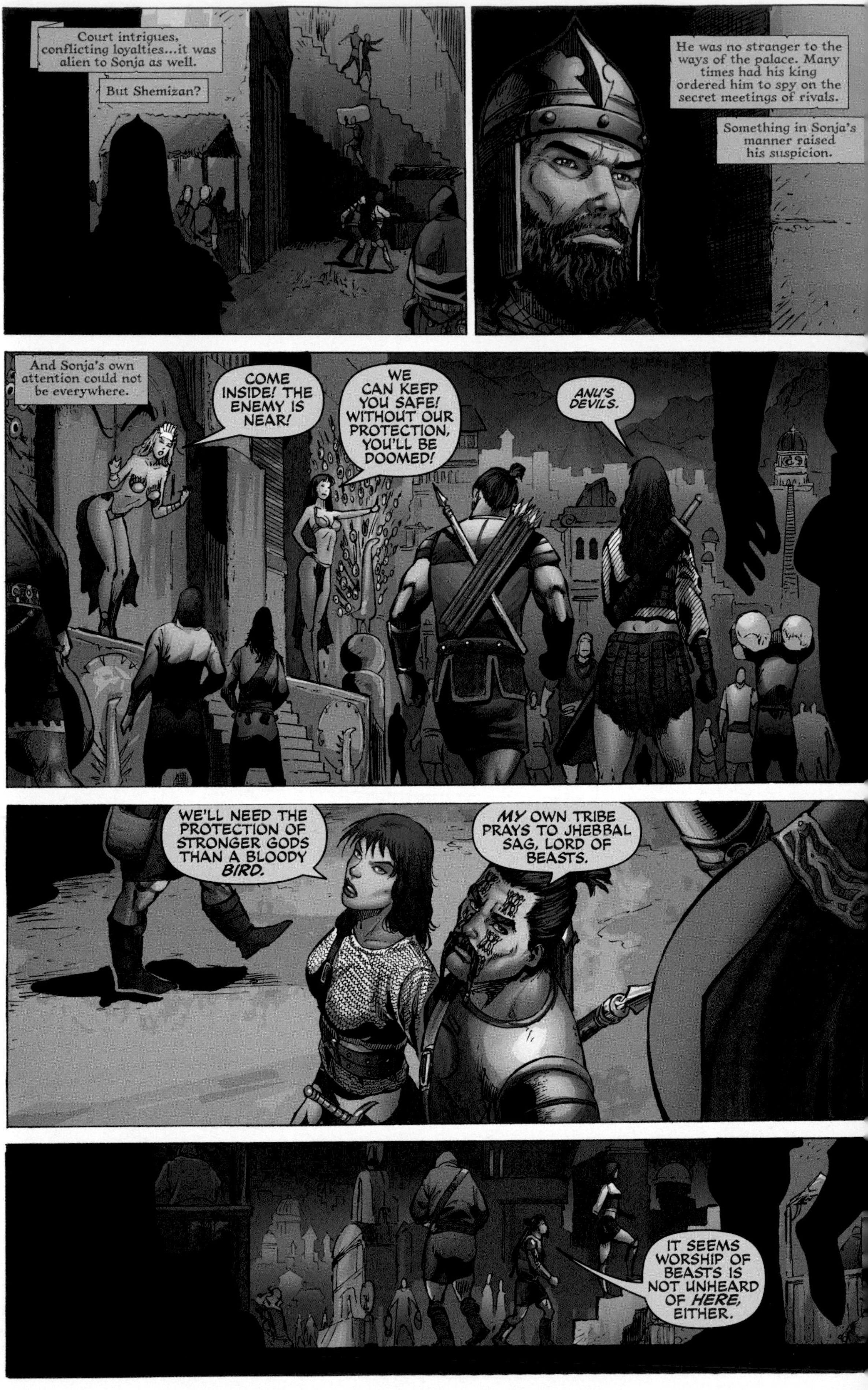
Court intrigues, conflicting loyalties...it was alien to Sonja as well.
But Shemizan?
He was no stranger to the ways of the palace. Many times had his king ordered him to spy on the secret meetings of rivals.
Something in Sonja's manner raised his suspicion.
And Sonja's own attention could not be everywhere.
COME INSIDE! THE ENEMY IS NEAR!
WE CAN KEEP YOU SAFE! WITHOUT OUR PROTECTION, YOU'LL BE DOOMED!
ANU'S DEVILS.
WE'LL NEED THE PROTECTION OF STRONGER GODS THAN A BLOODY BIRD.
MY OWN TRIBE PRAYS TO JHEBBAL SAG, LORD OF BEASTS.
IT SEEMS WORSHIP OF BEASTS IS NOT UNHEARD OF HERE, EITHER.

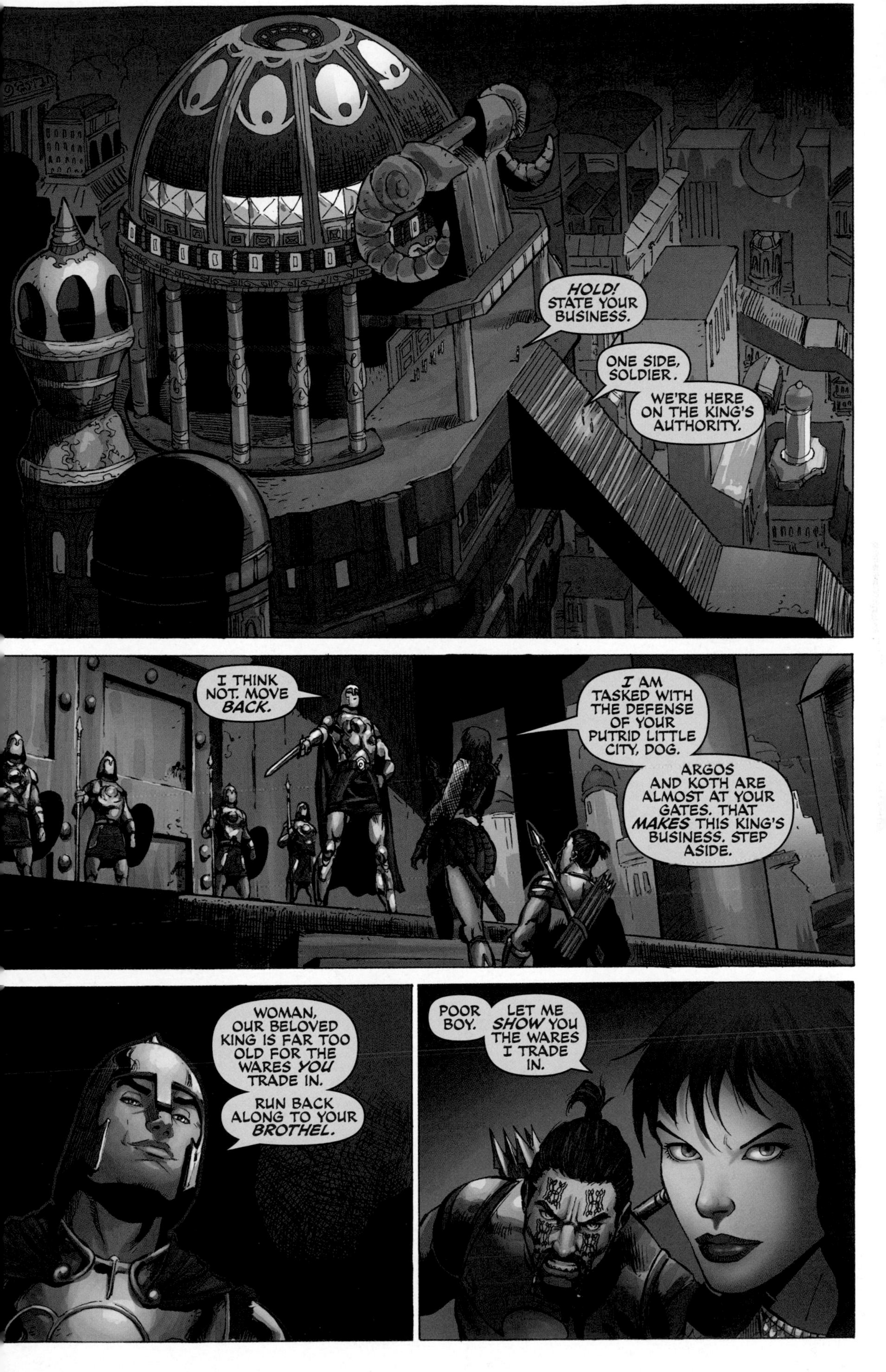
HOLD! STATE YOUR BUSINESS.
ONE SIDE, SOLDIER.
WE'RE HERE ON THE KING'S AUTHORITY.
I THINK NOT. MOVE BACK.
I AM TASKED WITH THE DEFENSE OF YOUR PUTRID LITTLE CITY, DOG.
ARGOS AND KOTH ARE ALMOST AT YOUR GATES. THAT MAKES THIS KING'S BUSINESS. STEP ASIDE.
WOMAN, OUR BELOVED KING IS FAR TOO OLD FOR THE WARES YOU TRADE IN.
RUN BACK ALONG TO YOUR BROTHEL.
POOR BOY.
LET ME SHOW YOU THE WARES I TRADE IN.

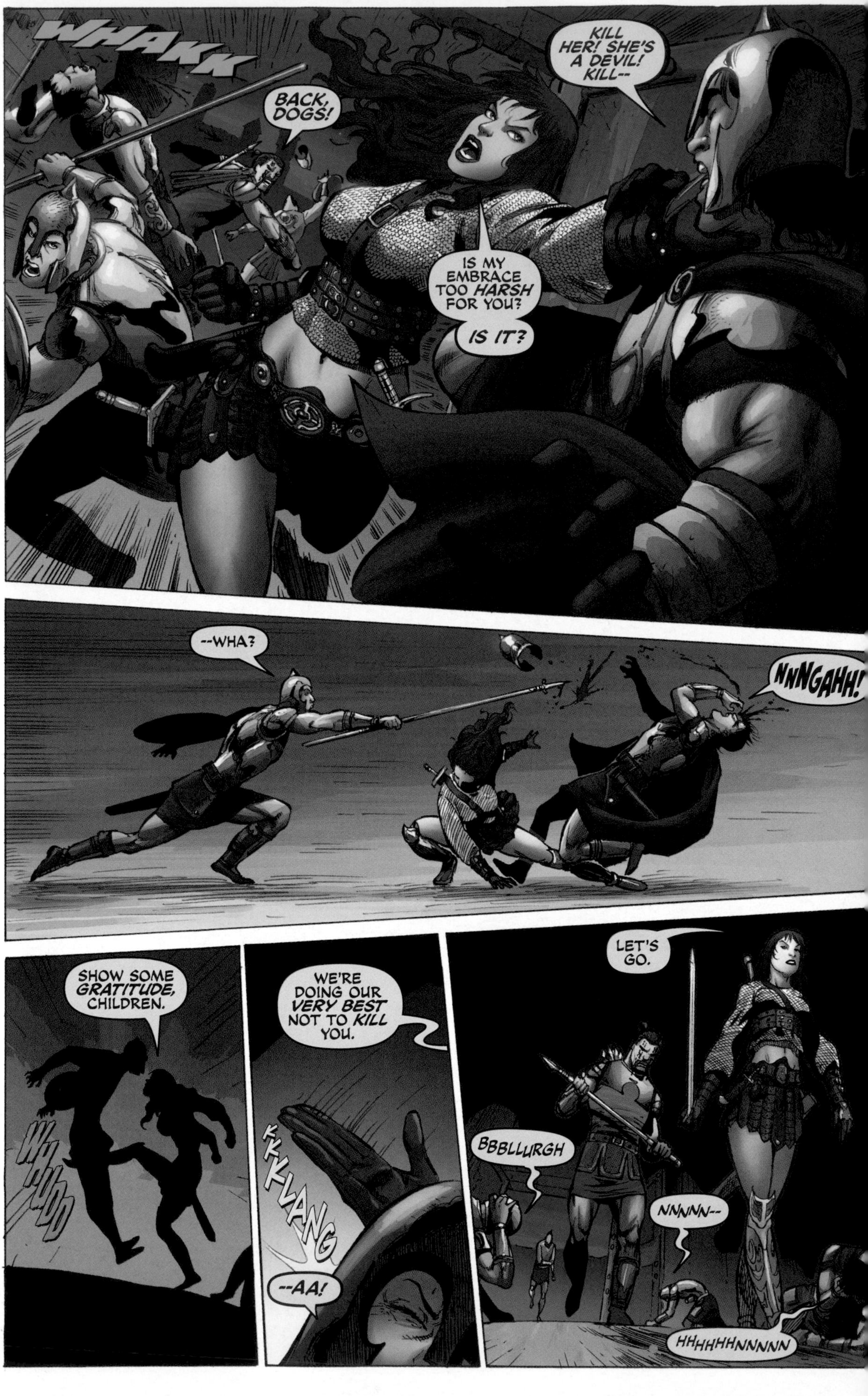
WHAKK
BACK, DOGS!
KILL HER! SHE'S A DEVIL! KILL--
IS MY EMBRACE TOO HARSH FOR YOU?
IS IT?
--WHA?
NNNGAHH!
SHOW SOME GRATITUDE, CHILDREN.
WHUDD
WE'RE DOING OUR VERY BEST NOT TO KILL YOU.
KKKLANG
--AA!
LET'S GO.
BBBLLURGH
NNNNN--
HHHHHHNNNNN

Sonja's anger cooled.

Something about the cathedral gave her pause. it's solemnity and silence, perhaps.

The room seemed home to grace.

...SWEET MITRA.

Precious metals and gems gleamed in the thin light.

Riches beyond imagining, adorning a monument to the elegant creatures immortalized in bronze, in marble, in gold.

FOUND SOMETHING. A HINGE MECHANISM, I THINK.

OPEN IT. *CAREFULLY.*

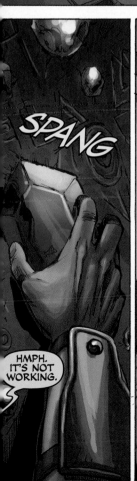

SPANG

HMPH. IT'S NOT WORKING.

TELL ME, WURKEST. ASIDE FROM THOSE TEMPLE WHORES, HAVE YOU SEEN ANY WOMEN IN THE CITY?

A FEW. NOT MANY. A TAVERN WENCH, SOME PEASANTS--

--BUT NO QUEEN, NO NOBLEWOMAN, NO LADIES IN WAITING.

I WONDER IF ALL THIS NEEDS IS A *WOMAN'S* TOUCH.

KA-LATCH

JULLAH'S CLAWS...

I'D SAY YOU FOUND IT.

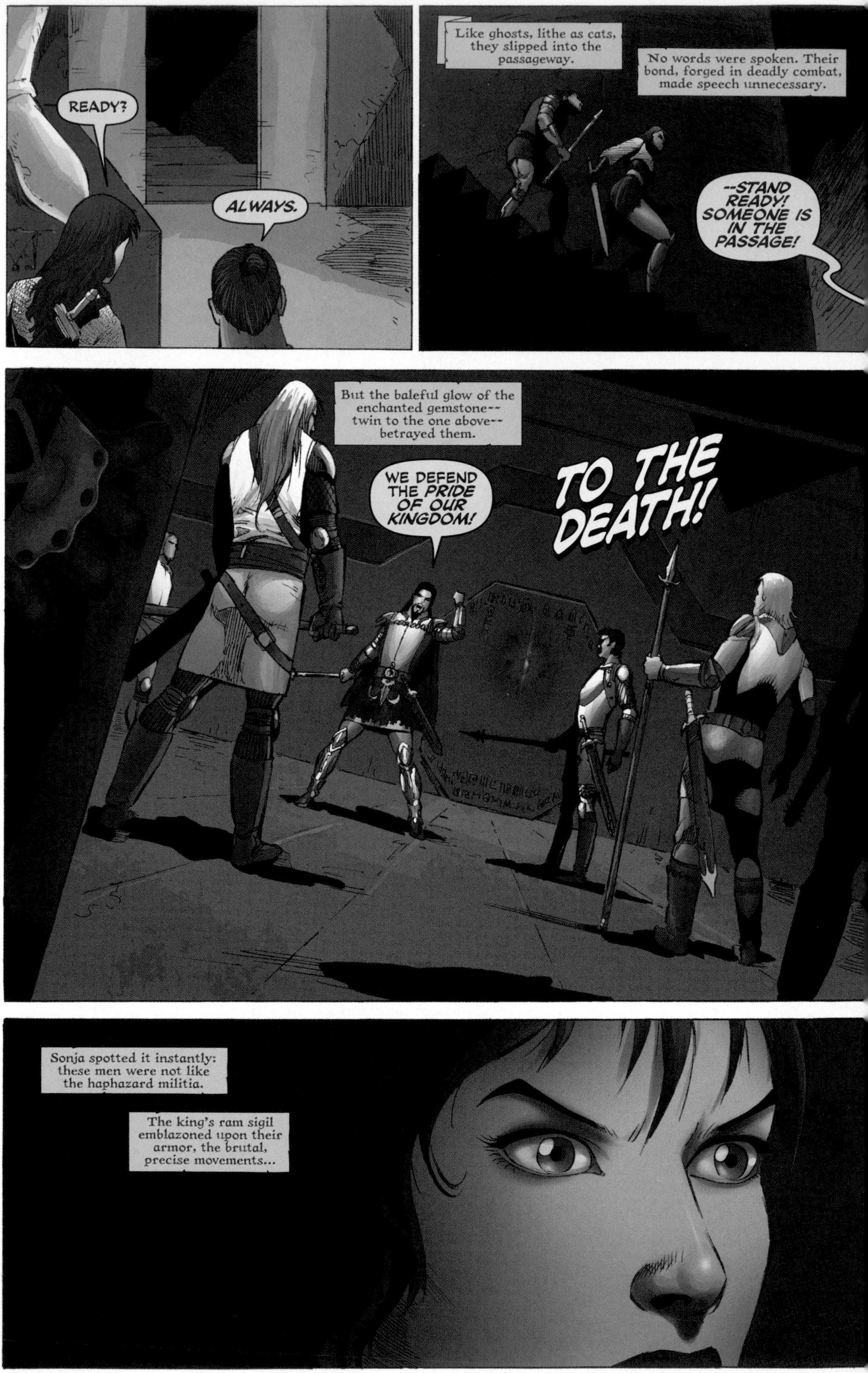
READY?
ALWAYS.
Like ghosts, lithe as cats, they slipped into the passageway.
No words were spoken. Their bond, forged in deadly combat, made speech unnecessary.
--STAND READY! SOMEONE IS IN THE PASSAGE!
But the baleful glow of the enchanted gemstone-- twin to the one above-- betrayed them.
WE DEFEND THE *PRIDE* OF OUR KINGDOM!
TO THE DEATH!
Sonja spotted it instantly: these men were not like the haphazard militia.
The king's ram sigil emblazoned upon their armor, the brutal, precise movements...

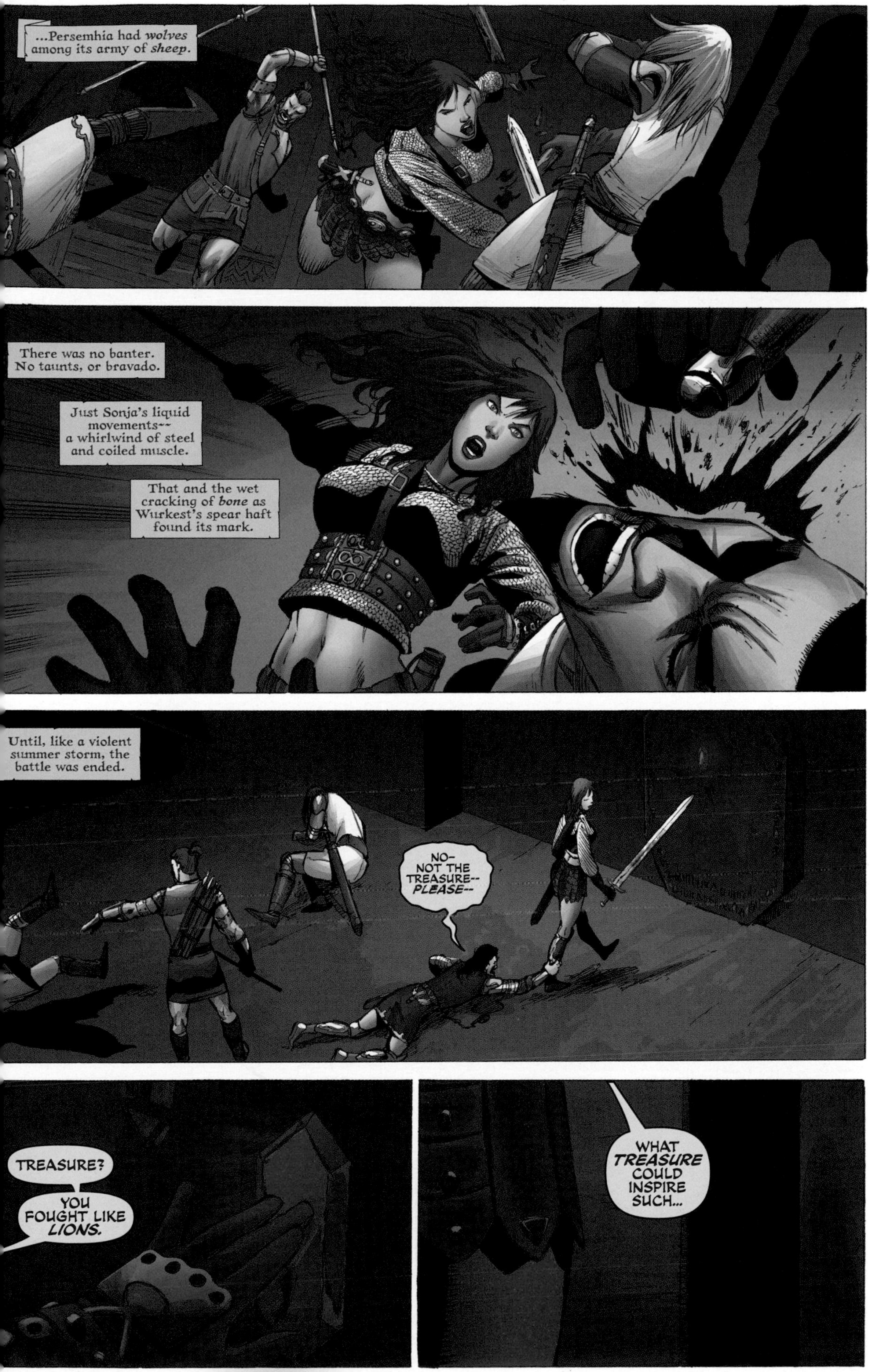
...Persemhia had *wolves* among its army of *sheep*.
There was no banter. No taunts, or bravado.
Just Sonja's liquid movements-- a whirlwind of steel and coiled muscle.
That and the wet cracking of *bone* as Wurkest's spear haft found its mark.
Until, like a violent summer storm, the battle was ended.
NO-- NOT THE TREASURE-- *PLEASE*--
TREASURE?
YOU FOUGHT LIKE *LIONS.*
WHAT *TREASURE* COULD INSPIRE SUCH...

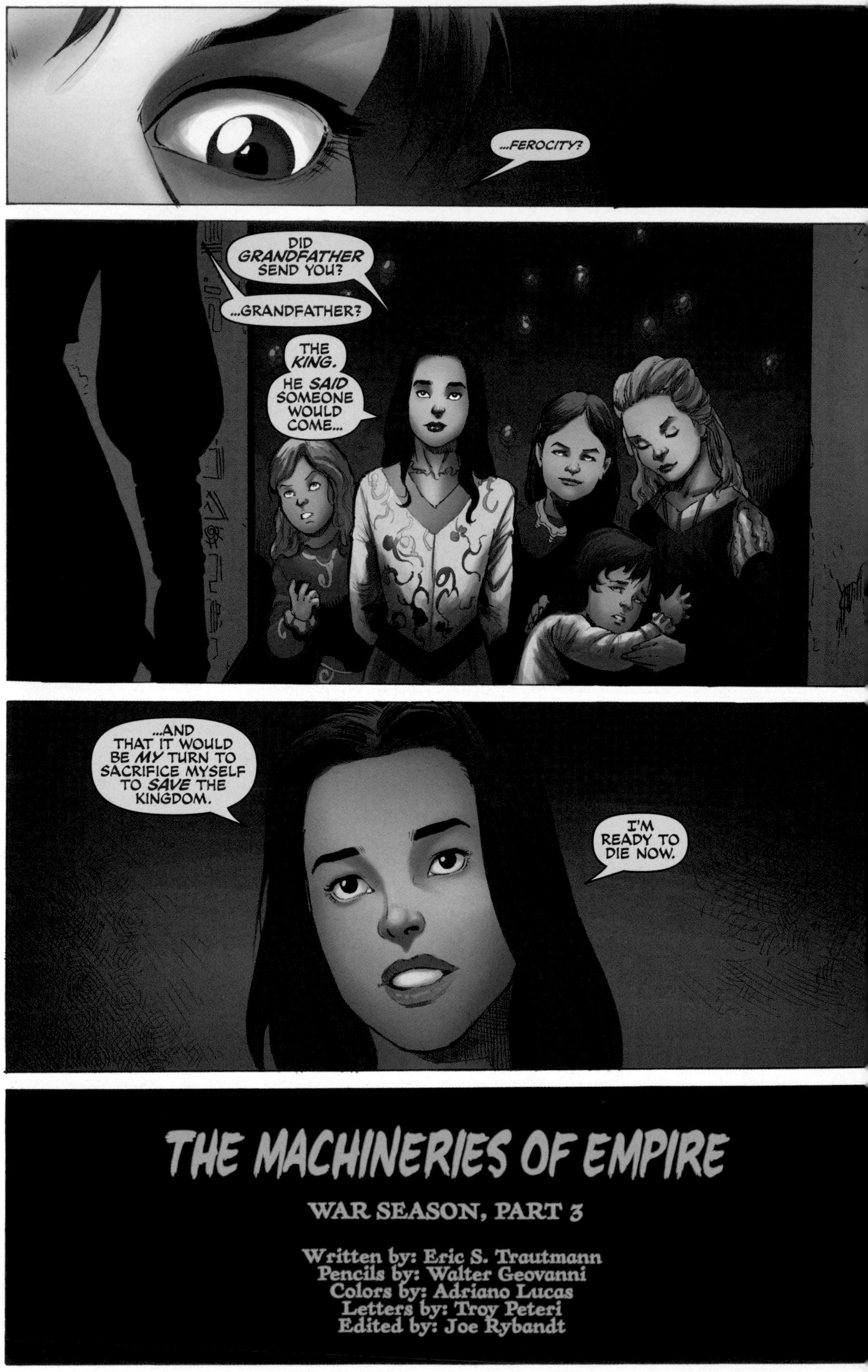
...FEROCITY?
DID GRANDFATHER SEND YOU?
...GRANDFATHER?
THE KING. HE SAID SOMEONE WOULD COME...
...AND THAT IT WOULD BE MY TURN TO SACRIFICE MYSELF TO SAVE THE KINGDOM.
I'M READY TO DIE NOW.

THE MACHINERIES OF EMPIRE

WAR SEASON, PART 3

Written by: Eric S. Trautmann
Pencils by: Walter Geovanni
Colors by: Adriano Lucas
Letters by: Troy Peteri
Edited by: Joe Rybandt

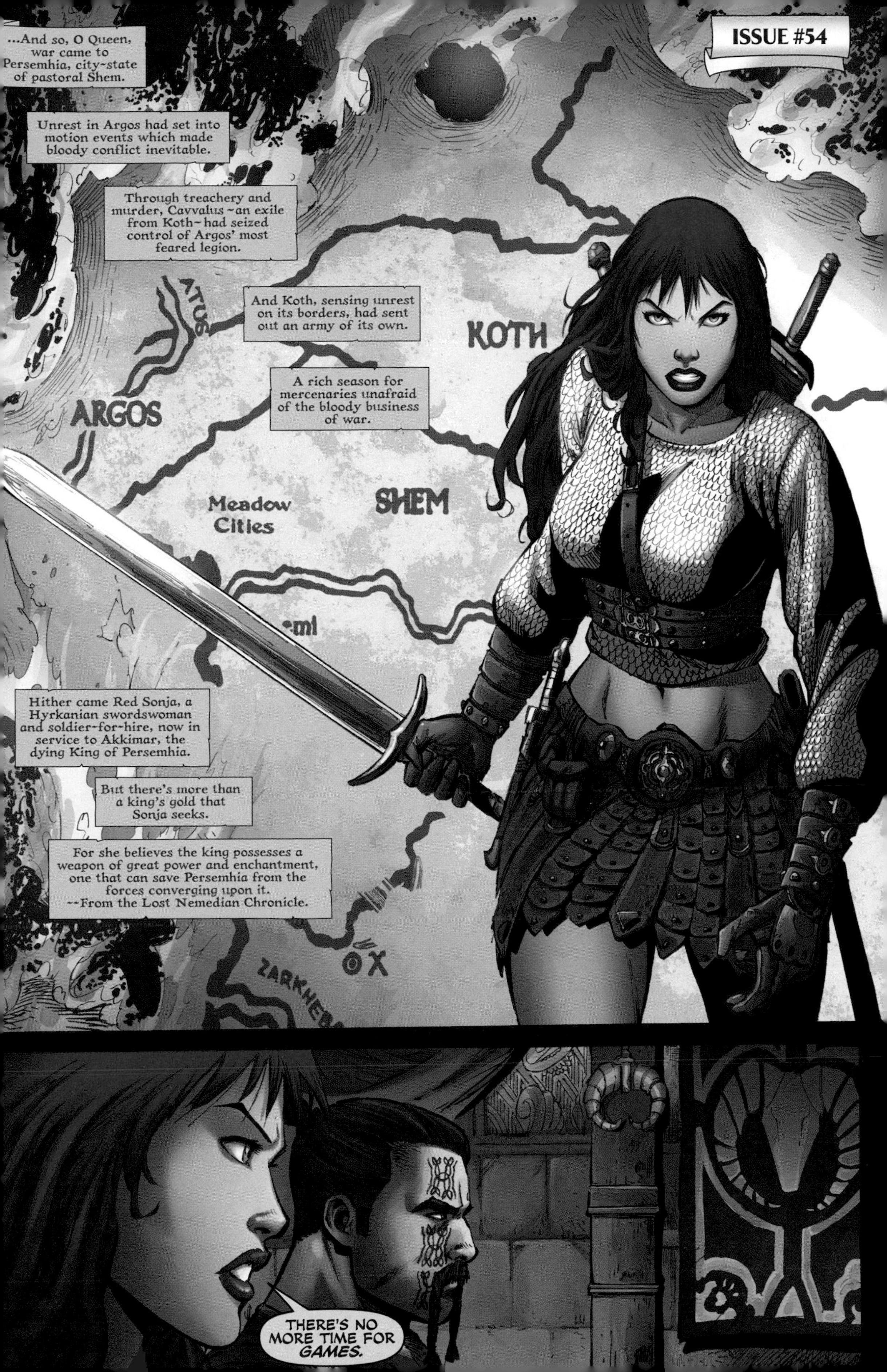
ISSUE #54
...And so, O Queen, war came to Persemhia, city~state of pastoral Shem.
Unrest in Argos had set into motion events which made bloody conflict inevitable.
Through treachery and murder, Cavvalus ~an exile from Koth~ had seized control of Argos' most feared legion.
ATUS
And Koth, sensing unrest on its borders, had sent out an army of its own.
KOTH
A rich season for mercenaries unafraid of the bloody business of war.
ARGOS
Meadow Cities
SHEM
Hither came Red Sonja, a Hyrkanian swordswoman and soldier~for~hire, now in service to Akkimar, the dying King of Persemhia.
But there's more than a king's gold that Sonja seeks.
For she believes the king possesses a weapon of great power and enchantment, one that can save Persemhia from the forces converging upon it.
--From the Lost Nemedian Chronicle.
OX
THERE'S NO MORE TIME FOR *GAMES.*

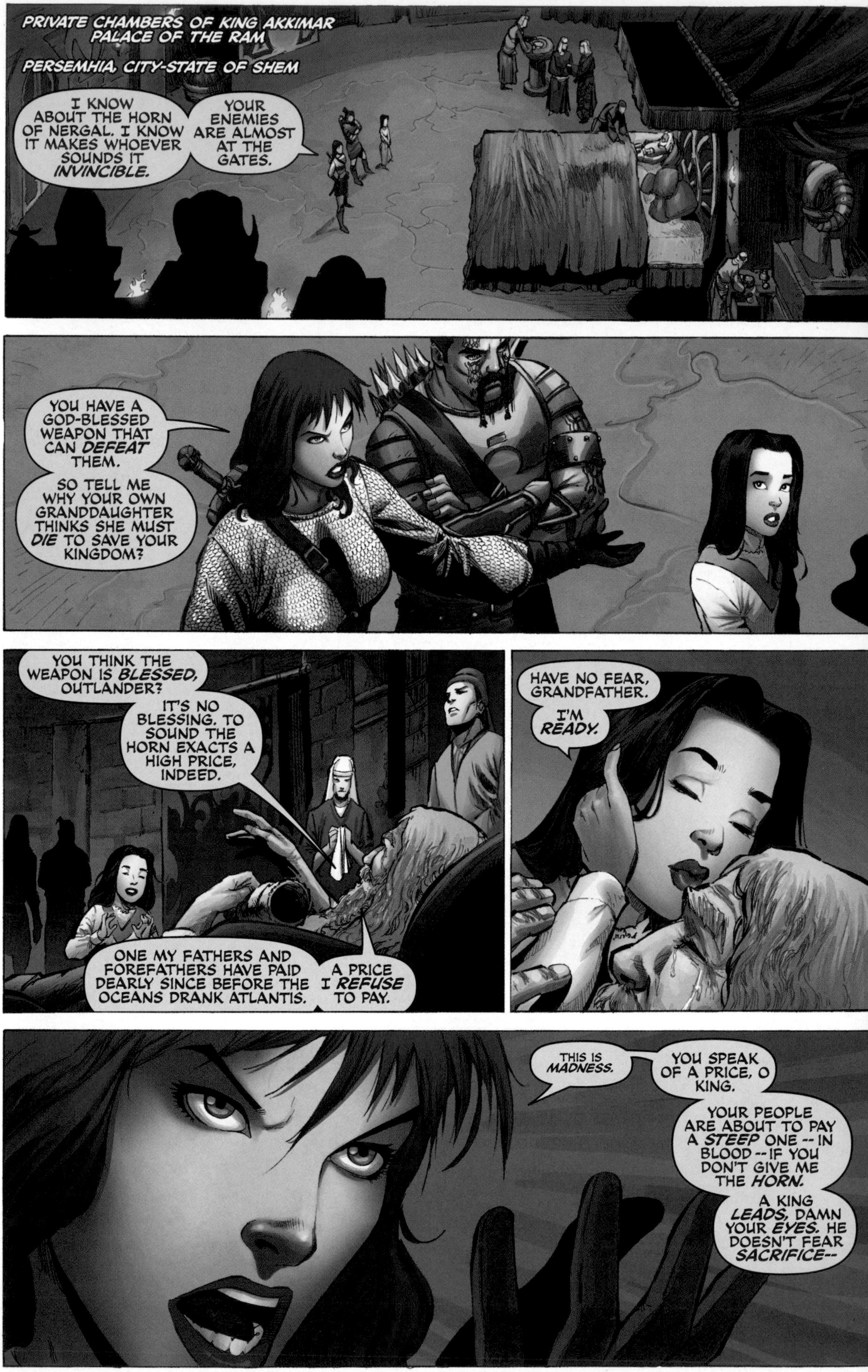
PRIVATE CHAMBERS OF KING AKKIMAR
PALACE OF THE RAM
PERSEMHIA, CITY-STATE OF SHEM
I KNOW ABOUT THE HORN OF NERGAL. I KNOW IT MAKES WHOEVER SOUNDS IT INVINCIBLE.
YOUR ENEMIES ARE ALMOST AT THE GATES.
YOU HAVE A GOD-BLESSED WEAPON THAT CAN DEFEAT THEM.
SO TELL ME WHY YOUR OWN GRANDDAUGHTER THINKS SHE MUST DIE TO SAVE YOUR KINGDOM?
YOU THINK THE WEAPON IS BLESSED, OUTLANDER?
IT'S NO BLESSING. TO SOUND THE HORN EXACTS A HIGH PRICE, INDEED.
ONE MY FATHERS AND FOREFATHERS HAVE PAID DEARLY SINCE BEFORE THE OCEANS DRANK ATLANTIS.
A PRICE I REFUSE TO PAY.
HAVE NO FEAR, GRANDFATHER.
I'M READY.
THIS IS MADNESS.
YOU SPEAK OF A PRICE, O KING.
YOUR PEOPLE ARE ABOUT TO PAY A STEEP ONE -- IN BLOOD -- IF YOU DON'T GIVE ME THE HORN.
A KING LEADS, DAMN YOUR EYES. HE DOESN'T FEAR SACRIFICE--

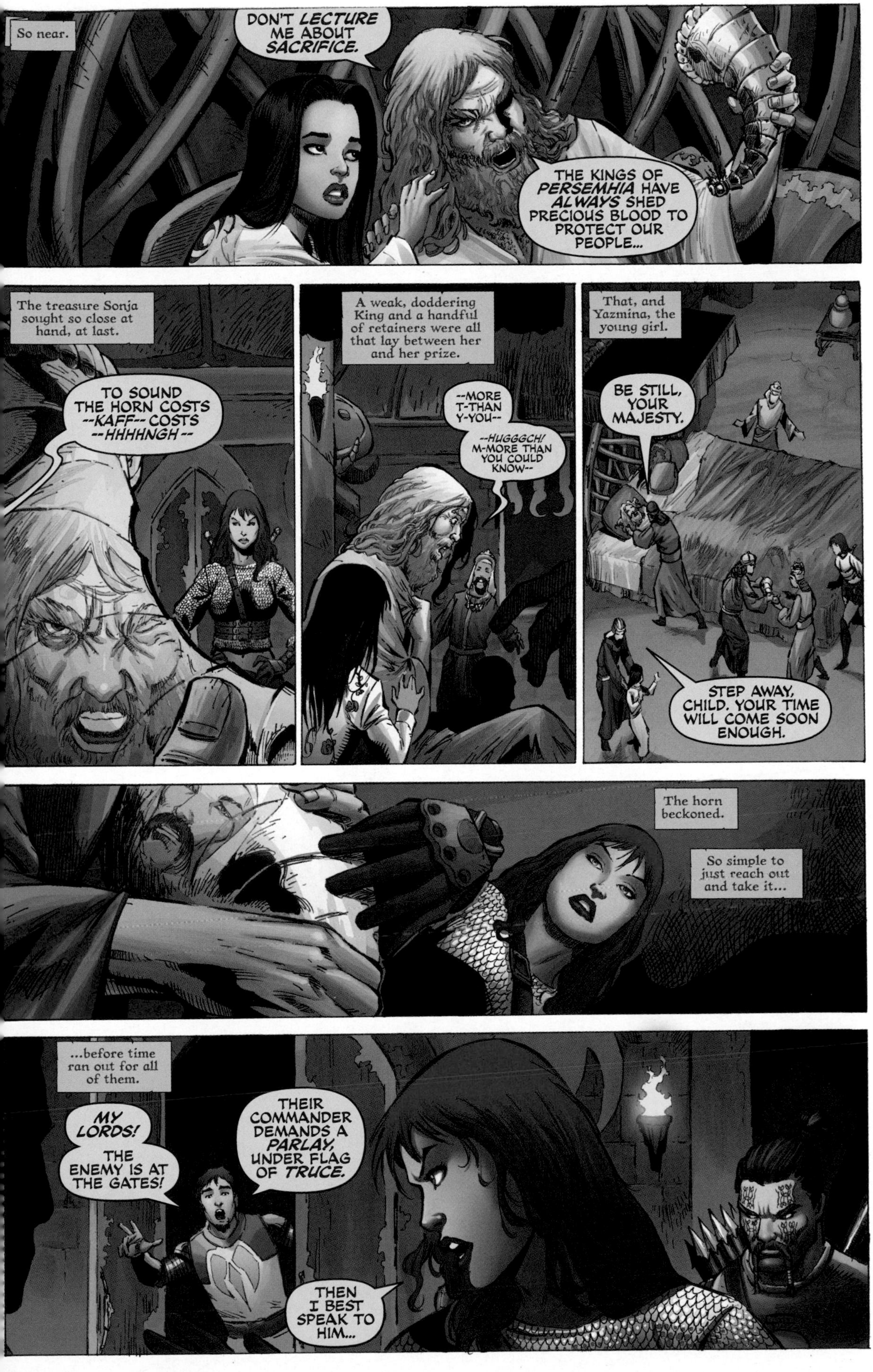
So near.
DON'T LECTURE ME ABOUT SACRIFICE.
THE KINGS OF PERSEMHIA HAVE ALWAYS SHED PRECIOUS BLOOD TO PROTECT OUR PEOPLE...
The treasure Sonja sought so close at hand, at last.
TO SOUND THE HORN COSTS --KAFF-- COSTS --HHHHNGH--
A weak, doddering King and a handful of retainers were all that lay between her and her prize.
--MORE T-THAN Y-YOU--
--HUGGGCH! M-MORE THAN YOU COULD KNOW--
That, and Yazmina, the young girl.
BE STILL, YOUR MAJESTY.
STEP AWAY, CHILD. YOUR TIME WILL COME SOON ENOUGH.
The horn beckoned.
So simple to just reach out and take it...
...before time ran out for all of them.
MY LORDS!
THE ENEMY IS AT THE GATES!
THEIR COMMANDER DEMANDS A PARLAY, UNDER FLAG OF TRUCE.
THEN I BEST SPEAK TO HIM...

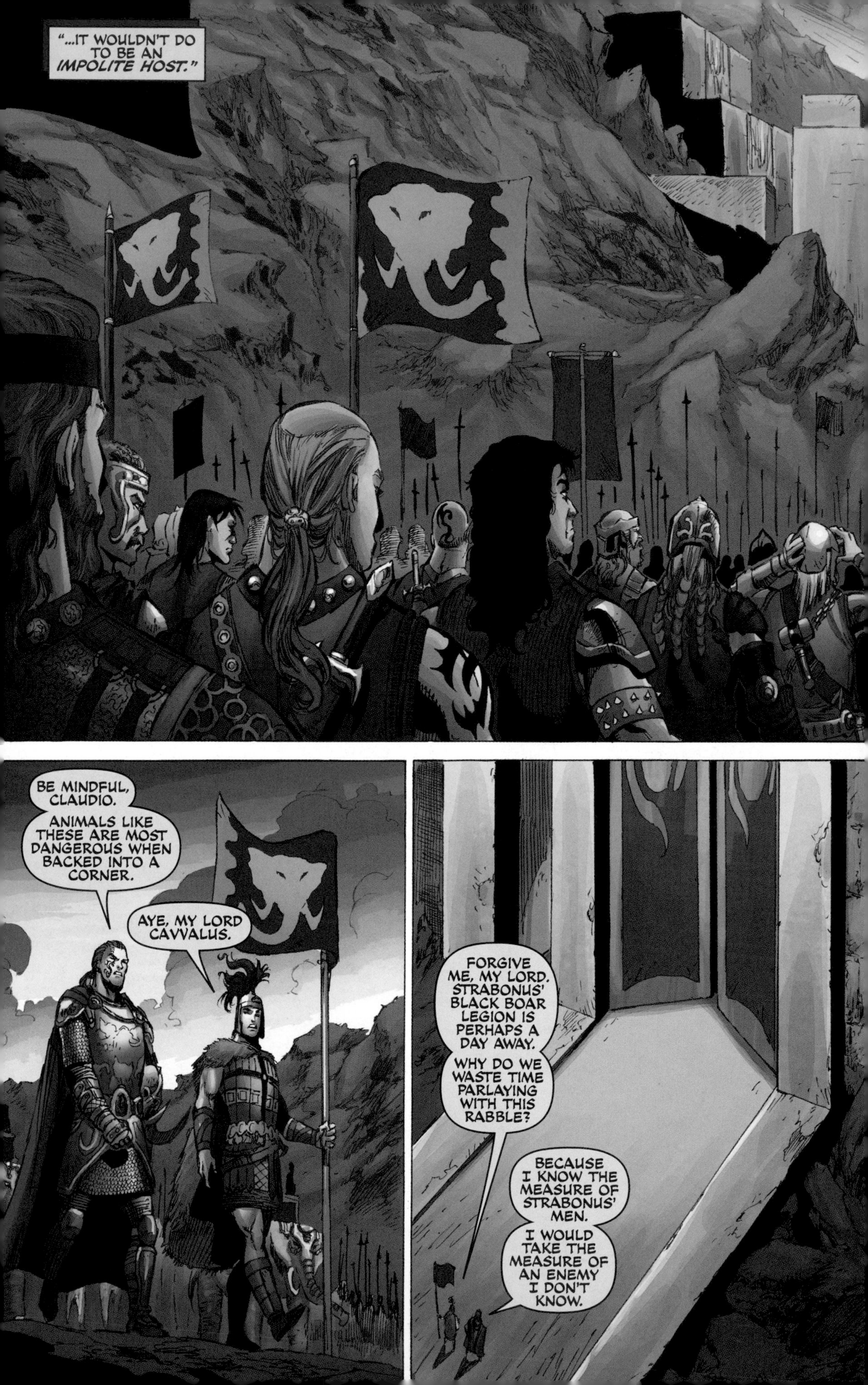
"...IT WOULDN'T DO TO BE AN *IMPOLITE HOST.*"
BE MINDFUL, CLAUDIO.
ANIMALS LIKE THESE ARE MOST DANGEROUS WHEN BACKED INTO A CORNER.
AYE, MY LORD CAVVALUS.
FORGIVE ME, MY LORD. STRABONUS' BLACK BOAR LEGION IS PERHAPS A DAY AWAY.
WHY DO WE WASTE TIME PARLAYING WITH THIS RABBLE?
BECAUSE I KNOW THE MEASURE OF STRABONUS' MEN.
I WOULD TAKE THE MEASURE OF AN ENEMY I DON'T KNOW.

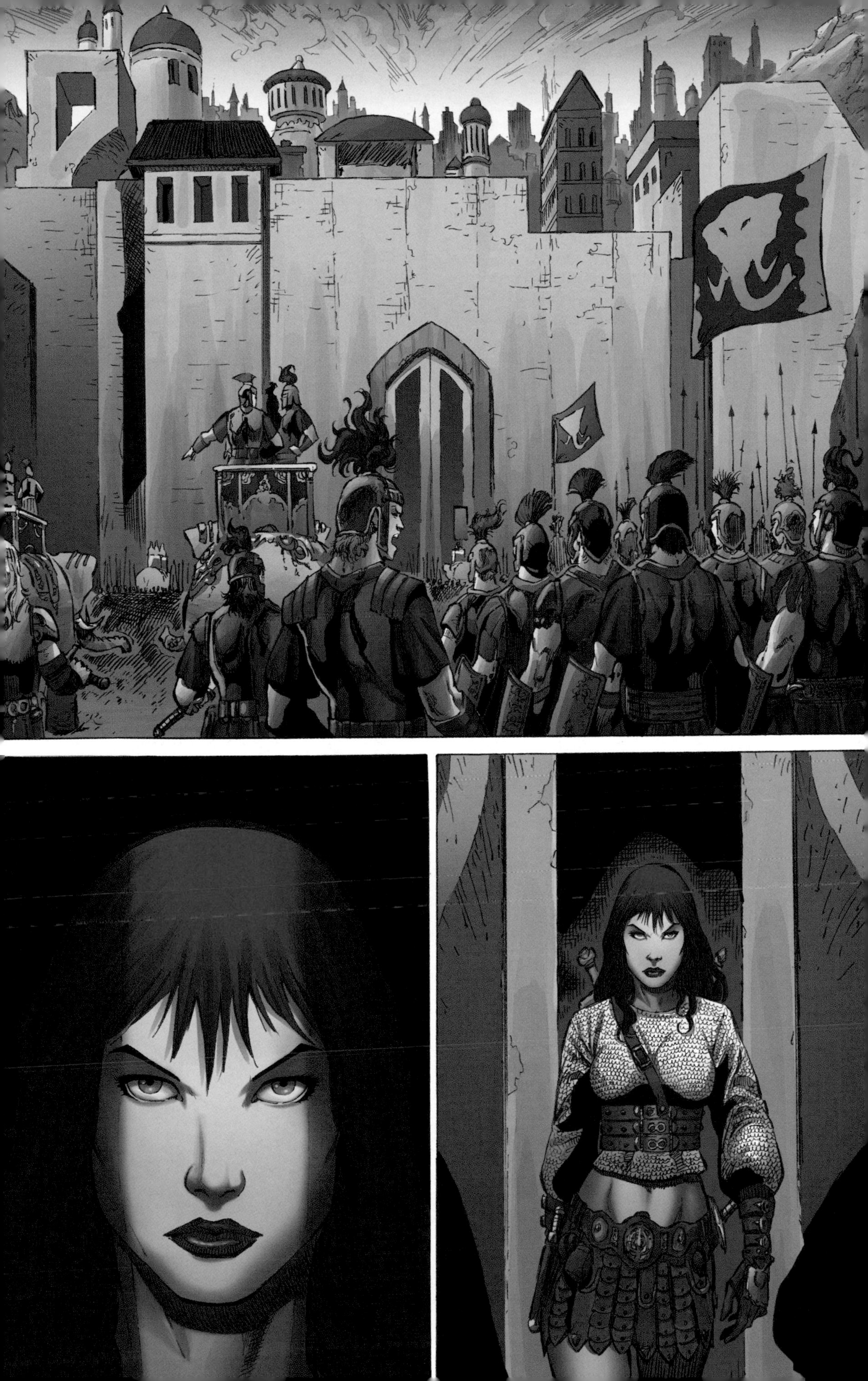

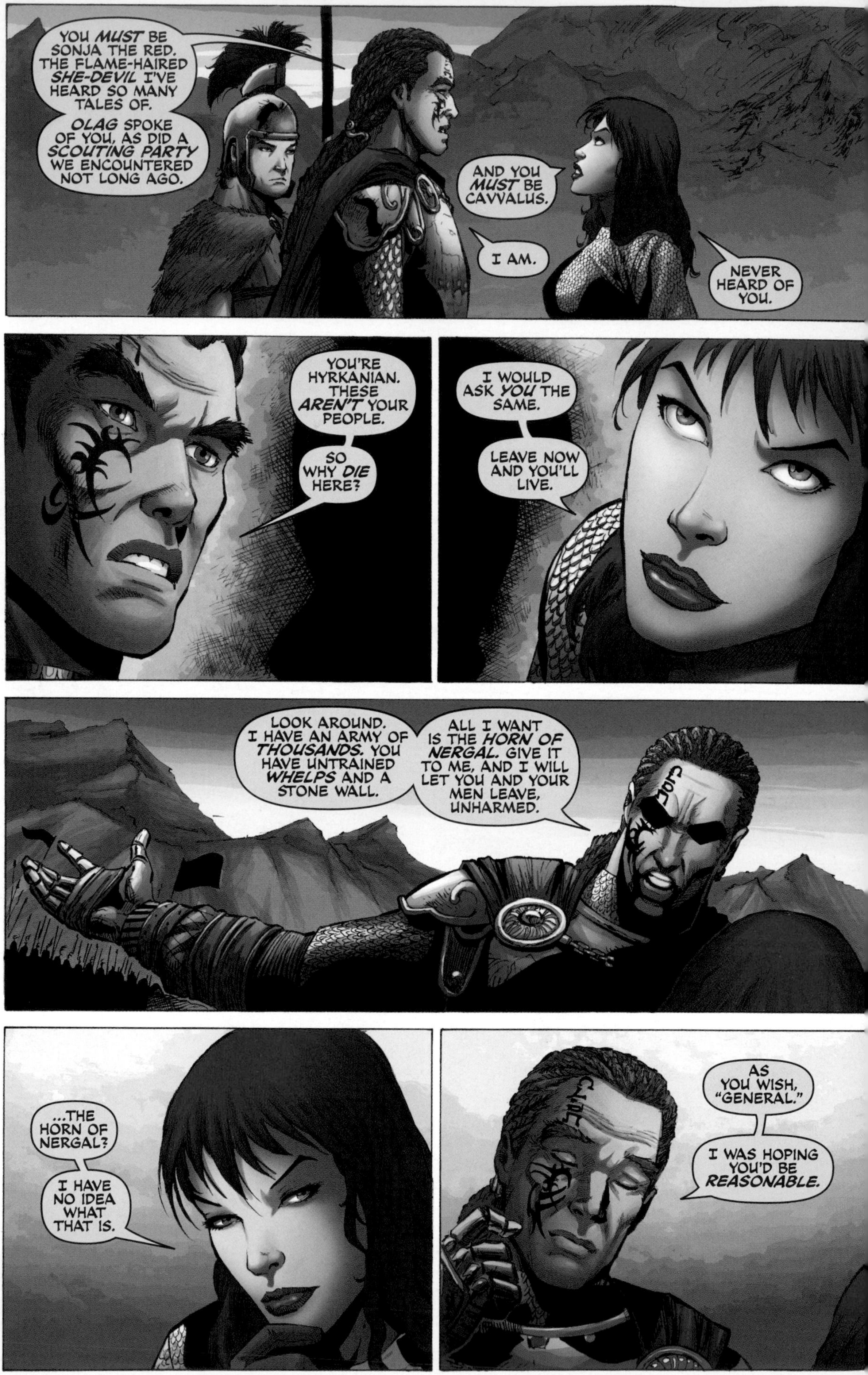

YOU MUST BE SONJA THE RED. THE FLAME-HAIRED SHE-DEVIL I'VE HEARD SO MANY TALES OF.
OLAG SPOKE OF YOU, AS DID A SCOUTING PARTY WE ENCOUNTERED NOT LONG AGO.
AND YOU MUST BE CAVVALUS.
I AM.
NEVER HEARD OF YOU.
YOU'RE HYRKANIAN. THESE AREN'T YOUR PEOPLE.
SO WHY DIE HERE?
I WOULD ASK YOU THE SAME.
LEAVE NOW AND YOU'LL LIVE.
LOOK AROUND. I HAVE AN ARMY OF THOUSANDS. YOU HAVE UNTRAINED WHELPS AND A STONE WALL.
ALL I WANT IS THE HORN OF NERGAL. GIVE IT TO ME, AND I WILL LET YOU AND YOUR MEN LEAVE, UNHARMED.
...THE HORN OF NERGAL?
I HAVE NO IDEA WHAT THAT IS.
AS YOU WISH, "GENERAL."
I WAS HOPING YOU'D BE REASONABLE.

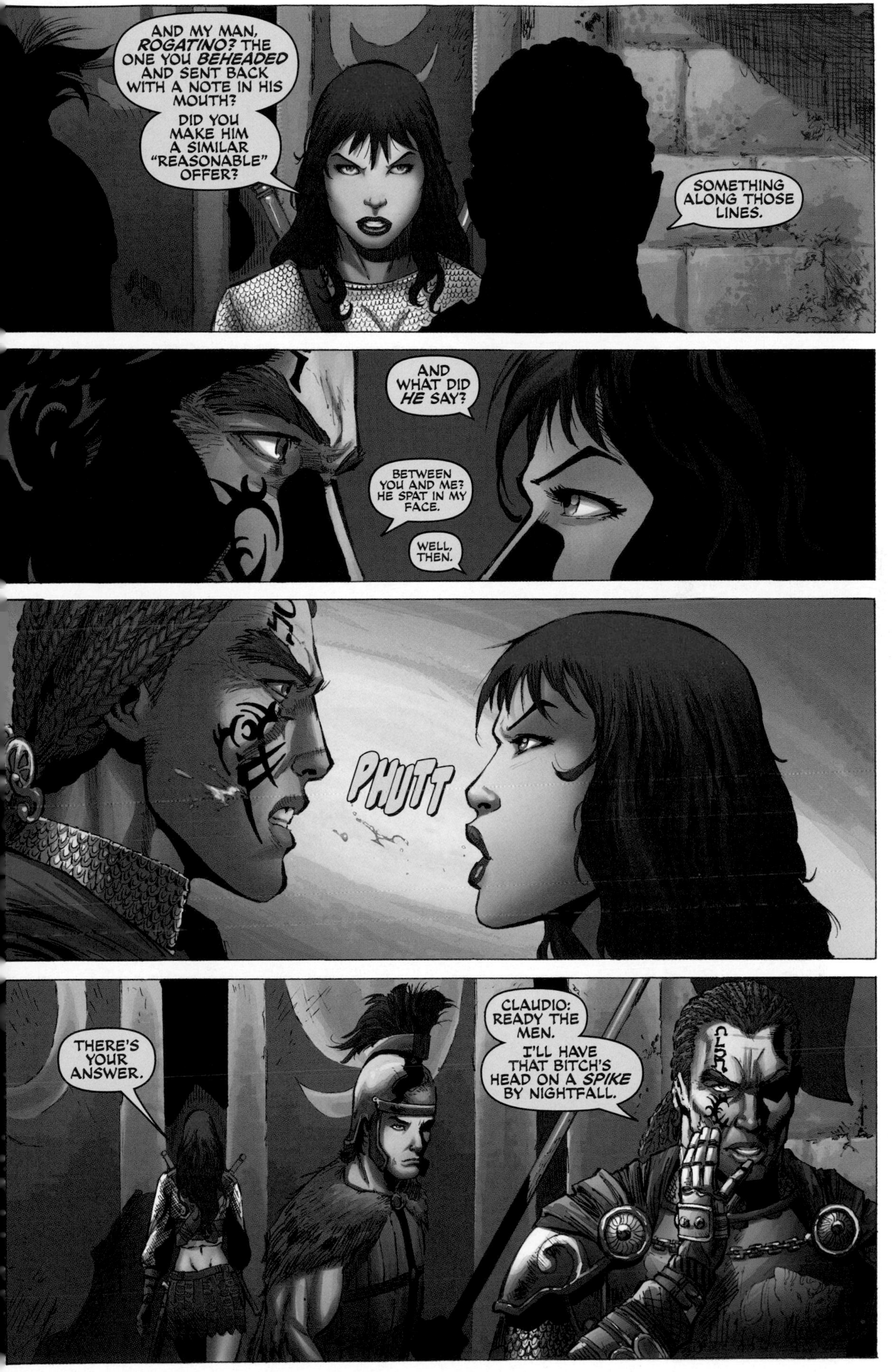

AND MY MAN, *ROGATINO?* THE ONE YOU *BEHEADED* AND SENT BACK WITH A NOTE IN HIS MOUTH?
DID YOU MAKE HIM A SIMILAR "REASONABLE" OFFER?
SOMETHING ALONG THOSE LINES.
AND WHAT DID *HE* SAY?
BETWEEN YOU AND ME? HE SPAT IN MY FACE.
WELL, THEN.
PHUTT
THERE'S YOUR ANSWER.
CLAUDIO: READY THE MEN.
I'LL HAVE THAT BITCH'S HEAD ON A *SPIKE* BY NIGHTFALL.

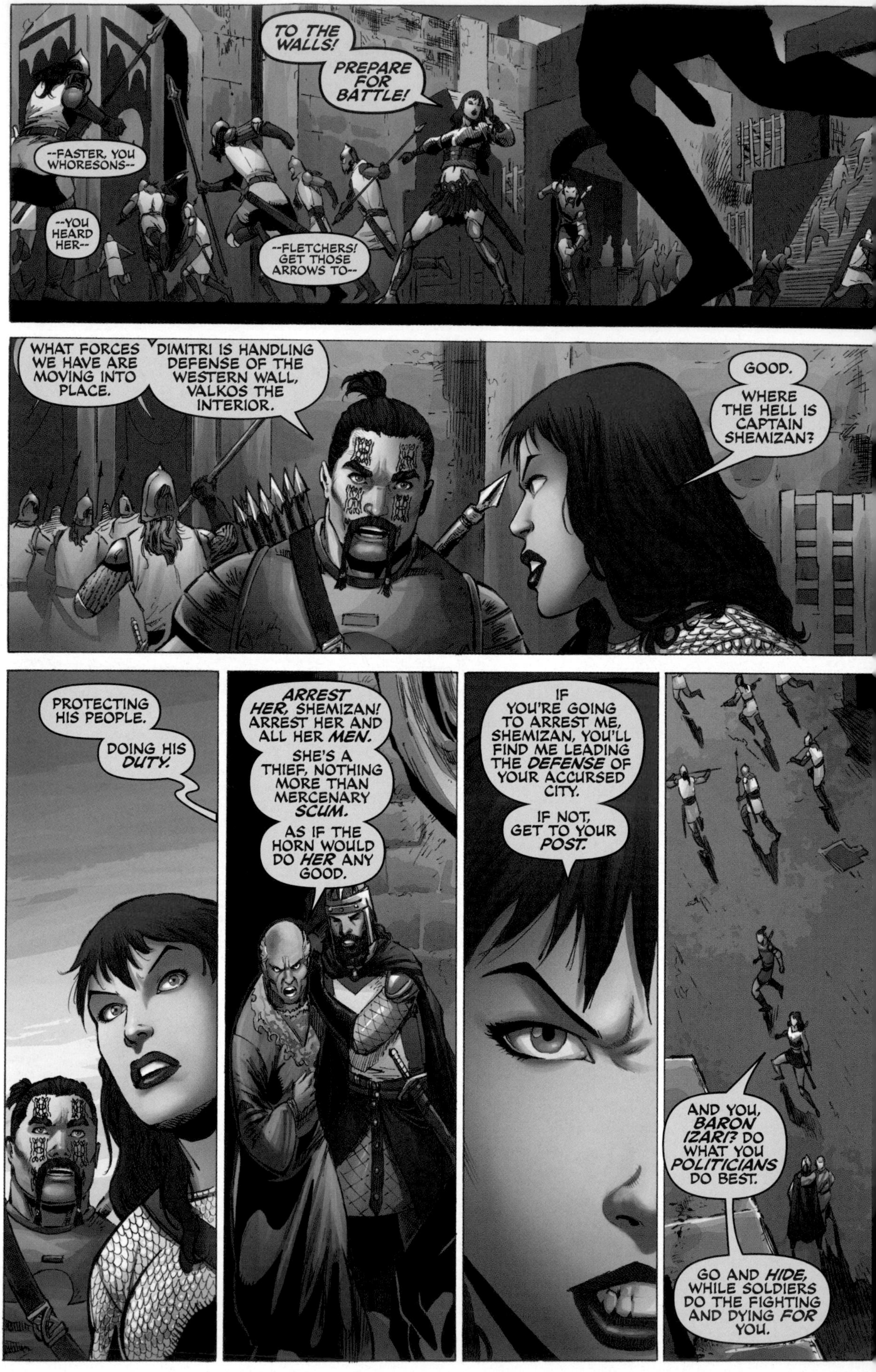
TO THE WALLS!
PREPARE FOR BATTLE!
--FASTER, YOU WHORESONS--
--YOU HEARD HER--
--FLETCHERS! GET THOSE ARROWS TO--
WHAT FORCES WE HAVE ARE MOVING INTO PLACE.
DIMITRI IS HANDLING DEFENSE OF THE WESTERN WALL, VALKOS THE INTERIOR.
GOOD.
WHERE THE HELL IS CAPTAIN SHEMIZAN?
PROTECTING HIS PEOPLE.
DOING HIS DUTY.
ARREST HER, SHEMIZAN! ARREST HER AND ALL HER MEN.
SHE'S A THIEF, NOTHING MORE THAN MERCENARY SCUM.
AS IF THE HORN WOULD DO HER ANY GOOD.
IF YOU'RE GOING TO ARREST ME, SHEMIZAN, YOU'LL FIND ME LEADING THE DEFENSE OF YOUR ACCURSED CITY.
IF NOT, GET TO YOUR POST.
AND YOU, BARON IZARI? DO WHAT YOU POLITICIANS DO BEST.
GO AND HIDE, WHILE SOLDIERS DO THE FIGHTING AND DYING FOR YOU.

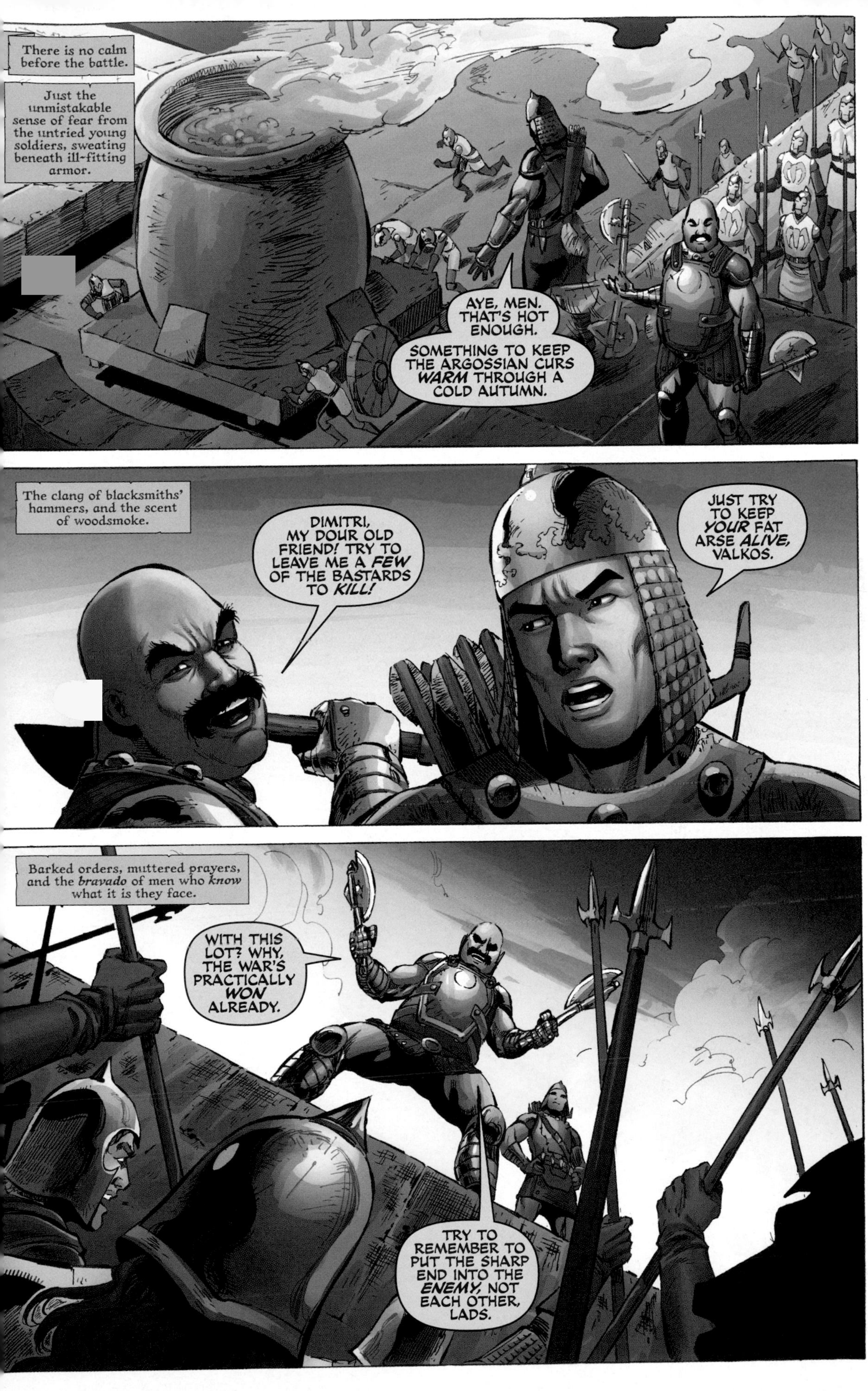
There is no calm before the battle.
Just the unmistakable sense of fear from the untried young soldiers, sweating beneath ill-fitting armor.
AYE, MEN. THAT'S HOT ENOUGH.
SOMETHING TO KEEP THE ARGOSSIAN CURS *WARM* THROUGH A COLD AUTUMN.
The clang of blacksmiths' hammers, and the scent of woodsmoke.
DIMITRI, MY DOUR OLD FRIEND! TRY TO LEAVE ME A *FEW* OF THE BASTARDS TO *KILL!*
JUST TRY TO KEEP *YOUR* FAT ARSE *ALIVE,* VALKOS.
Barked orders, muttered prayers, and the *bravado* of men who *know* what it is they face.
WITH THIS LOT? WHY, THE WAR'S PRACTICALLY *WON* ALREADY.
TRY TO REMEMBER TO PUT THE SHARP END INTO THE *ENEMY,* NOT EACH OTHER, LADS.

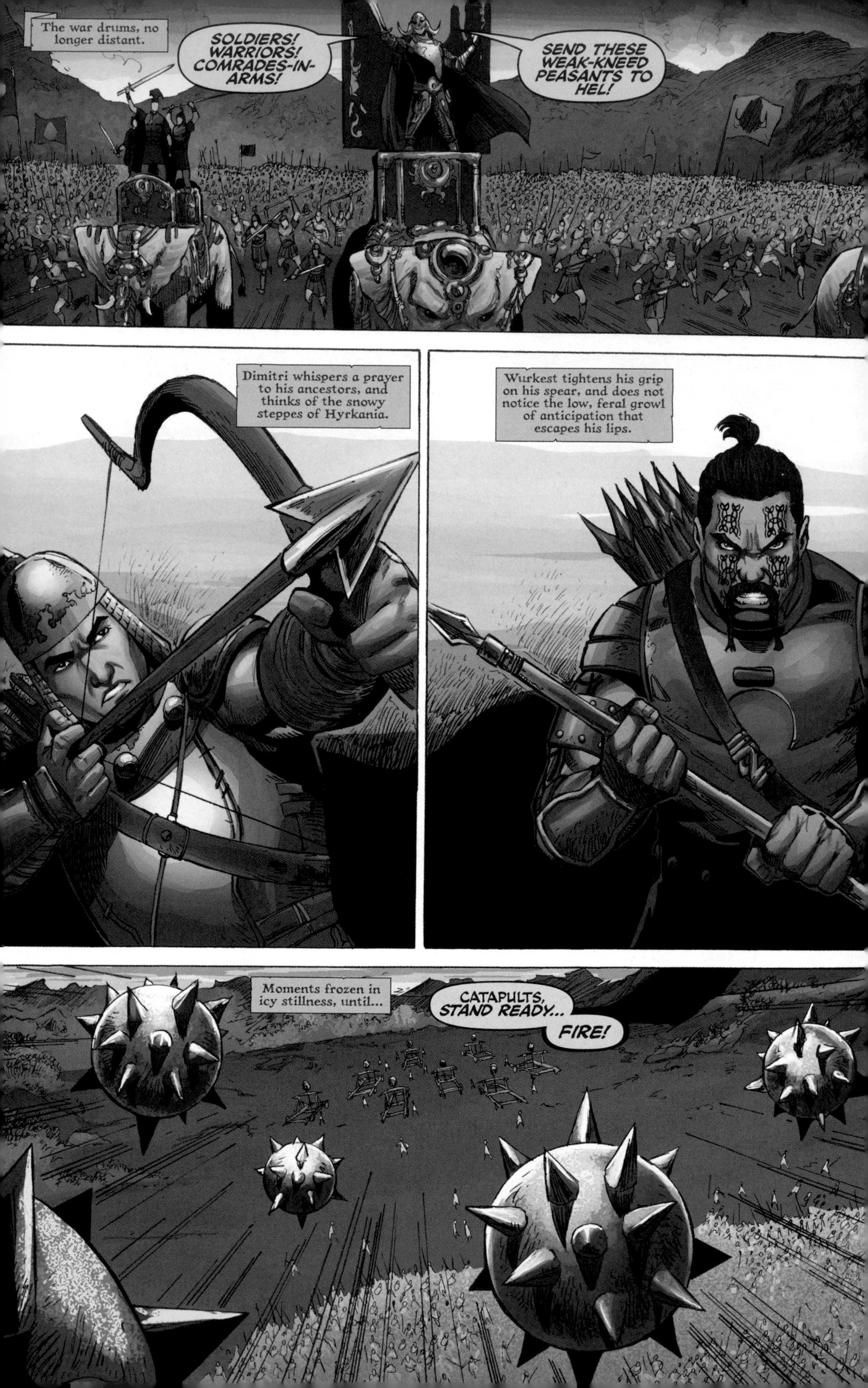

The war drums, no longer distant.
SOLDIERS! WARRIORS! COMRADES-IN-ARMS!
SEND THESE WEAK-KNEED PEASANTS TO HEL!
Dimitri whispers a prayer to his ancestors, and thinks of the snowy steppes of Hyrkania.
Wurkest tightens his grip on his spear, and does not notice the low, feral growl of anticipation that escapes his lips.
Moments frozen in icy stillness, until...
CATAPULTS, STAND READY...
FIRE!

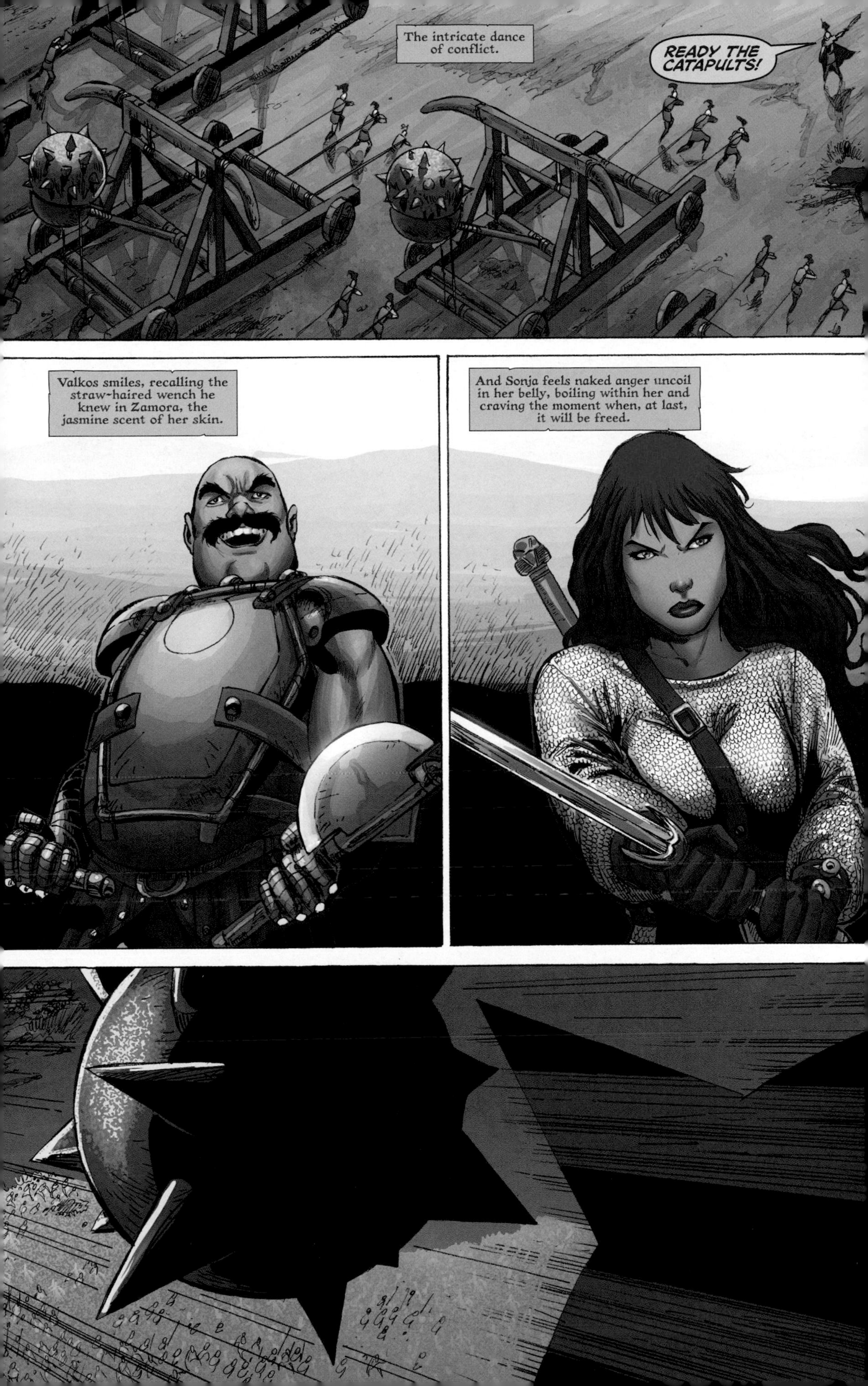
The intricate dance of conflict.
READY THE CATAPULTS!
Valkos smiles, recalling the straw-haired wench he knew in Zamora, the jasmine scent of her skin.
And Sonja feels naked anger uncoil in her belly, boiling within her and craving the moment when, at last, it will be freed.

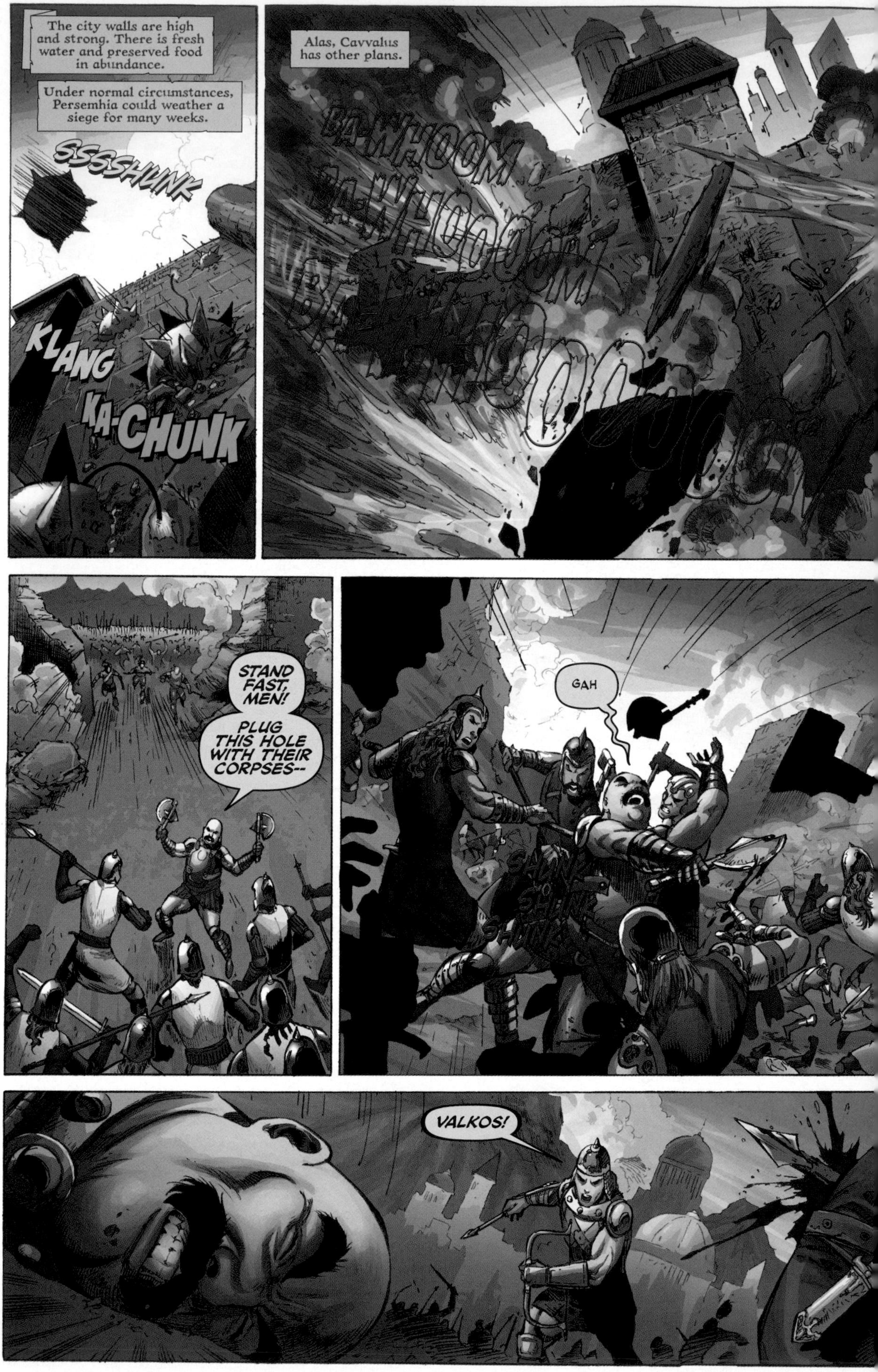

The city walls are high and strong. There is fresh water and preserved food in abundance.
Under normal circumstances, Persemhia could weather a siege for many weeks.
SSSSHUNK
KLANG
KA-CHUNK
Alas, Cavvalus has other plans.
BA-WHOOM
STAND FAST, MEN! PLUG THIS HOLE WITH THEIR CORPSES--
GAH
VALKOS!

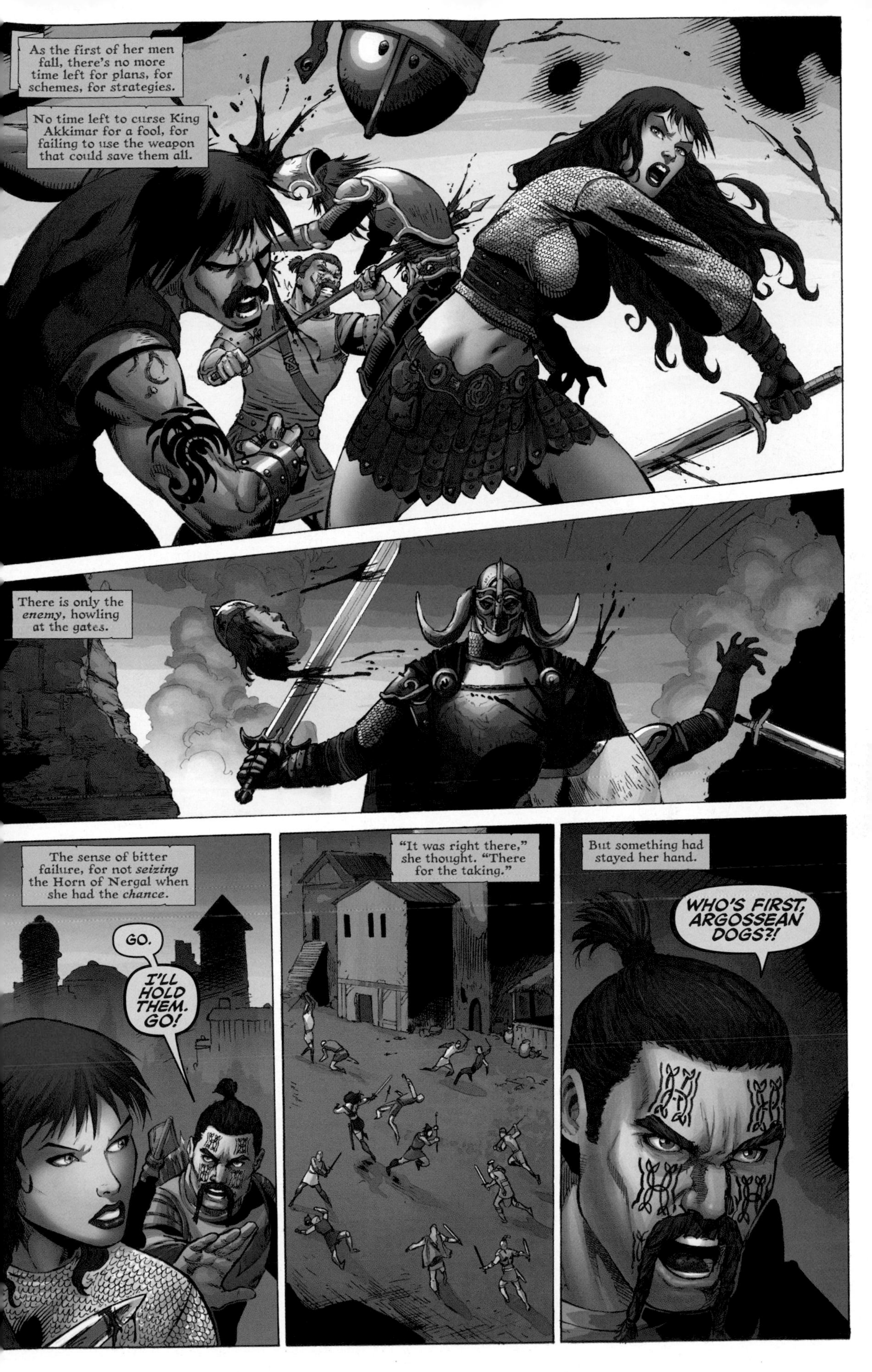
As the first of her men fall, there's no more time left for plans, for schemes, for strategies.
No time left to curse King Akkimar for a fool, for failing to use the weapon that could save them all.
There is only the *enemy*, howling at the gates.
The sense of bitter failure, for not *seizing* the Horn of Nergal when she had the *chance*.
GO.
I'LL HOLD THEM. GO!
"It was right there," she thought. "There for the taking."
But something had stayed her hand.
WHO'S FIRST, ARGOSSEAN DOGS?!

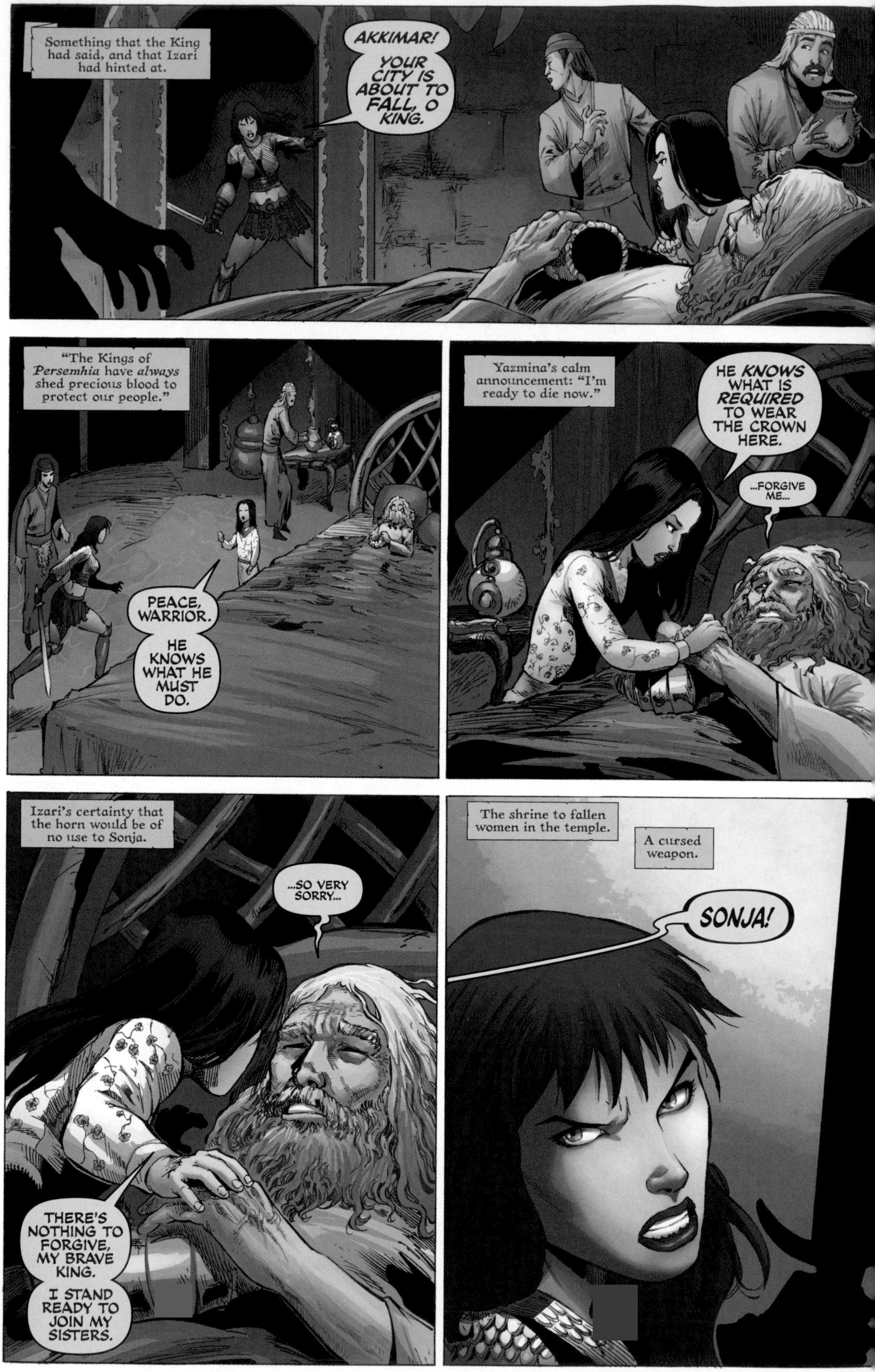
Something that the King had said, and that Izari had hinted at.
AKKIMAR! YOUR CITY IS ABOUT TO FALL, O KING.
"The Kings of *Persemhia* have *always* shed precious blood to protect our people."
PEACE, WARRIOR.
HE KNOWS WHAT HE MUST DO.
Yazmina's calm announcement: "I'm ready to die now."
HE *KNOWS* WHAT IS *REQUIRED* TO WEAR THE CROWN HERE.
...FORGIVE ME...
Izari's certainty that the horn would be of no use to Sonja.
...SO VERY SORRY...
THERE'S NOTHING TO FORGIVE, MY BRAVE KING.
I STAND READY TO JOIN MY SISTERS.
The shrine to fallen women in the temple.
A cursed weapon.
SONJA!

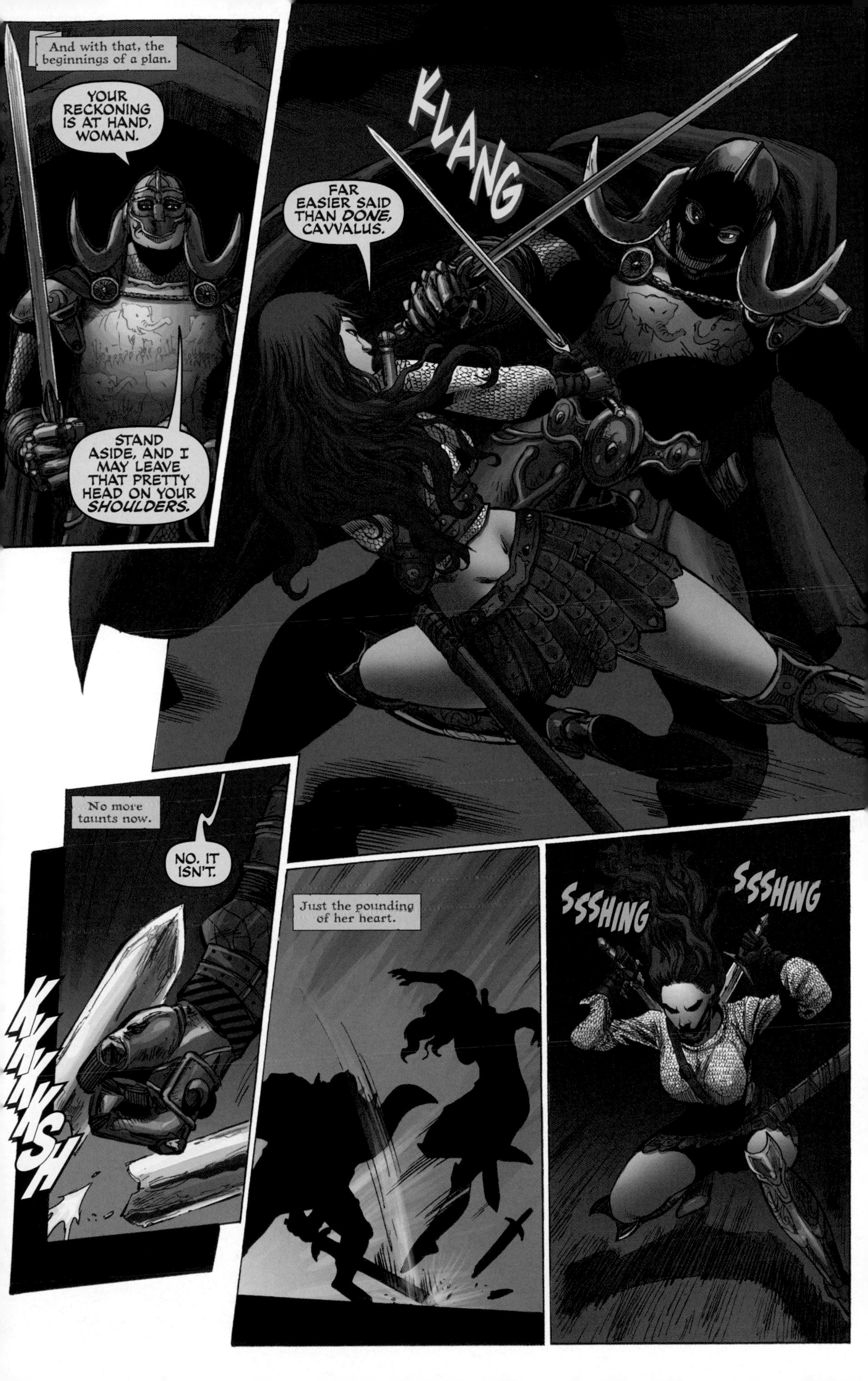
And with that, the beginnings of a plan.
YOUR RECKONING IS AT HAND, WOMAN.
STAND ASIDE, AND I MAY LEAVE THAT PRETTY HEAD ON YOUR SHOULDERS.
KLANG
FAR EASIER SAID THAN DONE, CAVVALUS.
No more taunts now.
NO. IT ISN'T.
KKKKSH
Just the pounding of her heart.
SSSHING
SSSHING

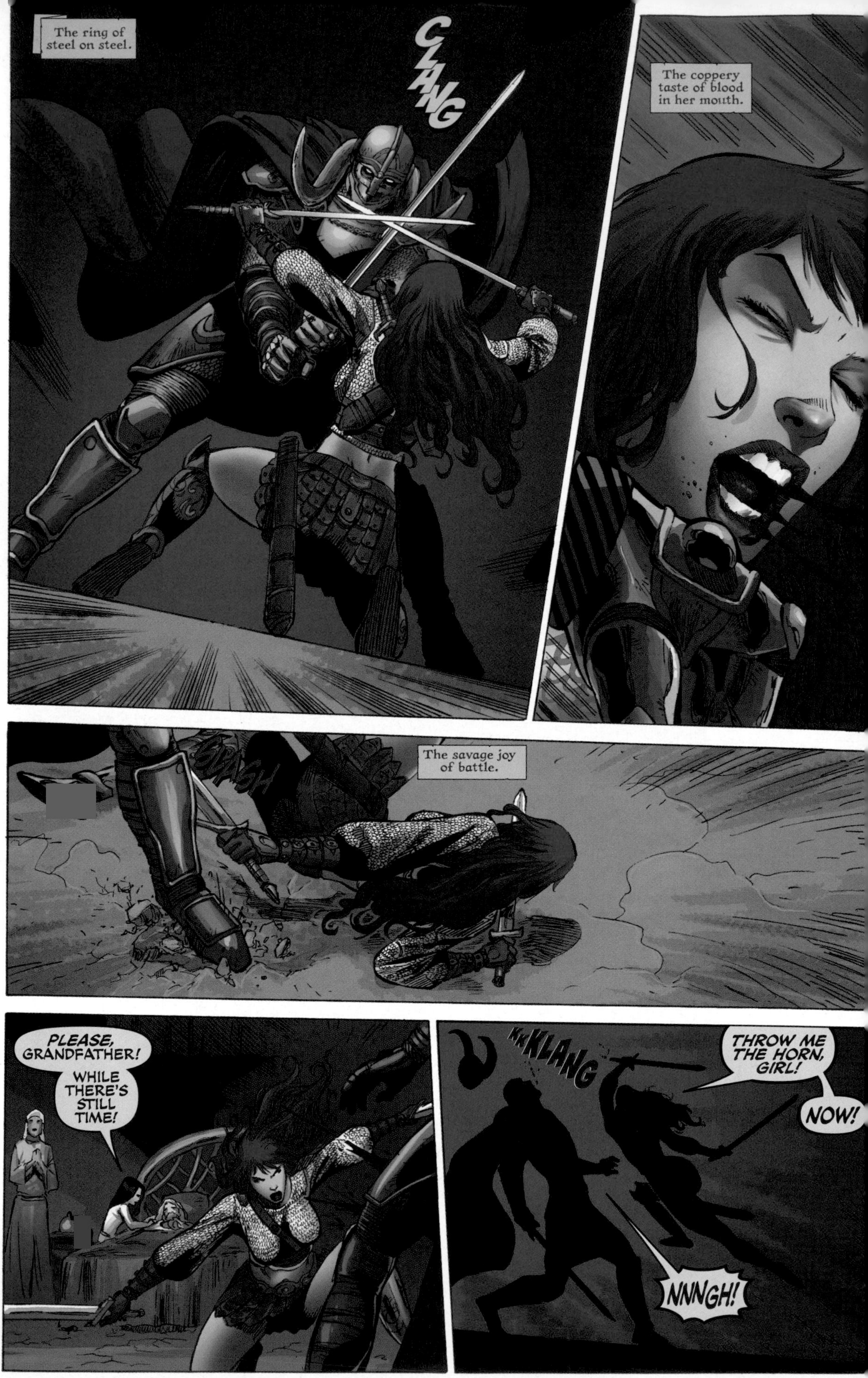
The ring of steel on steel.
CLANG
The coppery taste of blood in her mouth.
The savage joy of battle.
PLEASE, GRANDFATHER!
WHILE THERE'S STILL TIME!
KKKLANG
THROW ME THE HORN, GIRL!
NOW!
NNNGH!

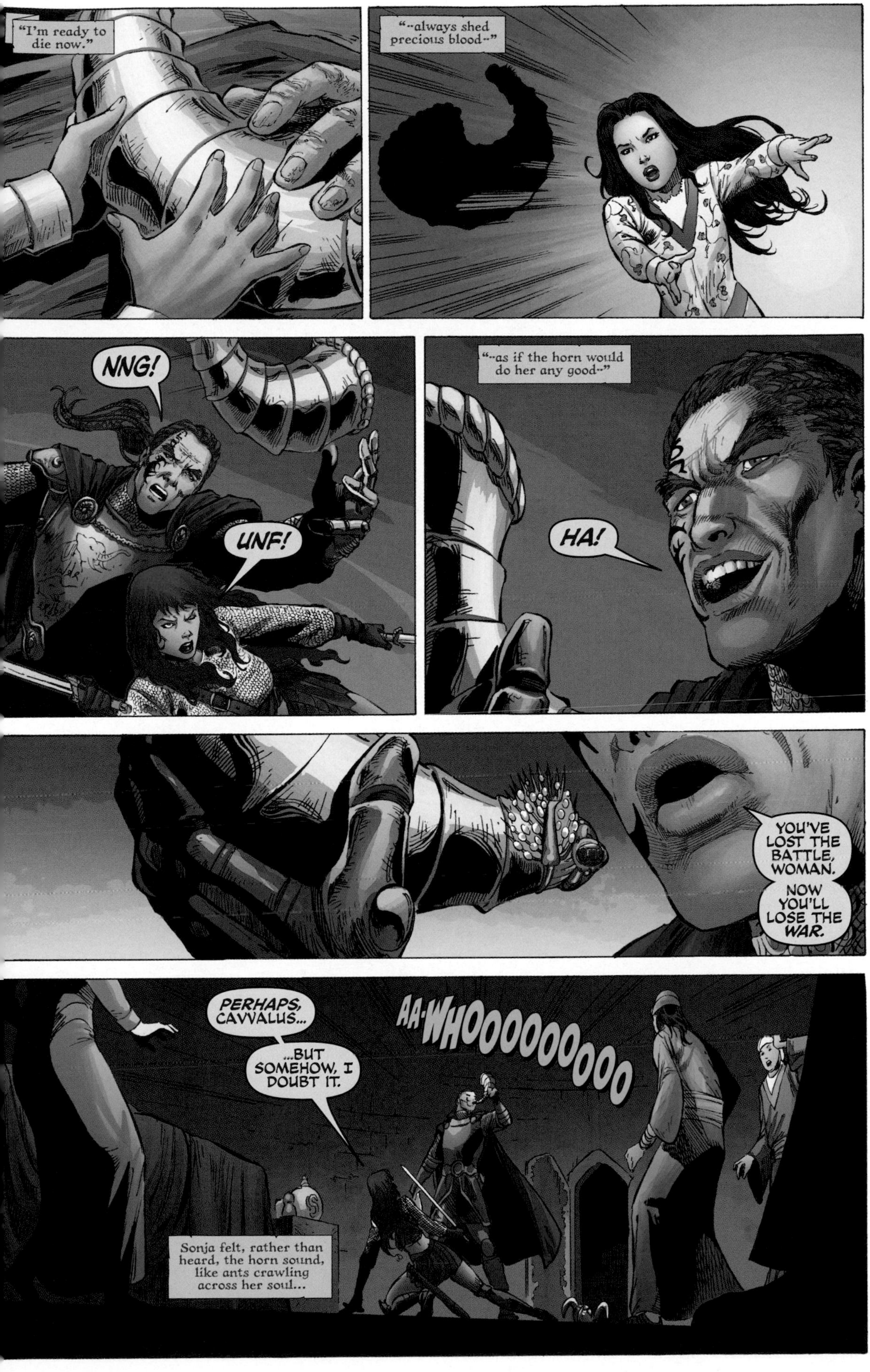
"I'm ready to die now."
"--always shed precious blood--"
NNG!
UNF!
"--as if the horn would do her any good--"
HA!
YOU'VE LOST THE BATTLE, WOMAN.
NOW YOU'LL LOSE THE WAR.
PERHAPS, CAVVALUS...
...BUT SOMEHOW, I DOUBT IT.
AA-WHOOOOOOOOOO
Sonja felt, rather than heard, the horn sound, like ants crawling across her soul...

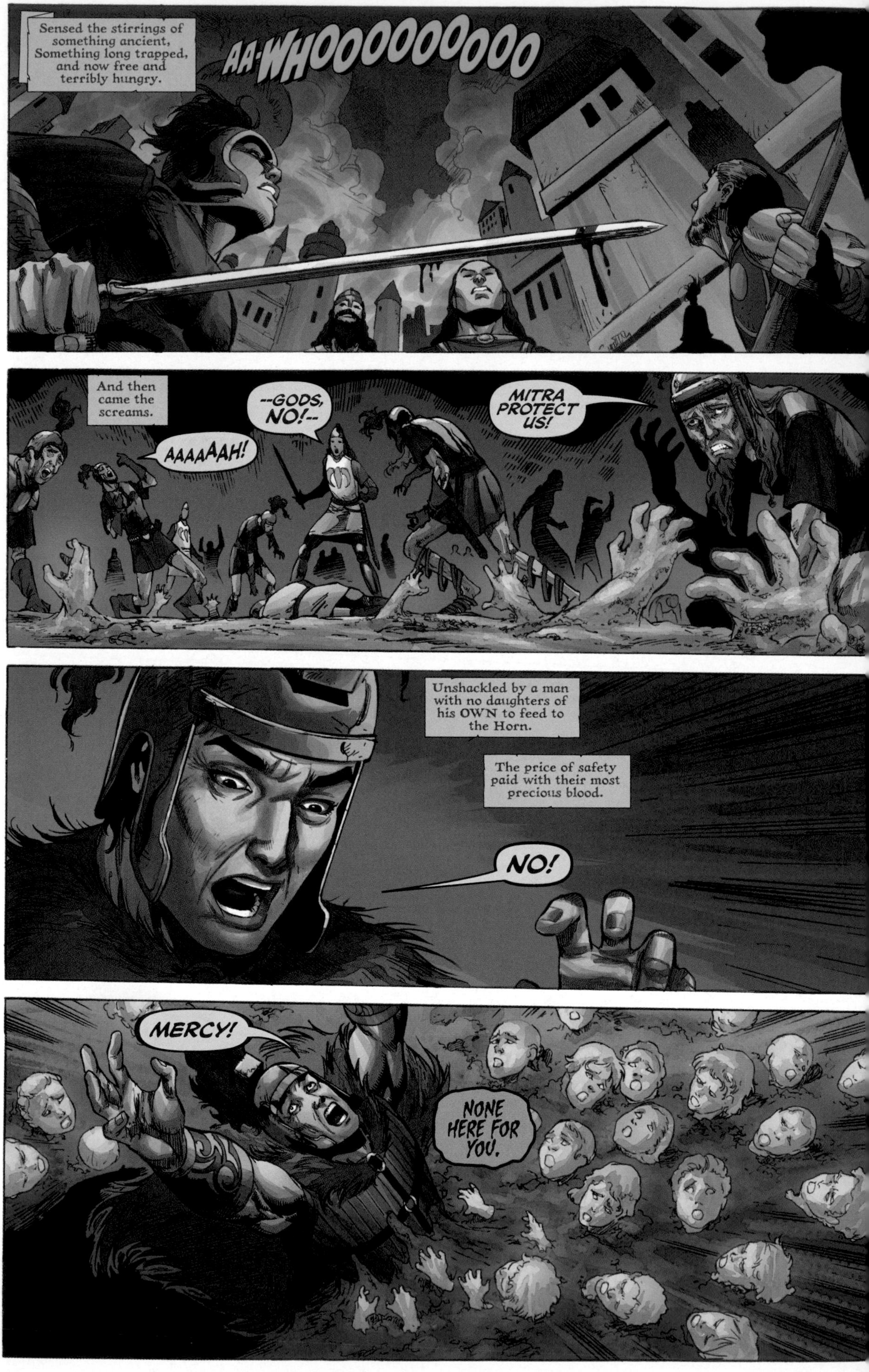

Sensed the stirrings of something ancient, Something long trapped, and now free and terribly hungry.
AA-WHOOOOOOOOOO
And then came the screams.
AAAAAAH!
--GODS, NO!--
MITRA PROTECT US!
Unshackled by a man with no daughters of his OWN to feed to the Horn.
The price of safety paid with their most precious blood.
NO!
MERCY!
NONE HERE FOR YOU.

The souls of Persemhia's royal daughters, trapped within the Horn for uncounted centuries.

Paying for the defense of the city with their very souls.

Released from their bondage by Cavvalus' rash action.

LOOK AWAY, CHILD.

KEEP YOUR EYES *SHUT.*

Unshackled by a man who had no daughters to feed to the horn.

NNNNNGHHH! NNNNNGG*GGAAAAAH!*

SSSHHHHHHHHHHK

And so, must suffer the *brunt* of the horn's *power.*

HHHHHGG*GLK*

WHUDD

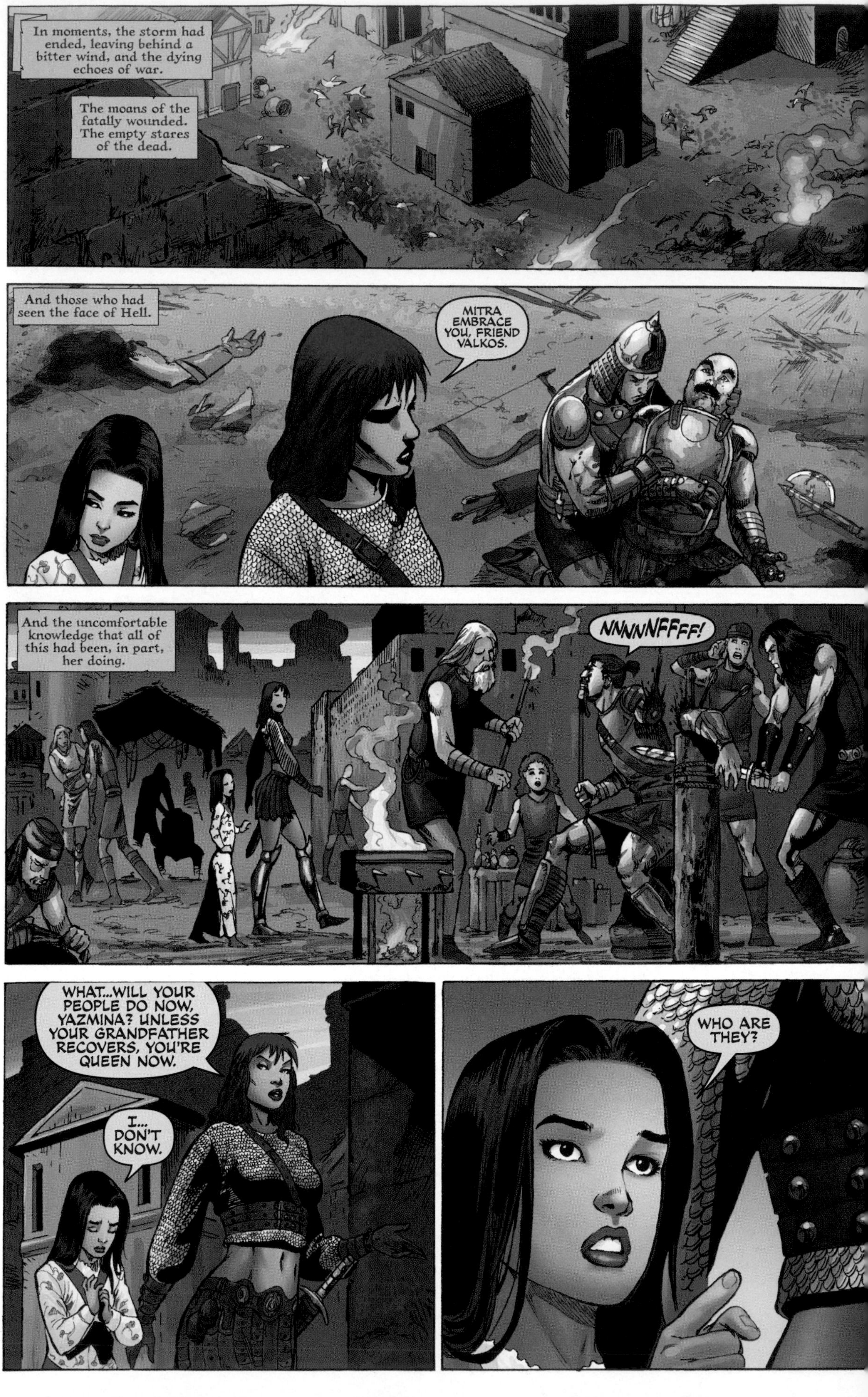
In moments, the storm had ended, leaving behind a bitter wind, and the dying echoes of war.
The moans of the fatally wounded. The empty stares of the dead.
And those who had seen the face of Hell.
MITRA EMBRACE YOU, FRIEND VALKOS.
And the uncomfortable knowledge that all of this had been, in part, her doing.
NNNNNFFFFF!
WHAT...WILL YOUR PEOPLE DO NOW, YAZMINA? UNLESS YOUR GRANDFATHER RECOVERS, YOU'RE QUEEN NOW.
I... DON'T KNOW.
WHO ARE THEY?

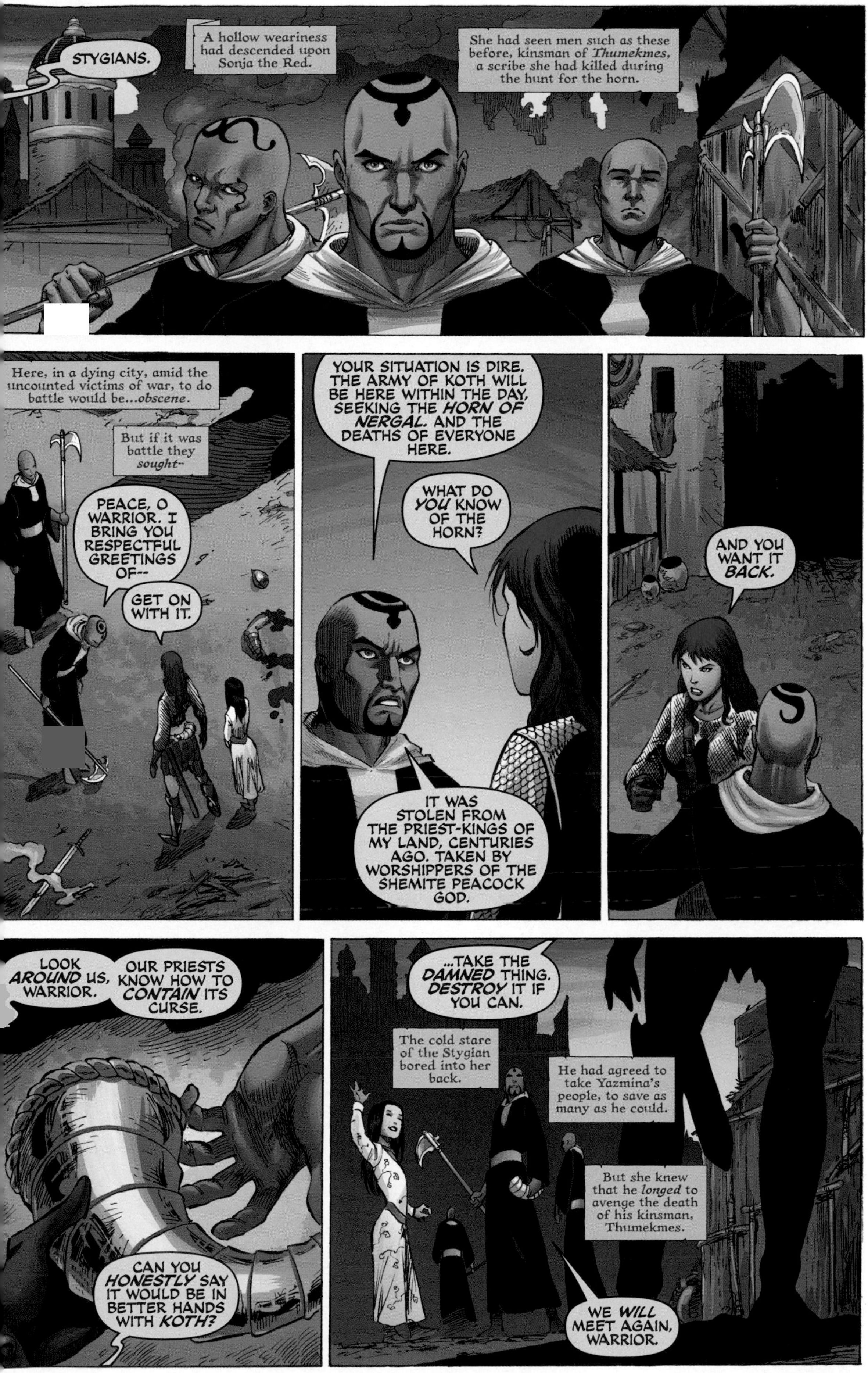
STYGIANS.
A hollow weariness had descended upon Sonja the Red.
She had seen men such as these before, kinsman of *Thumekmes*, a scribe she had killed during the hunt for the horn.
Here, in a dying city, amid the uncounted victims of war, to do battle would be...*obscene*.
But if it was battle they *sought*--
PEACE, O WARRIOR. I BRING YOU RESPECTFUL GREETINGS OF--
GET ON WITH IT.
YOUR SITUATION IS DIRE. THE ARMY OF KOTH WILL BE HERE WITHIN THE DAY, SEEKING THE *HORN OF NERGAL*. AND THE DEATHS OF EVERYONE HERE.
WHAT DO *YOU* KNOW OF THE HORN?
IT WAS STOLEN FROM THE PRIEST-KINGS OF MY LAND, CENTURIES AGO. TAKEN BY WORSHIPPERS OF THE SHEMITE PEACOCK GOD.
AND YOU WANT IT *BACK*.
LOOK *AROUND* US, WARRIOR.
OUR PRIESTS KNOW HOW TO *CONTAIN* ITS CURSE.
CAN YOU *HONESTLY* SAY IT WOULD BE IN BETTER HANDS WITH *KOTH*?
...TAKE THE *DAMNED* THING. *DESTROY* IT IF YOU CAN.
The cold stare of the Stygian bored into her back.
He had agreed to take Yazmina's people, to save as many as he could.
But she knew that he *longed* to avenge the death of his kinsman, Thumekmes.
WE *WILL* MEET AGAIN, WARRIOR.

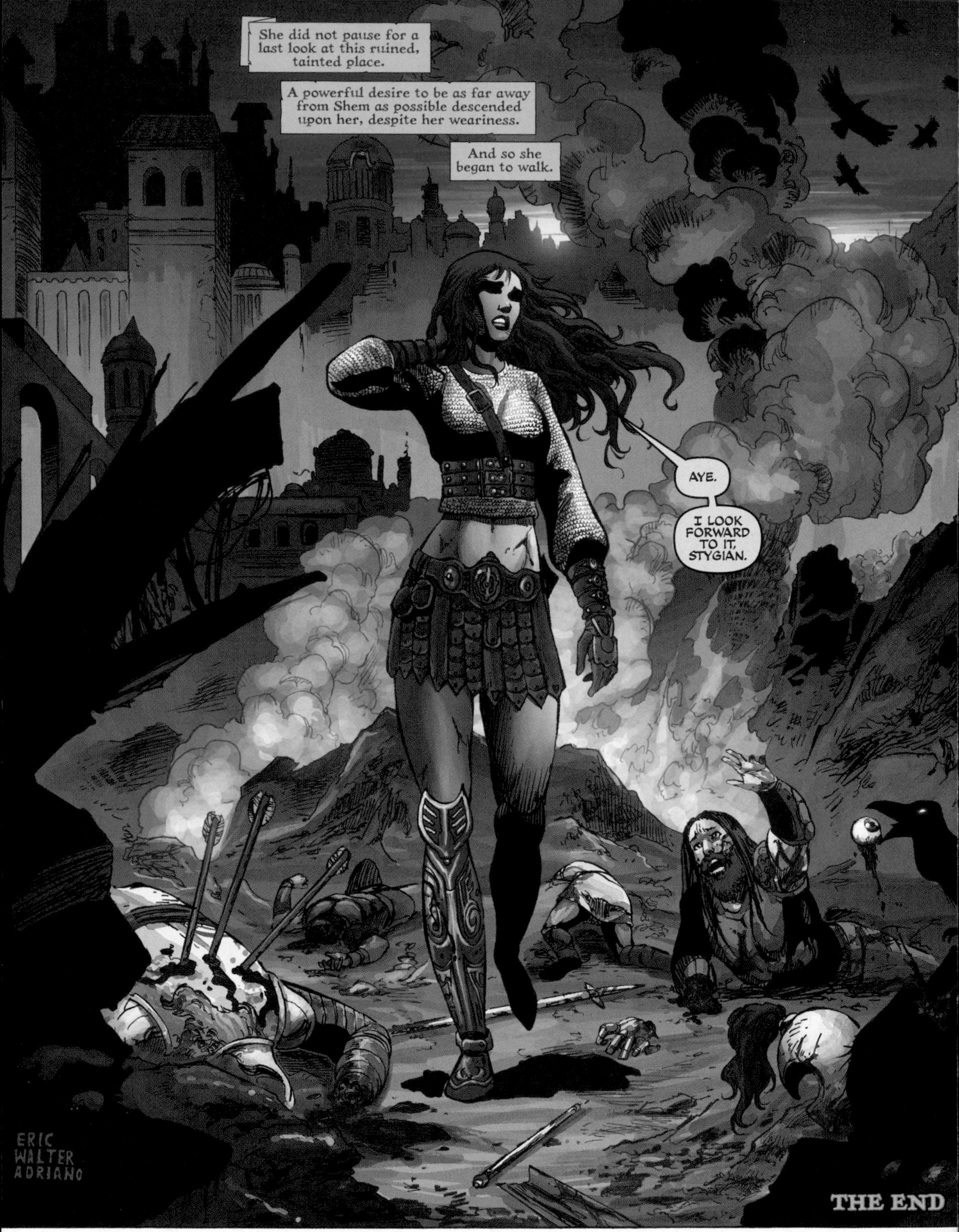
She did not pause for a last look at this ruined, tainted place.
A powerful desire to be as far away from Shem as possible descended upon her, despite her weariness.
And so she began to walk.
AYE.
I LOOK FORWARD TO IT, STYGIAN.
ERIC WALTER ADRIANO
THE END

DYING ECHOES

WAR SEASON, PART 4

Written by: Eric S. Trautmann
Pencils by: Walter Geovanni
Colors by: Adriano Lucas
Letters by: Troy Peteri
Edited by: Joe Rybandt

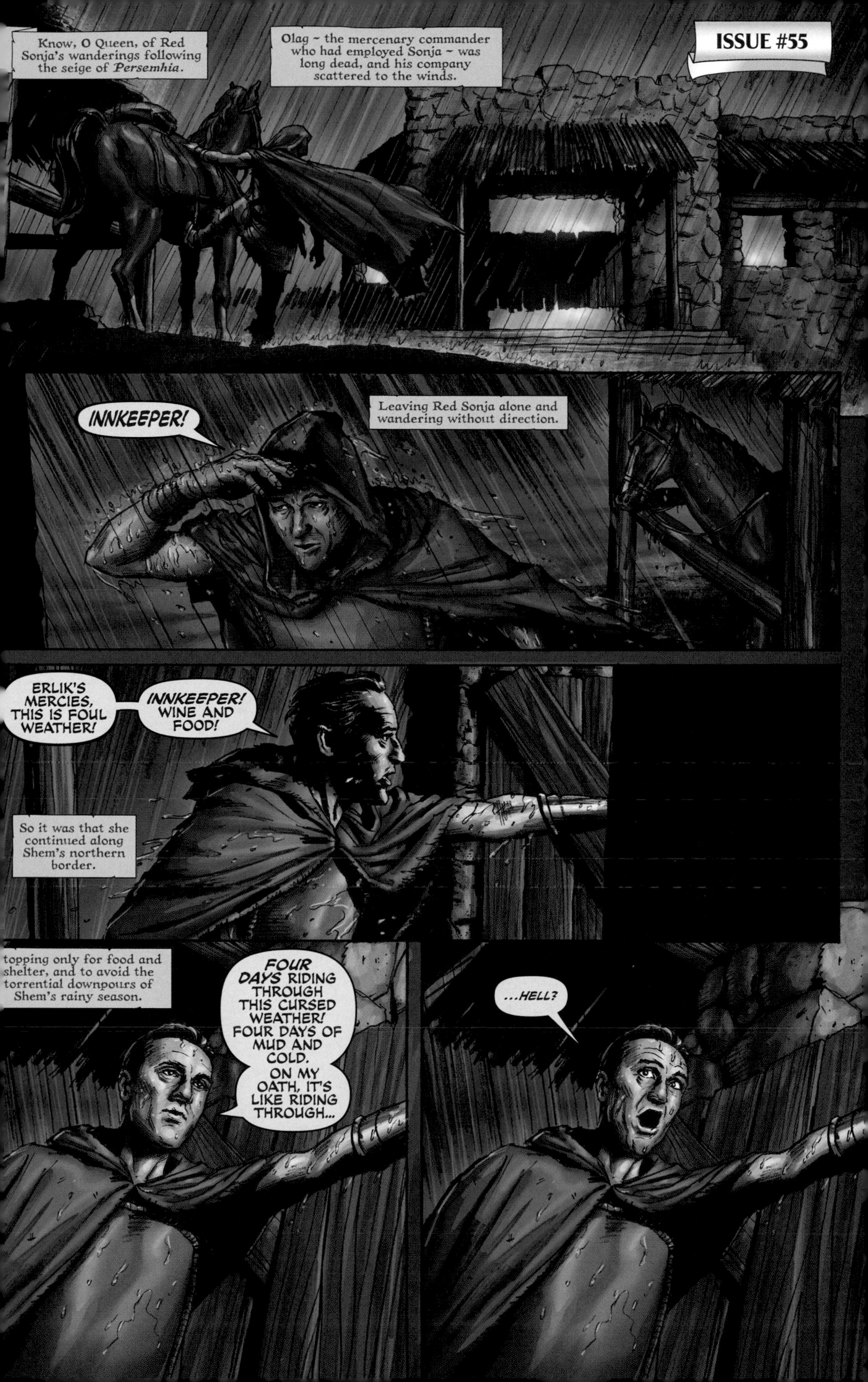
ISSUE #55
Know, O Queen, of Red Sonja's wanderings following the seige of *Persemhia*.
Olag ~ the mercenary commander who had employed Sonja ~ was long dead, and his company scattered to the winds.
Leaving Red Sonja alone and wandering without direction.
INNKEEPER!
ERLIK'S MERCIES, THIS IS FOUL WEATHER!
INNKEEPER! WINE AND FOOD!
So it was that she continued along Shem's northern border.
topping only for food and shelter, and to avoid the torrential downpours of Shem's rainy season.
FOUR DAYS RIDING THROUGH THIS CURSED WEATHER! FOUR DAYS OF MUD AND COLD. ON MY OATH, IT'S LIKE RIDING THROUGH...
...HELL?

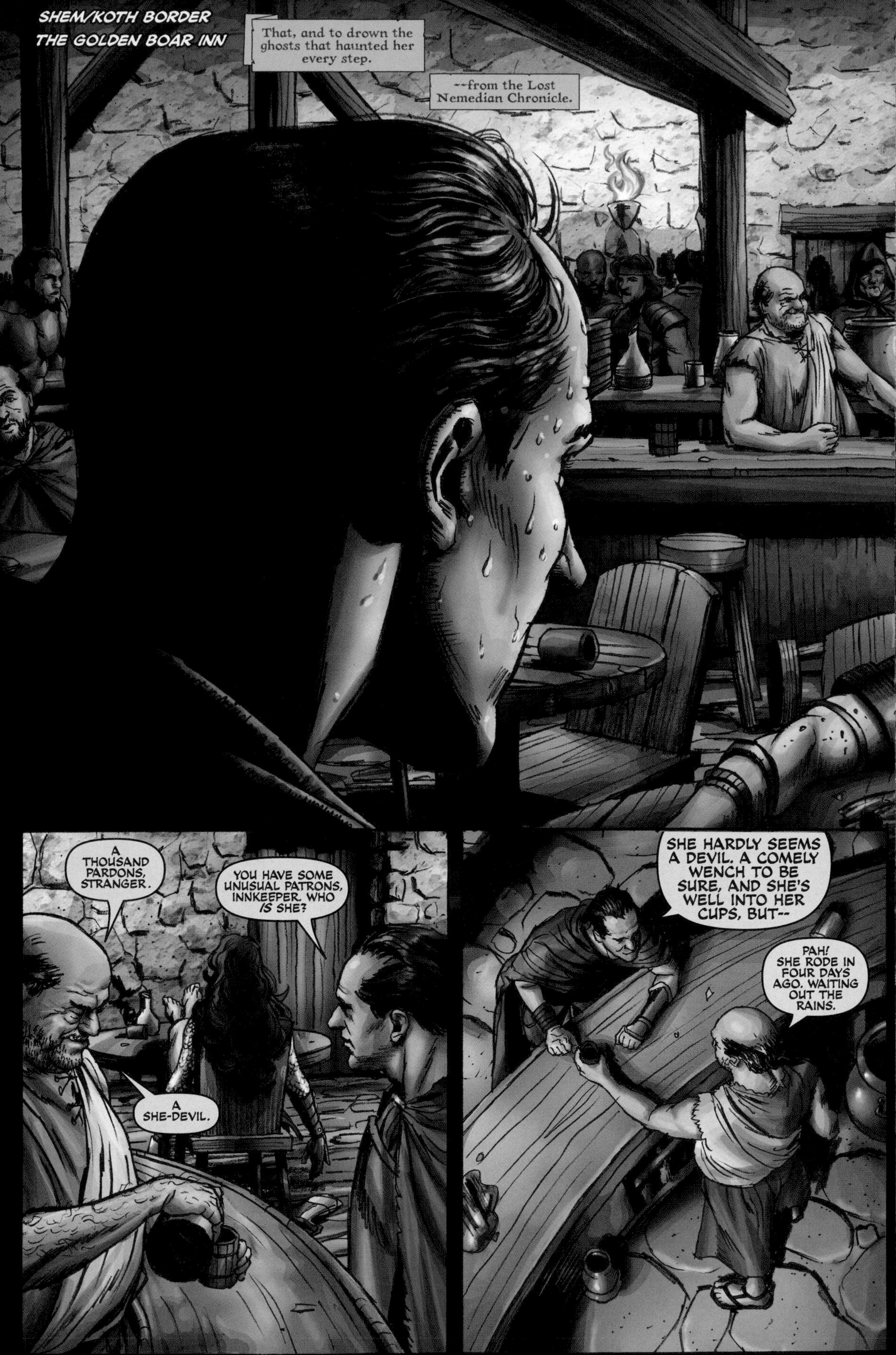
SHEM/KOTH BORDER
THE GOLDEN BOAR INN
That, and to drown the ghosts that haunted her every step.
--from the Lost Nemedian Chronicle.
A THOUSAND PARDONS, STRANGER.
YOU HAVE SOME UNUSUAL PATRONS, INNKEEPER. WHO *IS* SHE?
A SHE-DEVIL.
SHE HARDLY SEEMS A DEVIL. A COMELY WENCH TO BE SURE, AND SHE'S WELL INTO HER CUPS, BUT--
PAH! SHE RODE IN FOUR DAYS AGO. WAITING OUT THE RAINS.

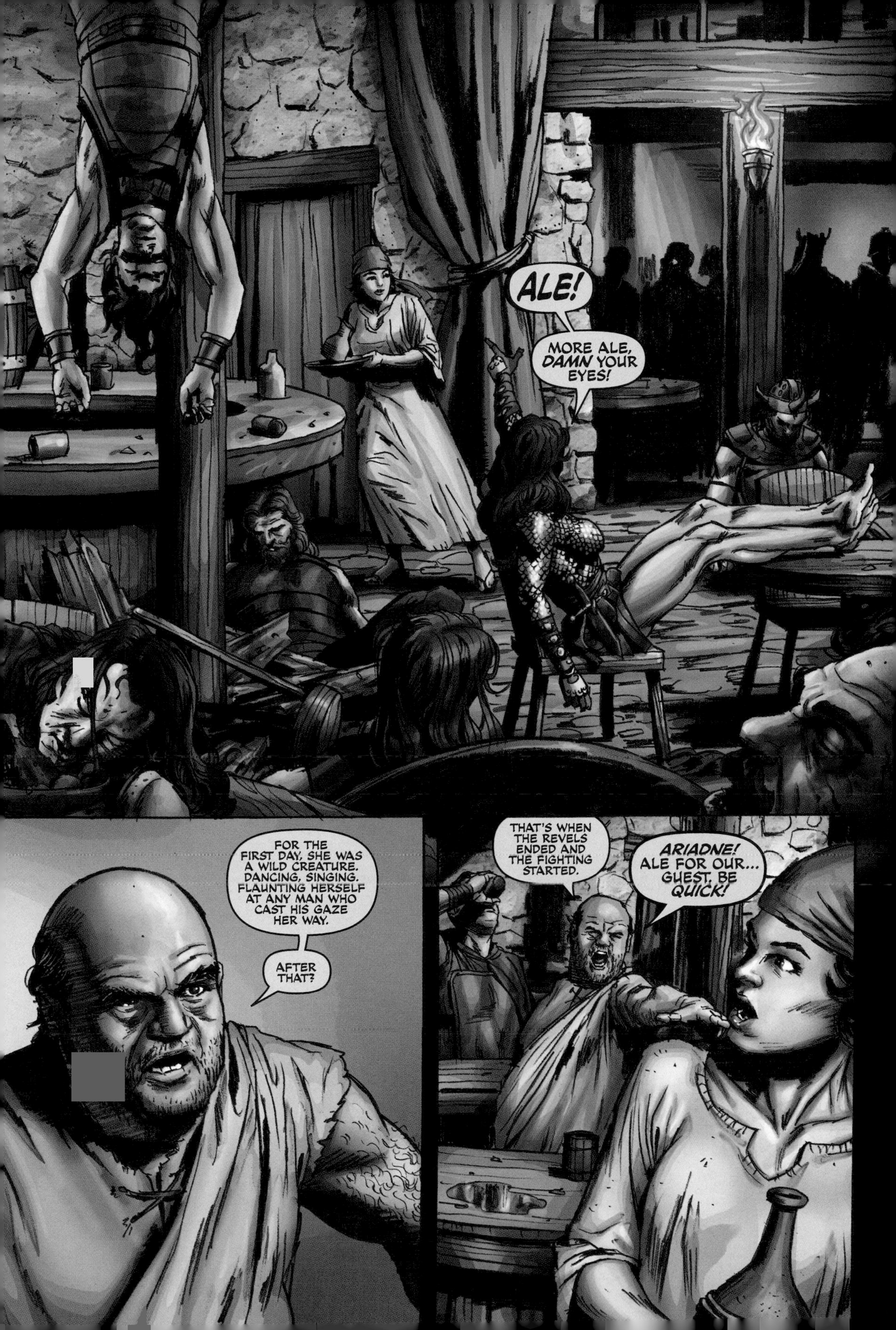
ALE!
MORE ALE, DAMN YOUR EYES!
FOR THE FIRST DAY, SHE WAS A WILD CREATURE. DANCING, SINGING. FLAUNTING HERSELF AT ANY MAN WHO CAST HIS GAZE HER WAY.
AFTER THAT?
THAT'S WHEN THE REVELS ENDED AND THE FIGHTING STARTED.
ARIADNE! ALE FOR OUR... GUEST. BE QUICK!

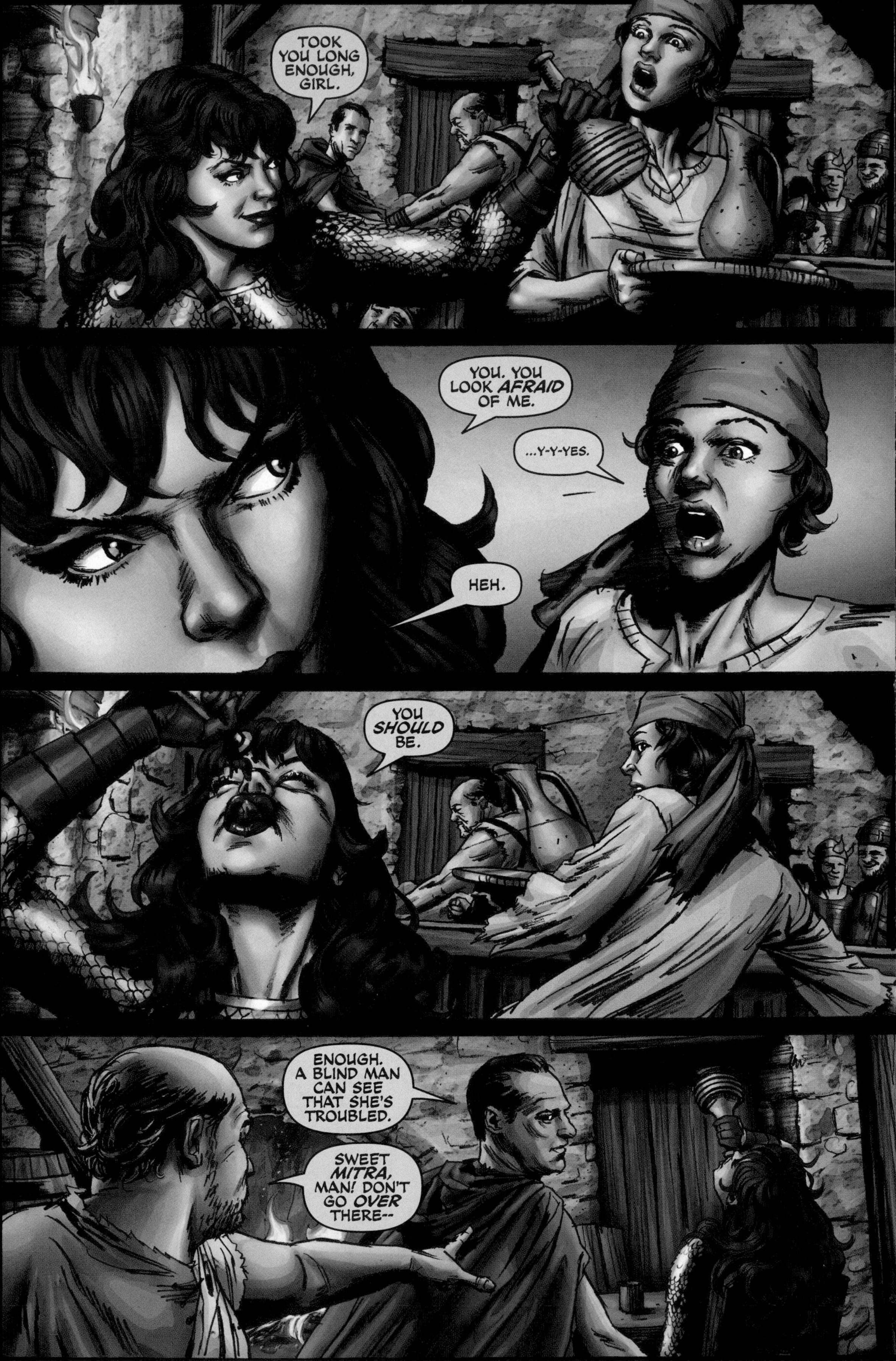
TOOK YOU LONG ENOUGH, GIRL.
YOU. YOU LOOK *AFRAID* OF ME.
...Y-Y-YES.
HEH.
YOU *SHOULD* BE.
ENOUGH. A BLIND MAN CAN SEE THAT SHE'S TROUBLED.
SWEET *MITRA*, MAN! DON'T GO *OVER* THERE--

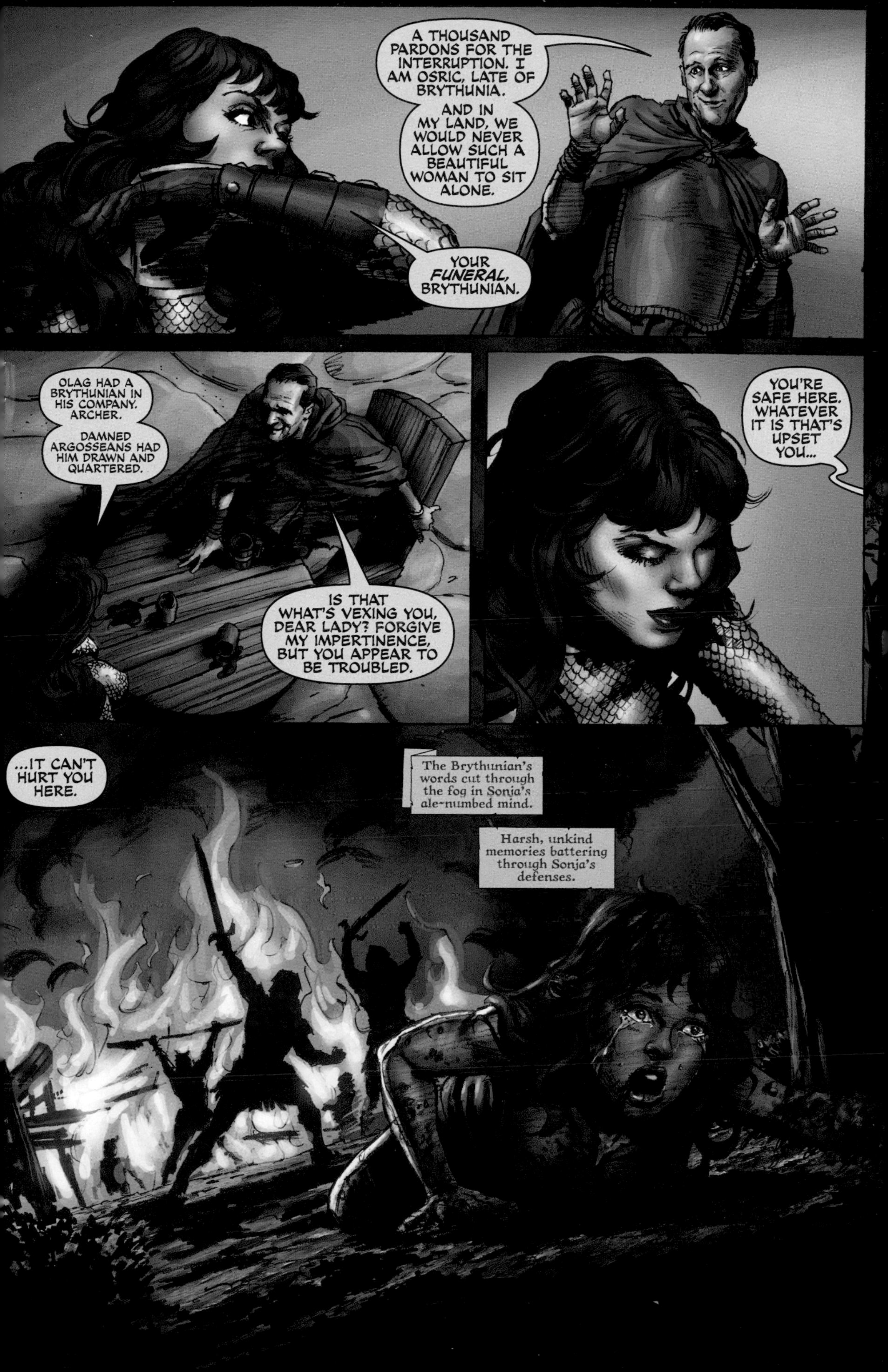
A THOUSAND PARDONS FOR THE INTERRUPTION. I AM OSRIC, LATE OF BRYTHUNIA.
AND IN MY LAND, WE WOULD NEVER ALLOW SUCH A BEAUTIFUL WOMAN TO SIT ALONE.
YOUR FUNERAL, BRYTHUNIAN.
OLAG HAD A BRYTHUNIAN IN HIS COMPANY. ARCHER.
DAMNED ARGOSSEANS HAD HIM DRAWN AND QUARTERED.
IS THAT WHAT'S VEXING YOU, DEAR LADY? FORGIVE MY IMPERTINENCE, BUT YOU APPEAR TO BE TROUBLED.
YOU'RE SAFE HERE. WHATEVER IT IS THAT'S UPSET YOU...
...IT CAN'T HURT YOU HERE.
The Brythunian's words cut through the fog in Sonja's ale-numbed mind.
Harsh, unkind memories battering through Sonja's defenses.

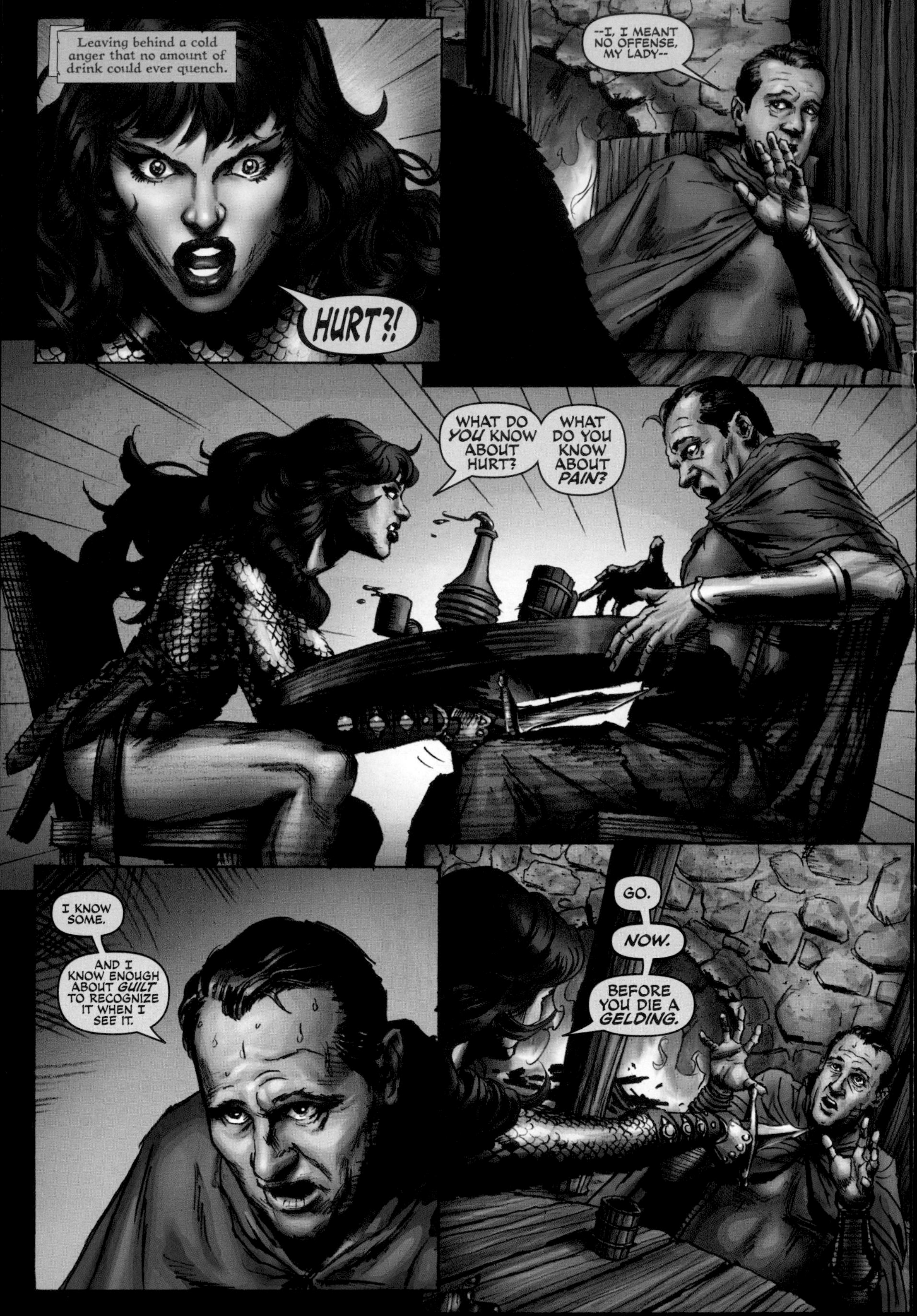
Leaving behind a cold anger that no amount of drink could ever quench.
HURT?!
--I, I MEANT NO OFFENSE, MY LADY--
WHAT DO YOU KNOW ABOUT HURT?
WHAT DO YOU KNOW ABOUT PAIN?
I KNOW SOME.
AND I KNOW ENOUGH ABOUT GUILT TO RECOGNIZE IT WHEN I SEE IT.
GO.
NOW.
BEFORE YOU DIE A GELDING.

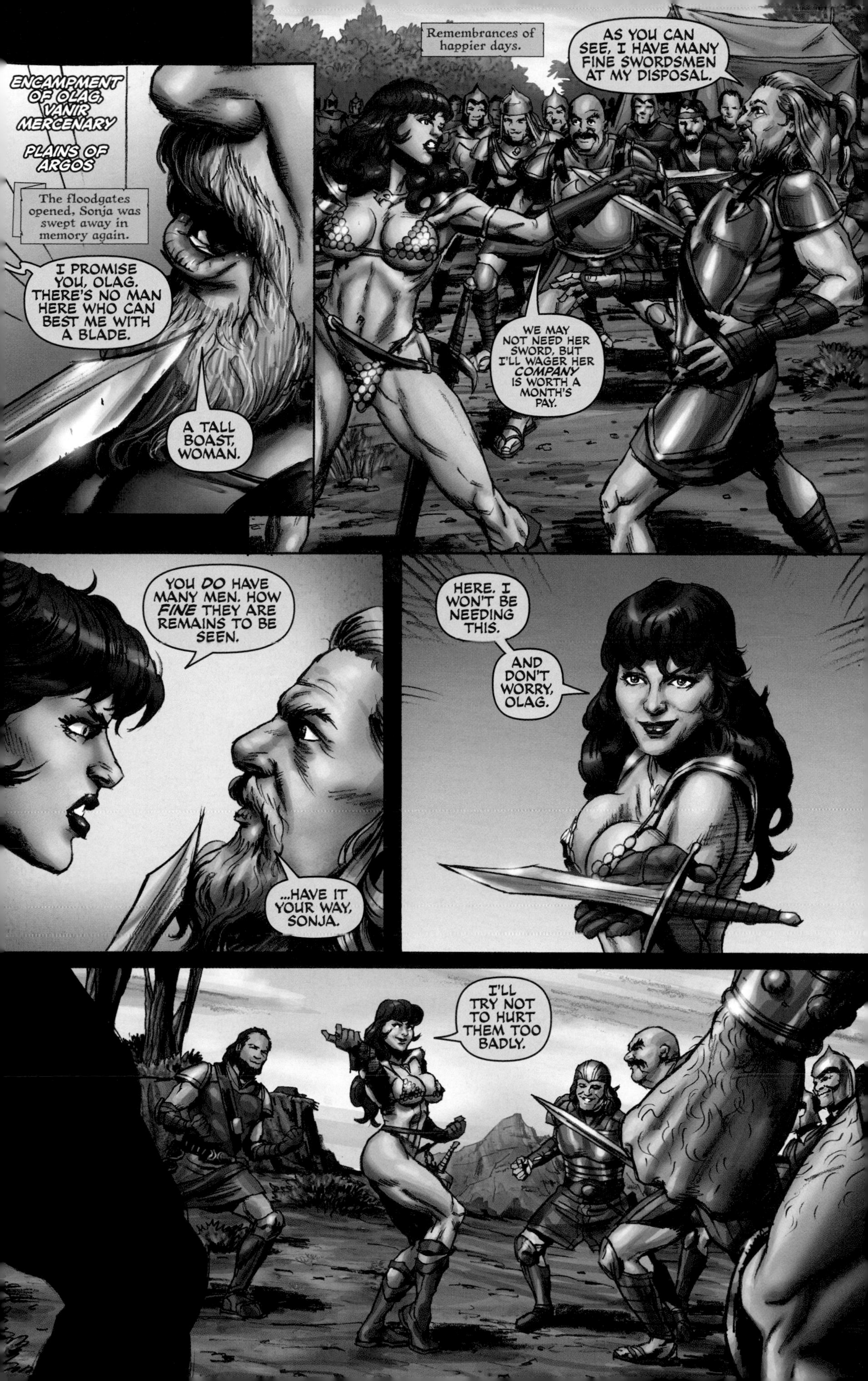
Encampment of Olag, Vanir Mercenary
Plains of Argos
The floodgates opened, Sonja was swept away in memory again.
Remembrances of happier days.
AS YOU CAN SEE, I HAVE MANY FINE SWORDSMEN AT MY DISPOSAL.
I PROMISE YOU, OLAG. THERE'S NO MAN HERE WHO CAN BEST ME WITH A BLADE.
A TALL BOAST, WOMAN.
WE MAY NOT NEED HER SWORD, BUT I'LL WAGER HER COMPANY IS WORTH A MONTH'S PAY.
YOU DO HAVE MANY MEN. HOW FINE THEY ARE REMAINS TO BE SEEN.
...HAVE IT YOUR WAY, SONJA.
HERE. I WON'T BE NEEDING THIS.
AND DON'T WORRY, OLAG.
I'LL TRY NOT TO HURT THEM TOO BADLY.

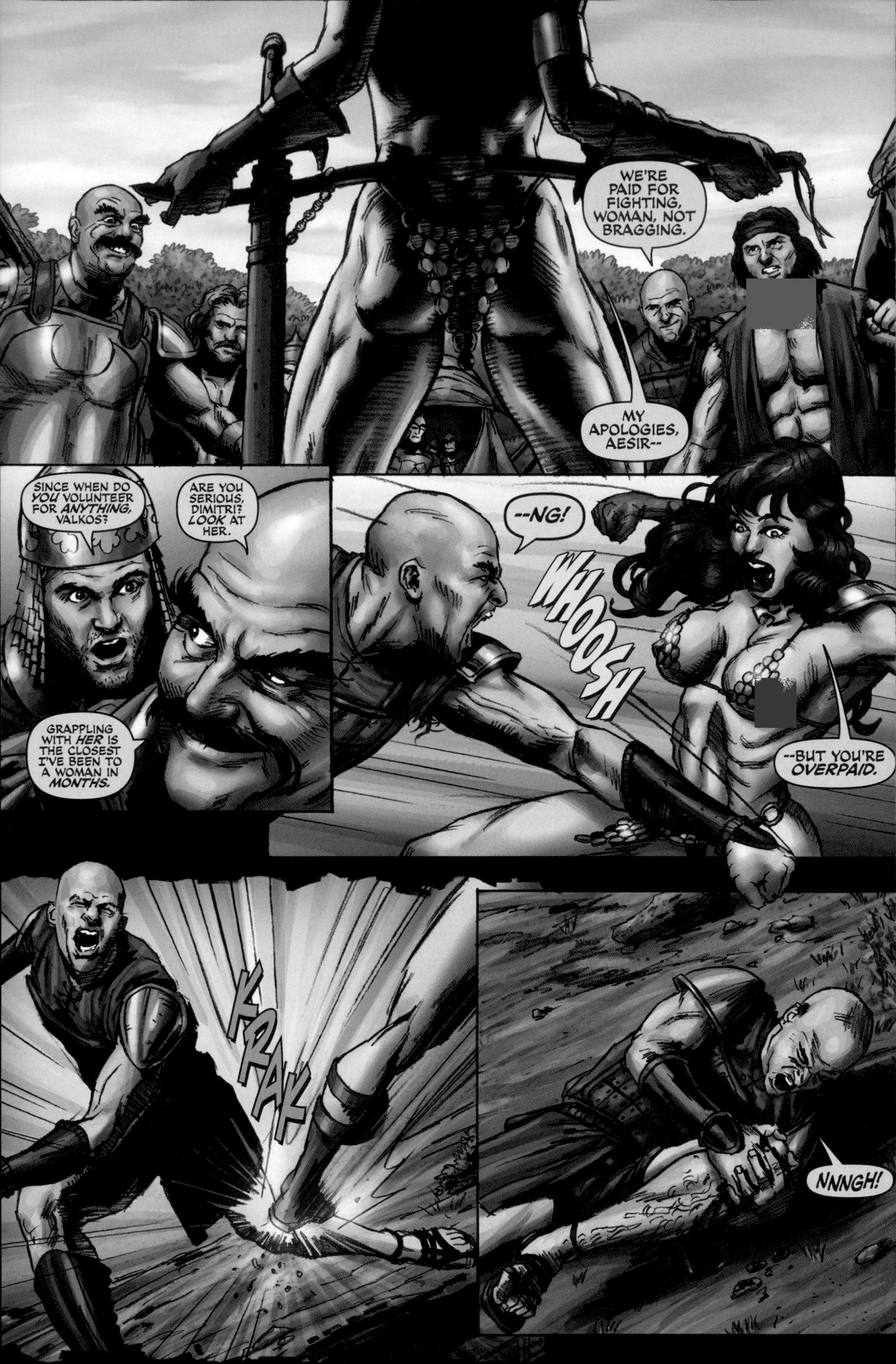

WE'RE PAID FOR FIGHTING, WOMAN, NOT BRAGGING.
MY APOLOGIES, AESIR--
SINCE WHEN DO YOU VOLUNTEER FOR ANYTHING, VALKOS?
ARE YOU SERIOUS, DIMITRI? LOOK AT HER.
GRAPPLING WITH HER IS THE CLOSEST I'VE BEEN TO A WOMAN IN MONTHS.
--NG!
WHOOSH
--BUT YOU'RE OVERPAID.
KRAK
NNNGH!

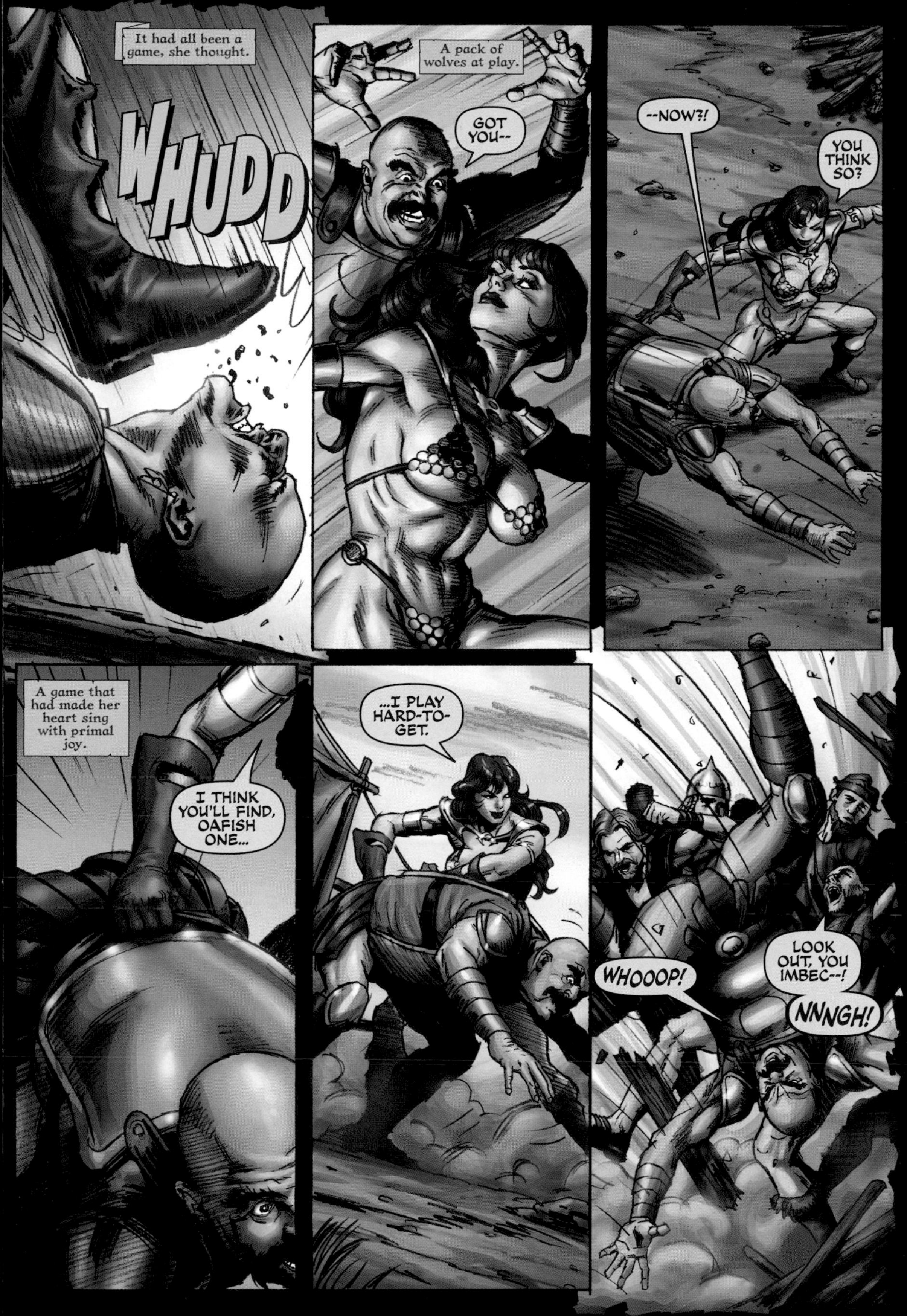
It had all been a game, she thought.
WHUDD
A pack of wolves at play.
GOT YOU--
--NOW?!
YOU THINK SO?
A game that had made her heart sing with primal joy.
I THINK YOU'LL FIND, OAFISH ONE...
...I PLAY HARD-TO-GET.
WHOOOP!
LOOK OUT, YOU IMBEC--!
NNNGH!

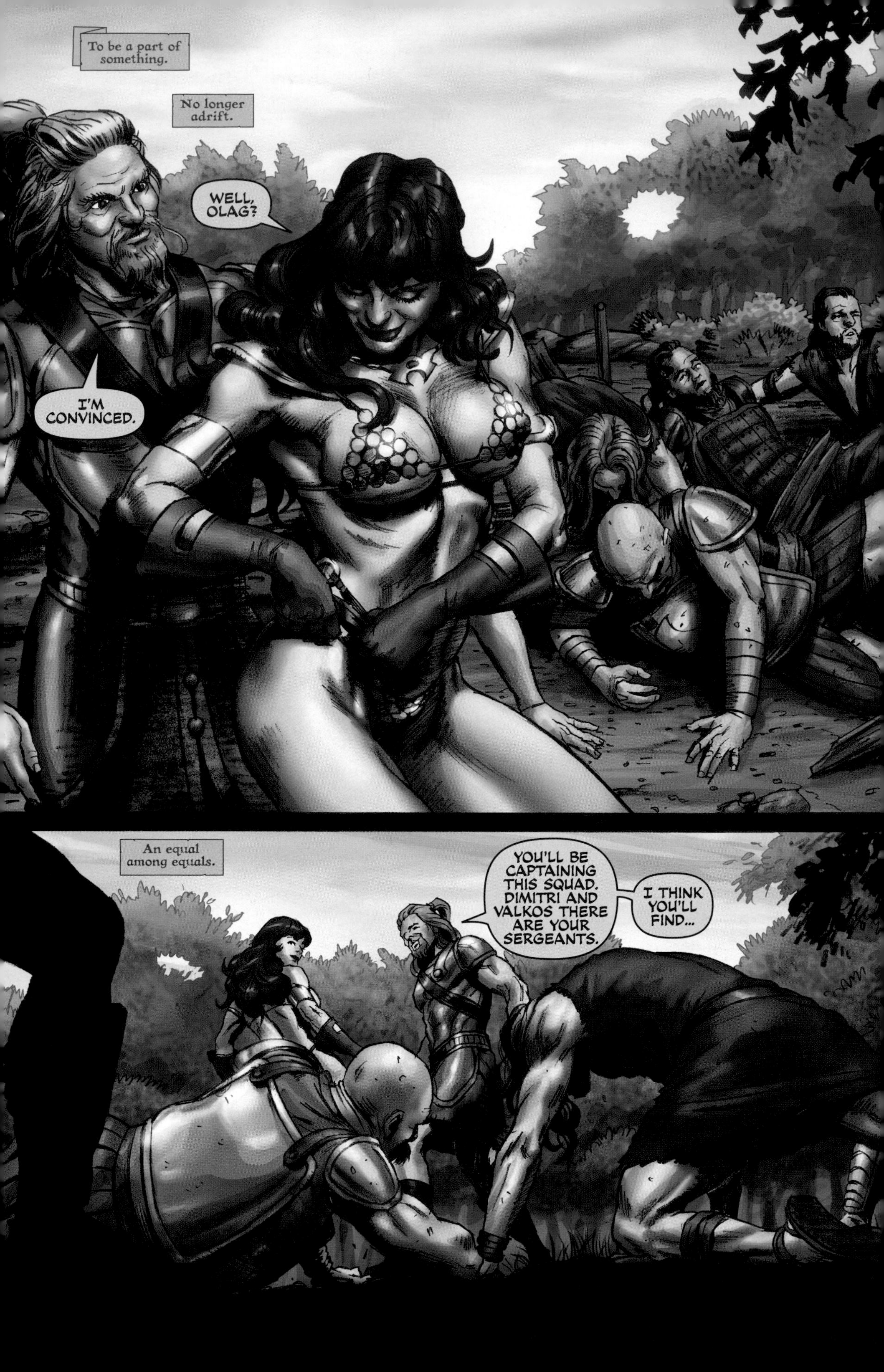
To be a part of something.
No longer adrift.
WELL, OLAG?
I'M CONVINCED.
An equal among equals.
YOU'LL BE CAPTAINING THIS SQUAD. DIMITRI AND VALKOS THERE ARE YOUR SERGEANTS.
I THINK YOU'LL FIND...

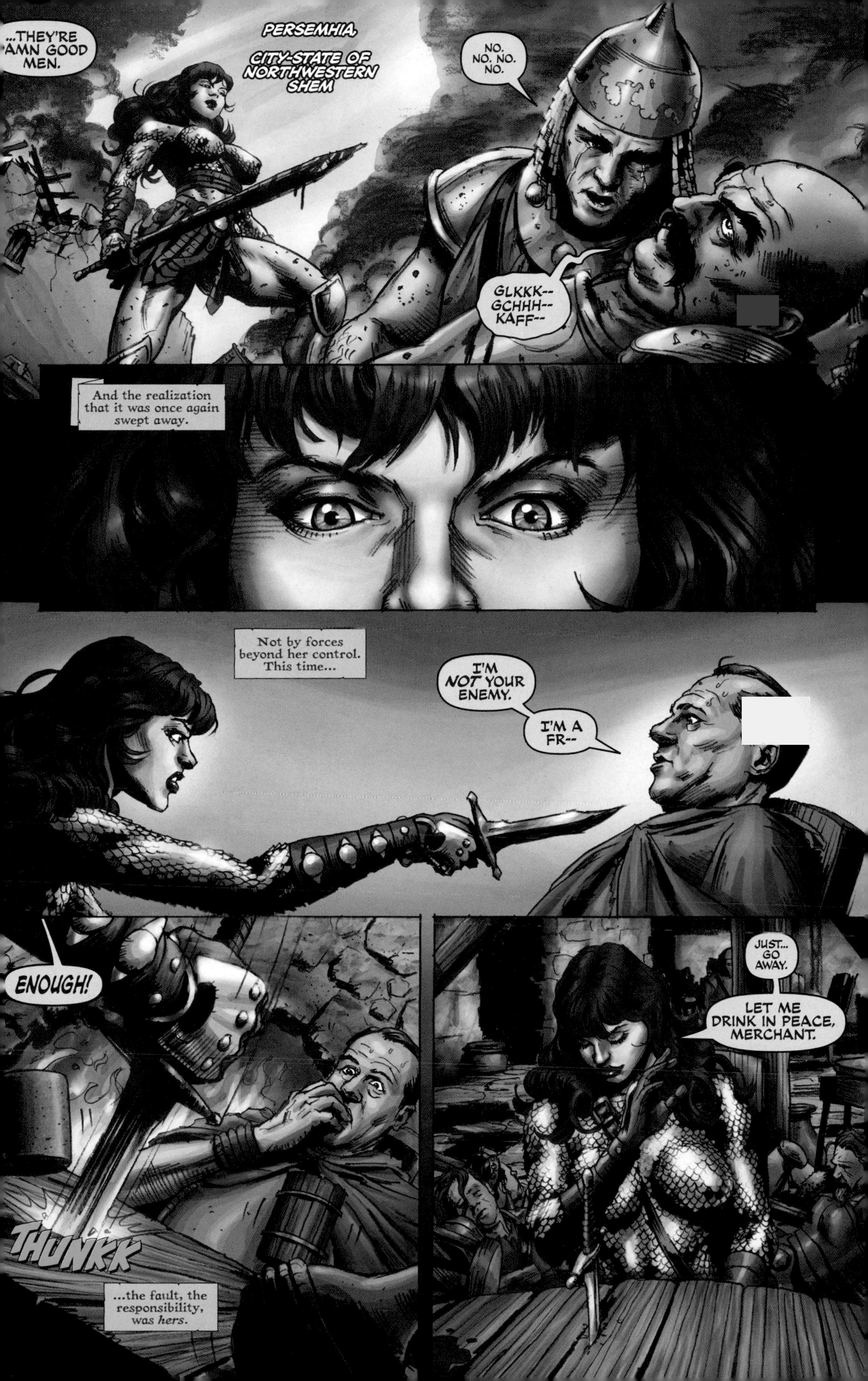

...THEY'RE AMN GOOD MEN.
PERSEMHIA,
CITY-STATE OF NORTHWESTERN SHEM
NO. NO. NO. NO.
GLKKK-- GCHHH-- KAFF--
And the realization that it was once again swept away.
Not by forces beyond her control. This time...
I'M *NOT* YOUR ENEMY.
I'M A FR--
ENOUGH!
THUNKK
...the fault, the responsibility, was *hers*.
JUST... GO AWAY.
LET ME DRINK IN PEACE, MERCHANT.

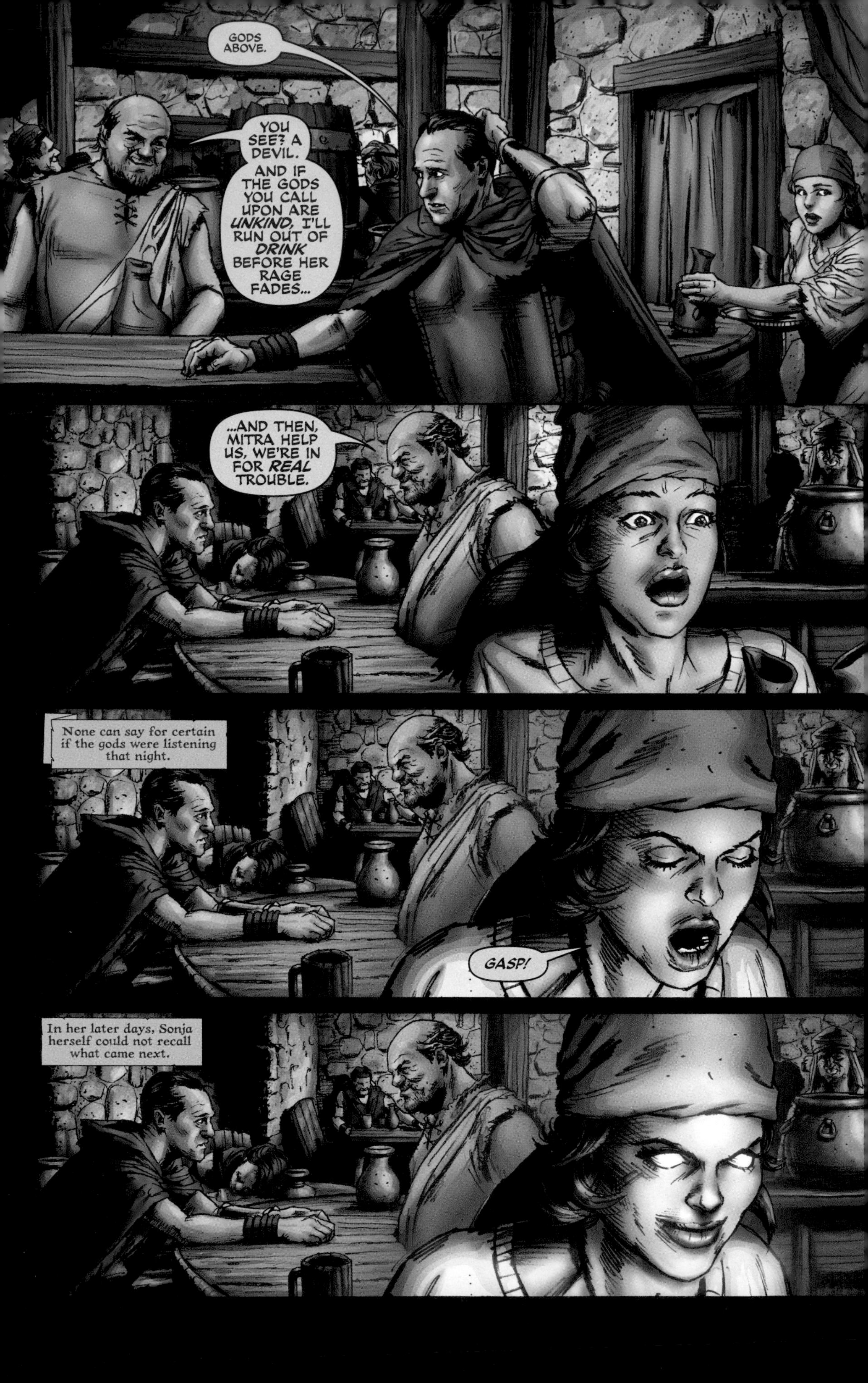
GODS ABOVE.
YOU SEE? A DEVIL. AND IF THE GODS YOU CALL UPON ARE *UNKIND,* I'LL RUN OUT OF *DRINK* BEFORE HER RAGE FADES...
...AND THEN, MITRA HELP US, WE'RE IN FOR *REAL* TROUBLE.
None can say for certain if the gods were listening that night.
GASP!
In her later days, Sonja herself could not recall what came next.

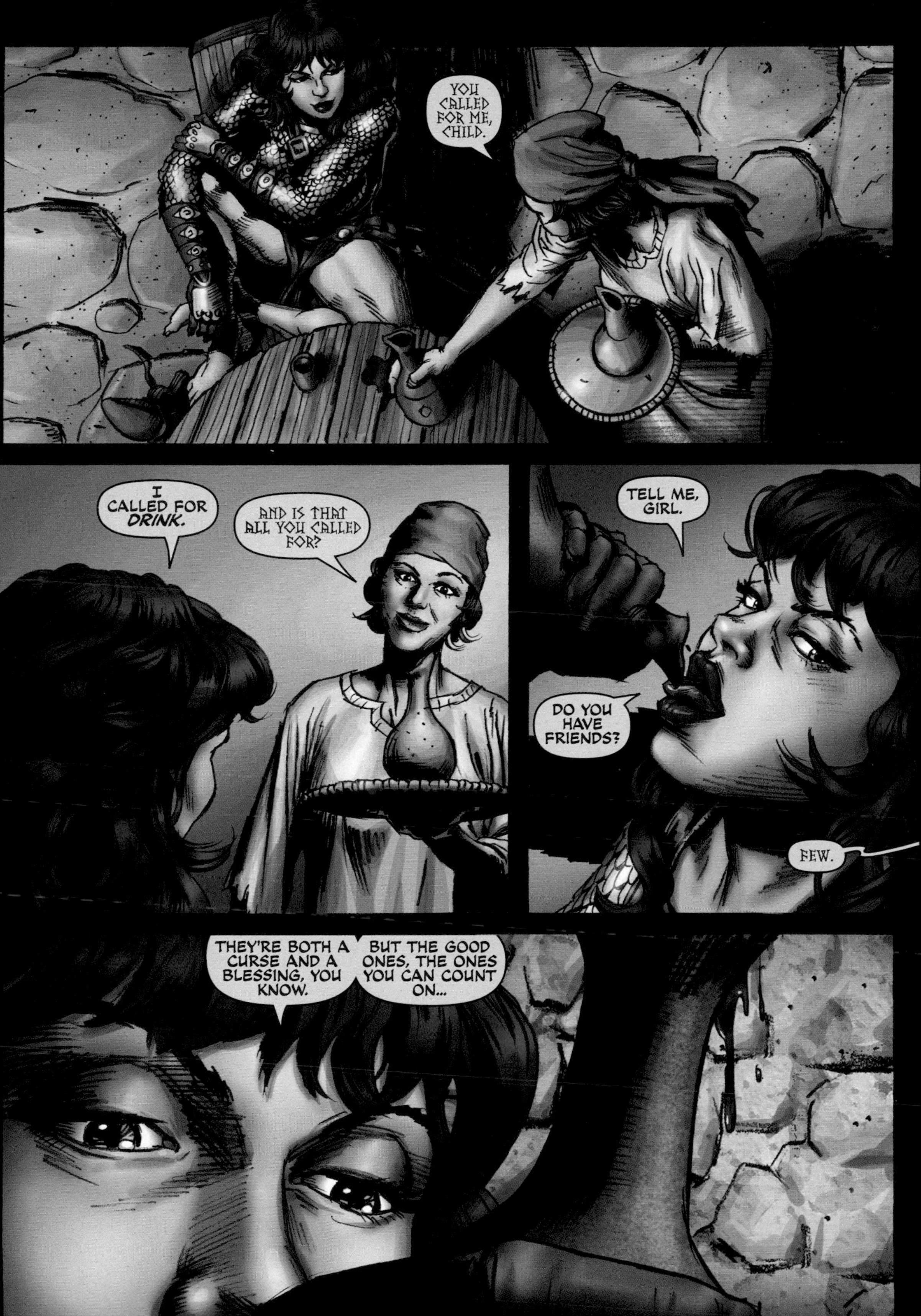
YOU CALLED FOR ME, CHILD.
I CALLED FOR DRINK.
AND IS THAT ALL YOU CALLED FOR?
TELL ME, GIRL.
DO YOU HAVE FRIENDS?
FEW.
THEY'RE BOTH A CURSE AND A BLESSING, YOU KNOW.
BUT THE GOOD ONES, THE ONES YOU CAN COUNT ON...

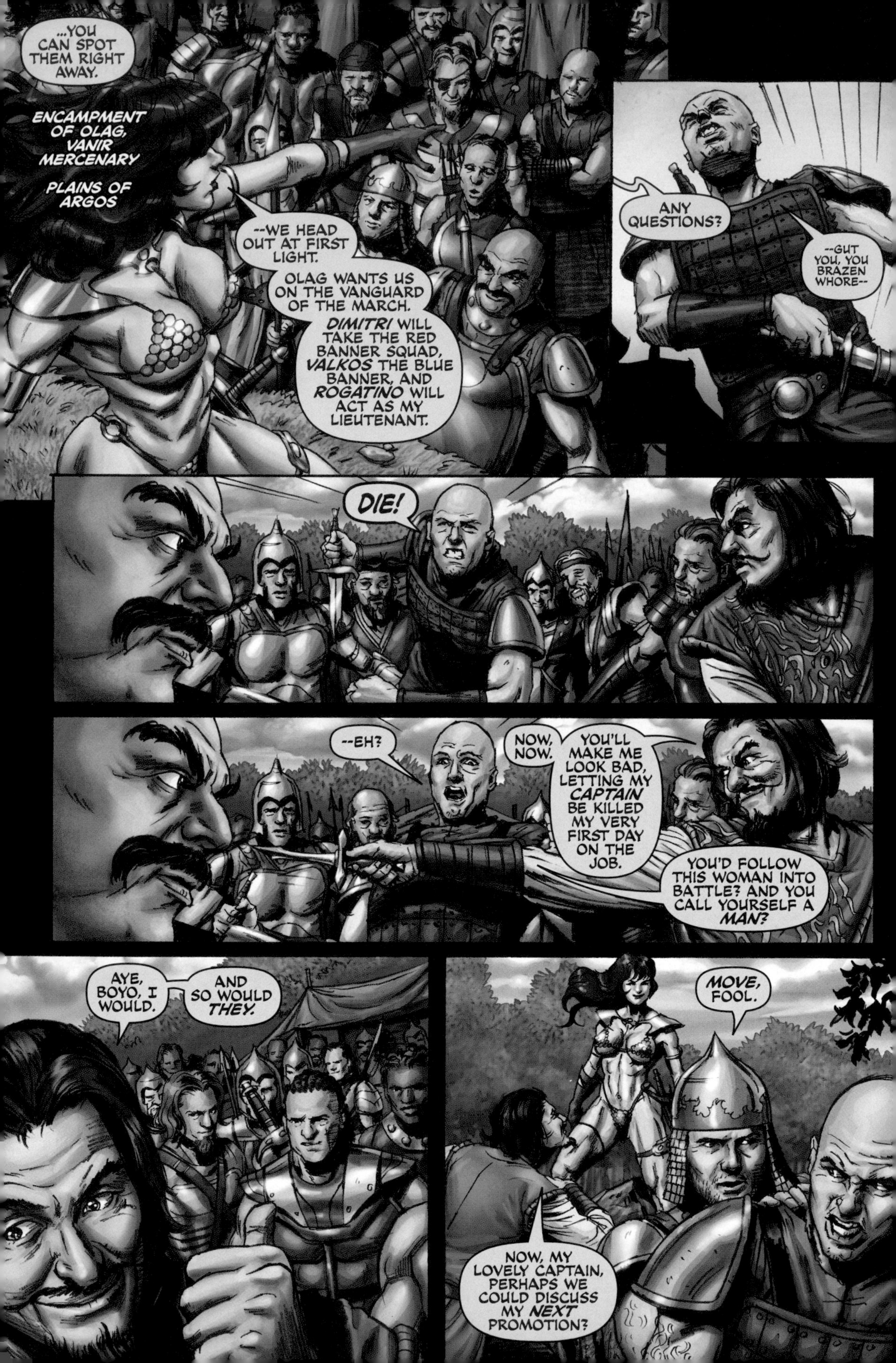
...YOU CAN SPOT THEM RIGHT AWAY.
ENCAMPMENT OF OLAG, VANIR MERCENARY
PLAINS OF ARGOS
--WE HEAD OUT AT FIRST LIGHT.
OLAG WANTS US ON THE VANGUARD OF THE MARCH.
DIMITRI WILL TAKE THE RED BANNER SQUAD, VALKOS THE BLUE BANNER, AND ROGATINO WILL ACT AS MY LIEUTENANT.
ANY QUESTIONS?
--GUT YOU, YOU BRAZEN WHORE--
DIE!
--EH?
NOW, NOW.
YOU'LL MAKE ME LOOK BAD, LETTING MY CAPTAIN BE KILLED MY VERY FIRST DAY ON THE JOB.
YOU'D FOLLOW THIS WOMAN INTO BATTLE? AND YOU CALL YOURSELF A MAN?
AYE, BOYO, I WOULD.
AND SO WOULD THEY.
MOVE, FOOL.
NOW, MY LOVELY CAPTAIN, PERHAPS WE COULD DISCUSS MY NEXT PROMOTION?

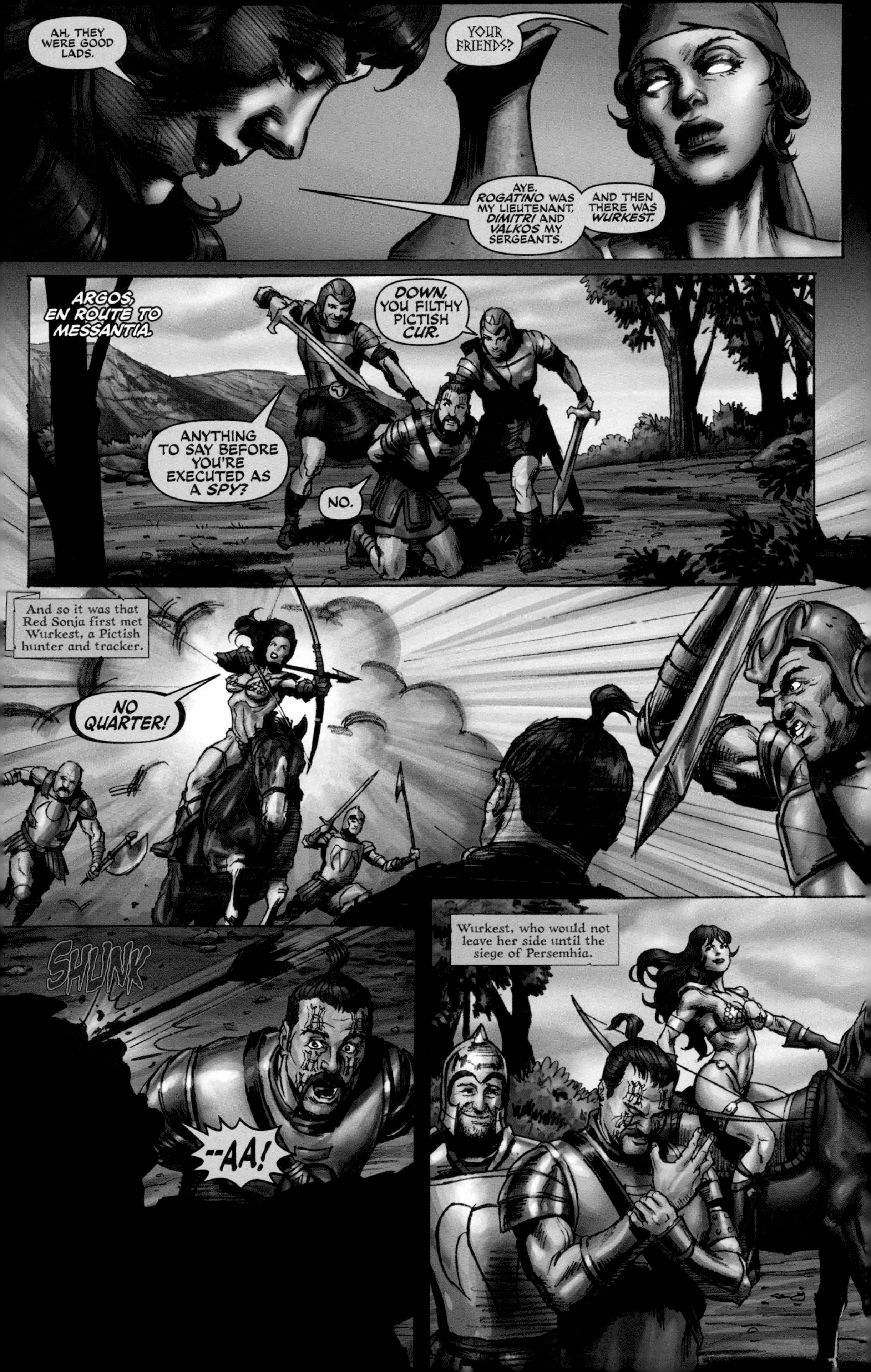
AH, THEY WERE GOOD LADS.
YOUR FRIENDS?
AYE. ROGATINO WAS MY LIEUTENANT, DIMITRI AND VALKOS MY SERGEANTS.
AND THEN THERE WAS WURKEST.
ARGOS, EN ROUTE TO MESSANTIA.
DOWN, YOU FILTHY PICTISH CUR.
ANYTHING TO SAY BEFORE YOU'RE EXECUTED AS A SPY?
NO.
And so it was that Red Sonja first met Wurkest, a Pictish hunter and tracker.
NO QUARTER!
SHUNK
--AA!
Wurkest, who would not leave her side until the siege of Persemhia.

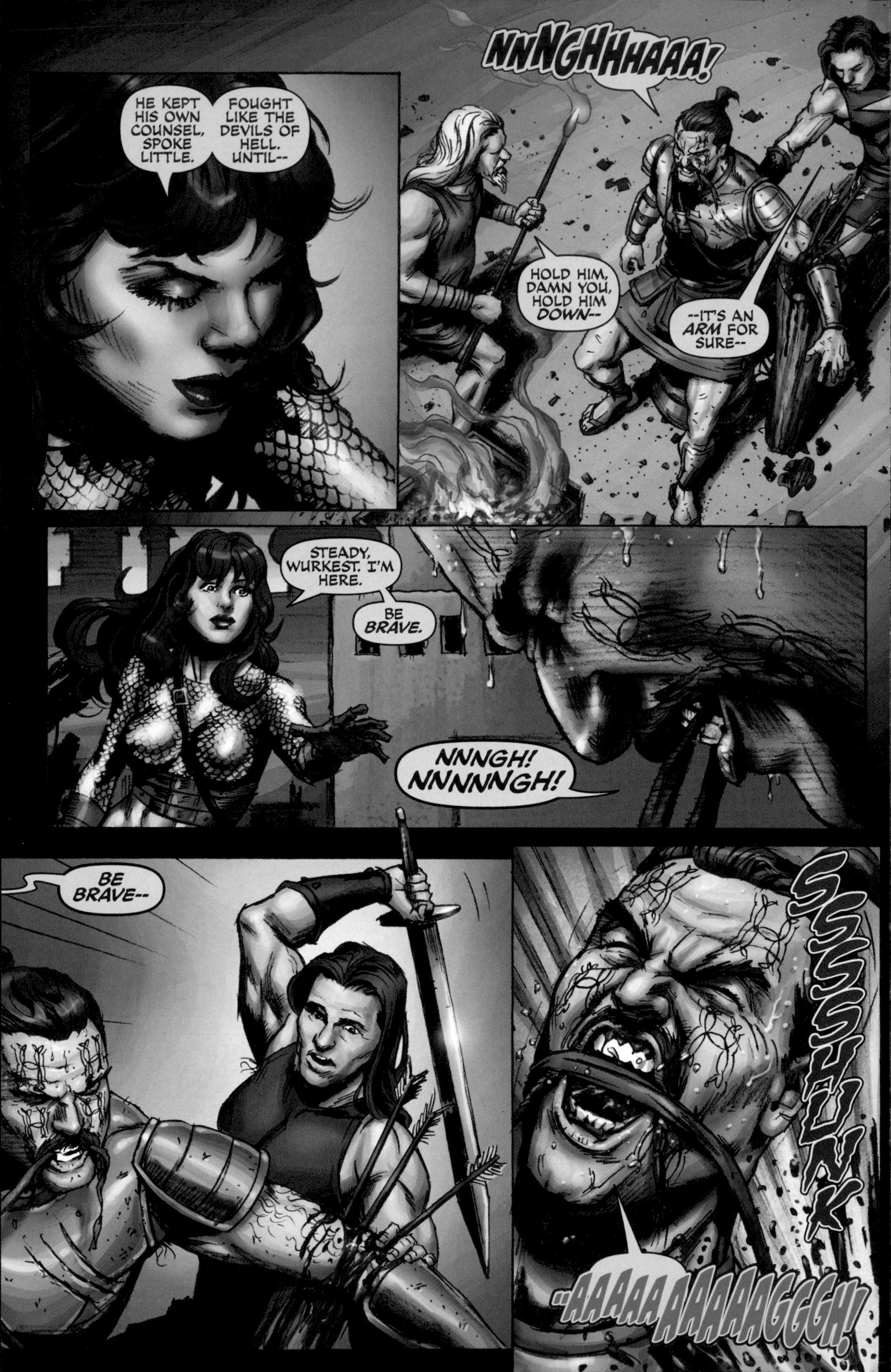
HE KEPT HIS OWN COUNSEL, SPOKE LITTLE.
FOUGHT LIKE THE DEVILS OF HELL. UNTIL--
NNNGHHHAAA!
HOLD HIM, DAMN YOU, HOLD HIM DOWN--
--IT'S AN ARM FOR SURE--
STEADY, WURKEST. I'M HERE.
BE BRAVE.
NNNGH! NNNNNGH!
BE BRAVE--
SSSSHUNK!
--AAAAAAAAAAGGGH!

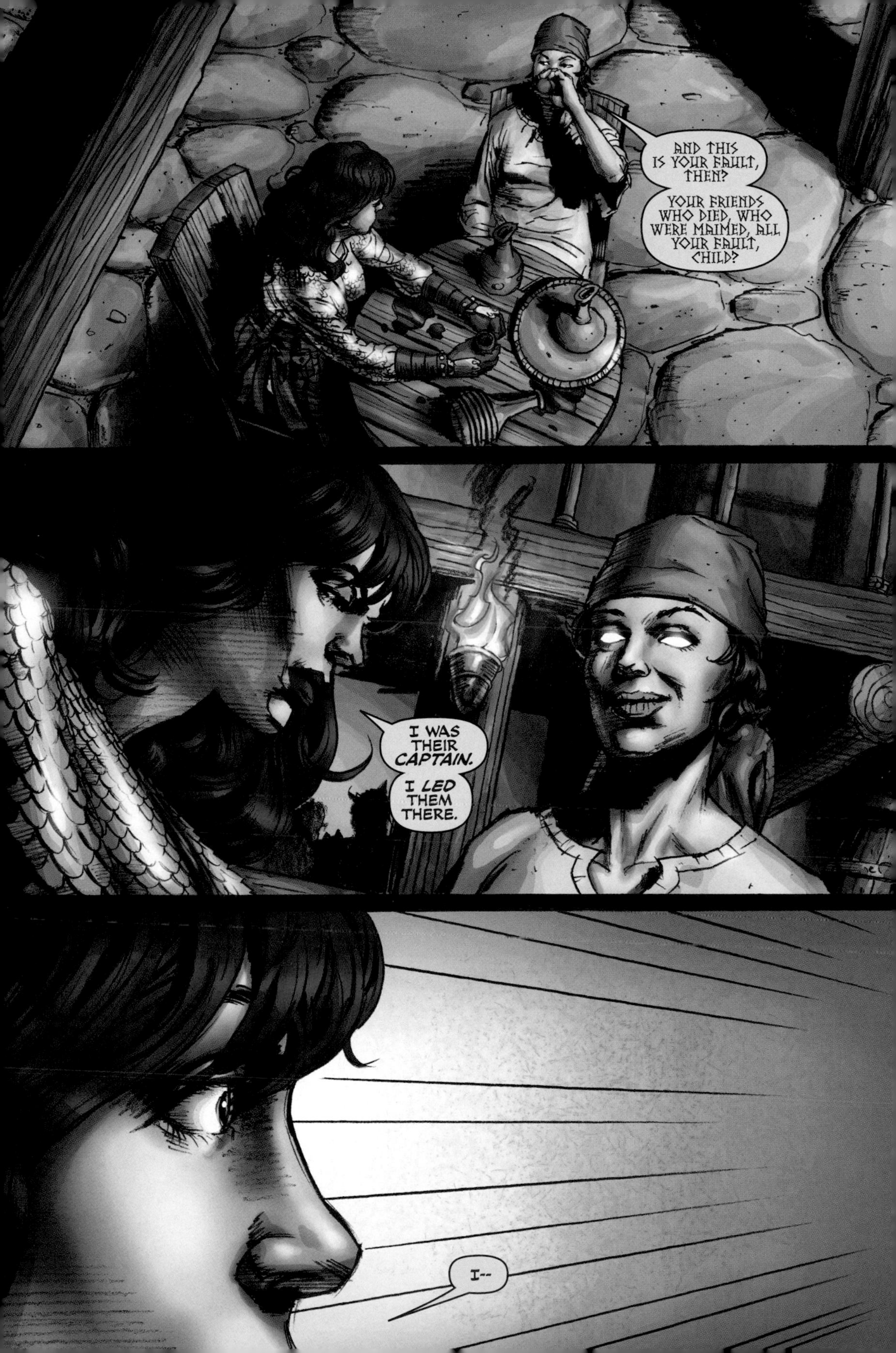
AND THIS IS YOUR FAULT, THEN?
YOUR FRIENDS WHO DIED, WHO WERE MAIMED, ALL YOUR FAULT, CHILD?
I WAS THEIR *CAPTAIN.*
I *LED* THEM THERE.
I--

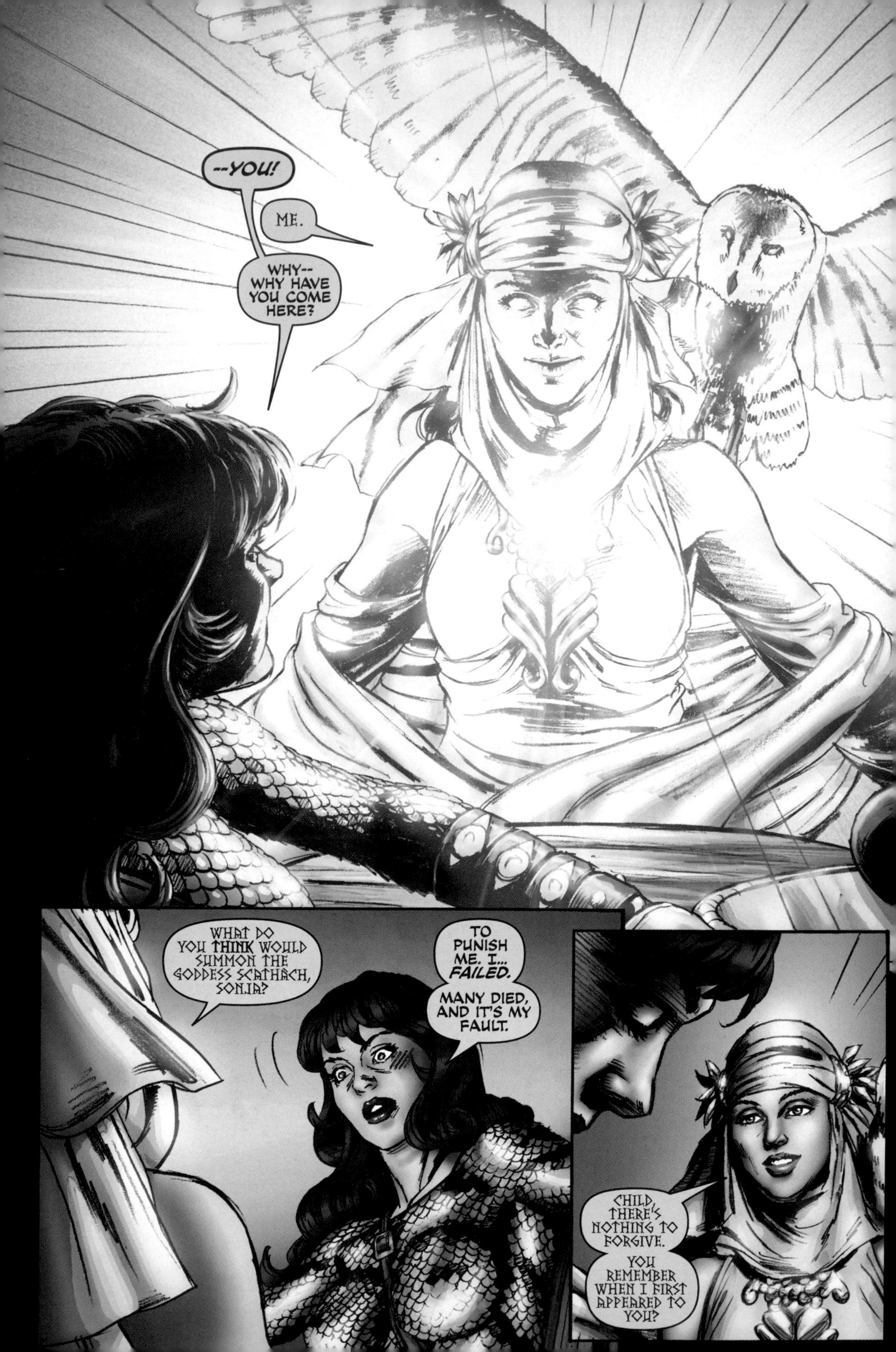
--YOU!
ME.
WHY-- WHY HAVE YOU COME HERE?
WHAT DO YOU THINK WOULD SUMMON THE GODDESS SCATHACH, SONJA?
TO PUNISH ME. I... FAILED.
MANY DIED, AND IT'S MY FAULT.
CHILD, THERE'S NOTHING TO FORGIVE.
YOU REMEMBER WHEN I FIRST APPEARED TO YOU?

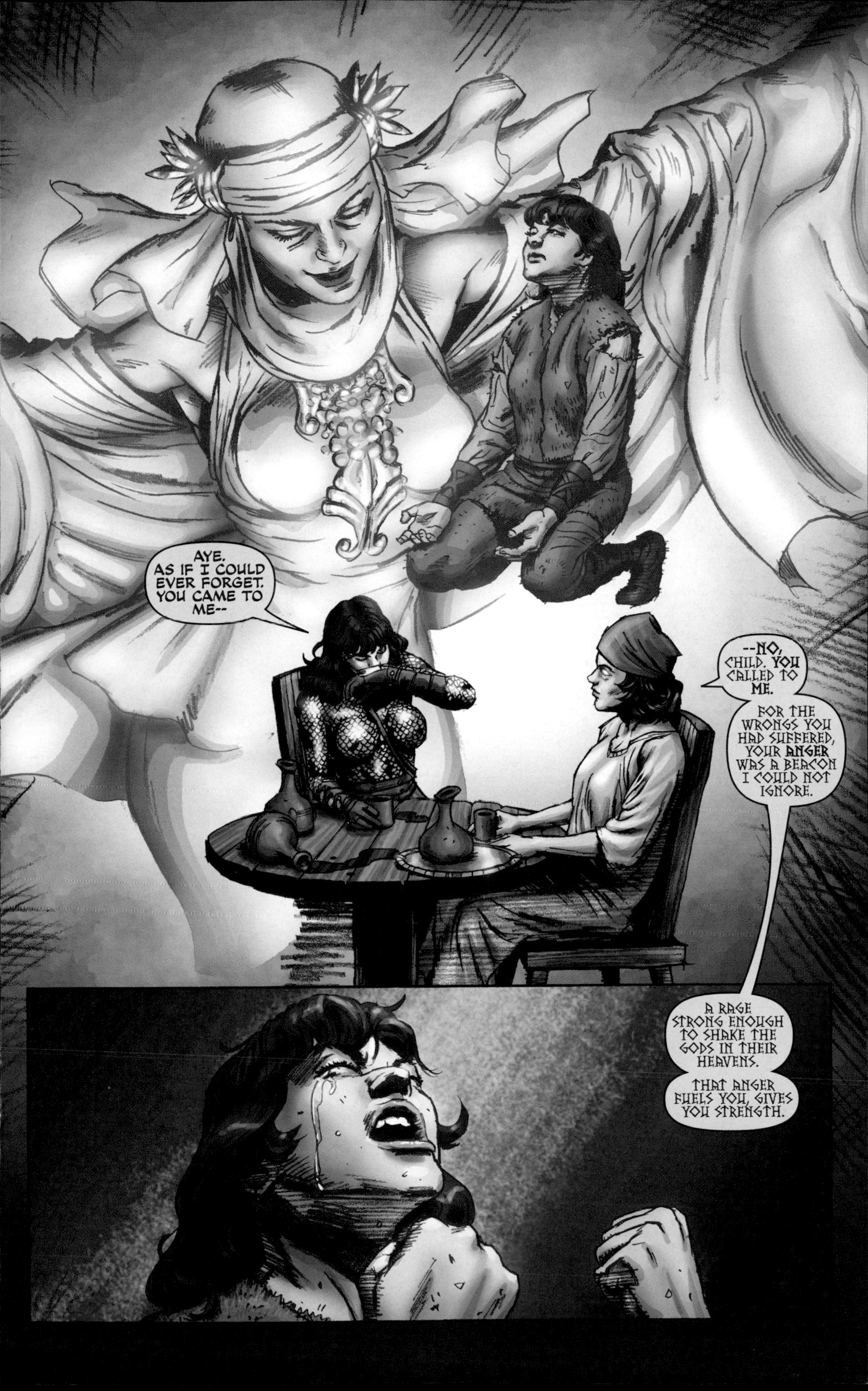
AYE. AS IF I COULD EVER FORGET. YOU CAME TO ME--
--NO, CHILD. YOU CALLED TO ME.
FOR THE WRONGS YOU HAD SUFFERED, YOUR ANGER WAS A BEACON I COULD NOT IGNORE.
A RAGE STRONG ENOUGH TO SHAKE THE GODS IN THEIR HEAVENS.
THAT ANGER FUELS YOU, GIVES YOU STRENGTH.

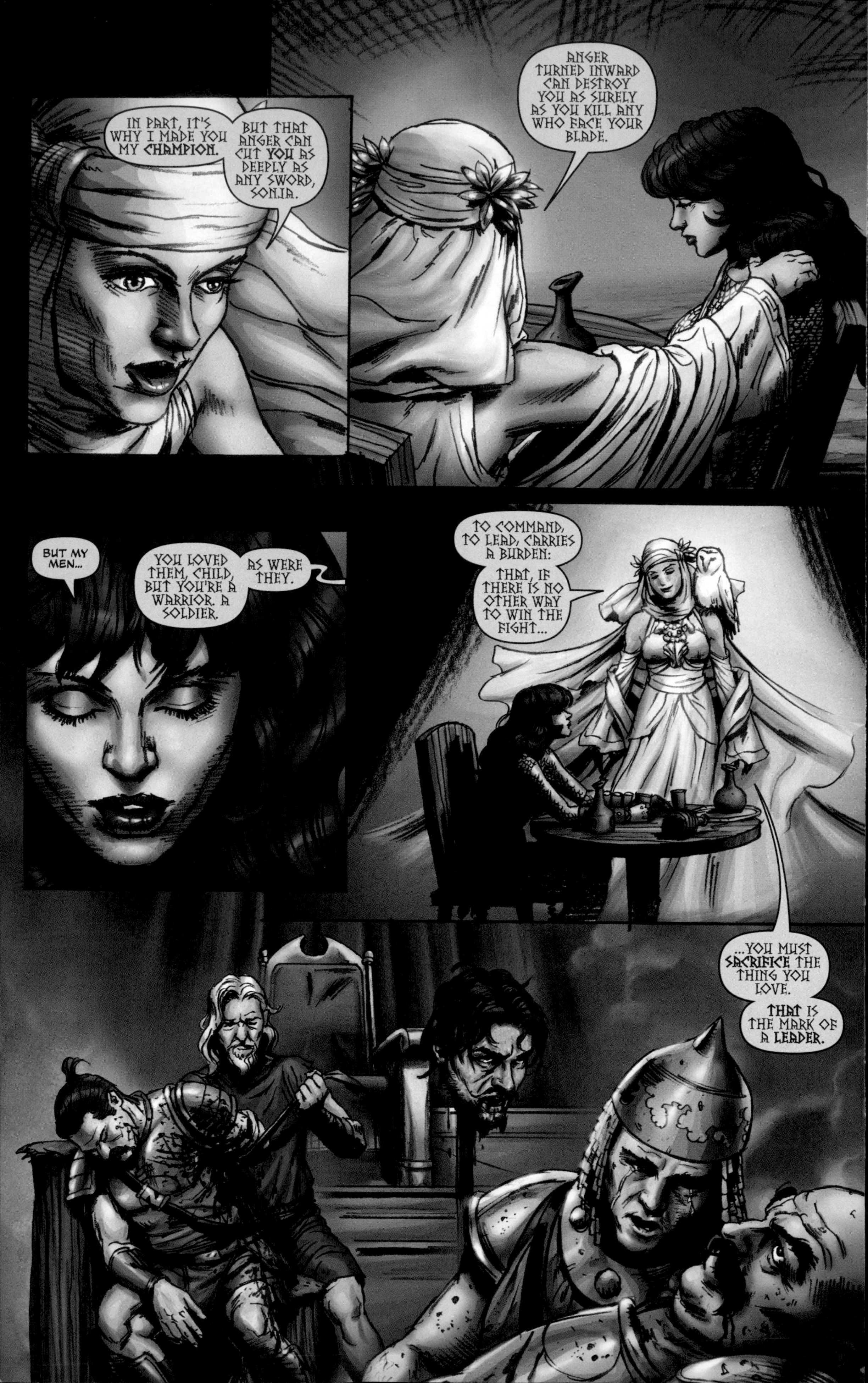

IN PART, IT'S WHY I MADE YOU MY CHAMPION.
BUT THAT ANGER CAN CUT YOU AS DEEPLY AS ANY SWORD, SONJA.
ANGER TURNED INWARD CAN DESTROY YOU AS SURELY AS YOU KILL ANY WHO FACE YOUR BLADE.
BUT MY MEN...
YOU LOVED THEM, CHILD, BUT YOU'RE A WARRIOR. A SOLDIER.
AS WERE THEY.
TO COMMAND, TO LEAD, CARRIES A BURDEN:
THAT, IF THERE IS NO OTHER WAY TO WIN THE FIGHT...
...YOU MUST SACRIFICE THE THING YOU LOVE.
THAT IS THE MARK OF A LEADER.

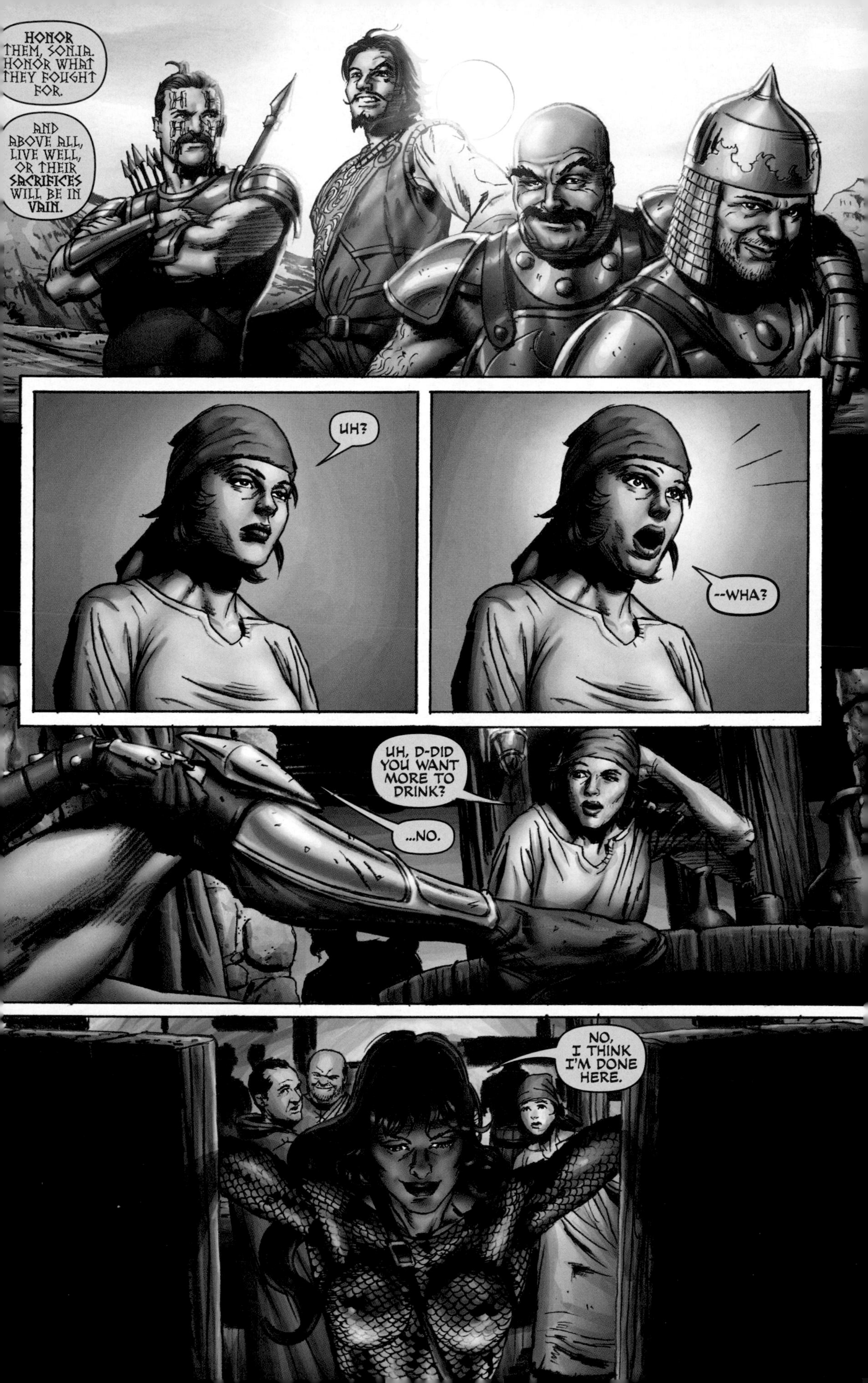
HONOR THEM, SONJA. HONOR WHAT THEY FOUGHT FOR.
AND ABOVE ALL, LIVE WELL, OR THEIR SACRIFICES WILL BE IN VAIN.
UH?
--WHA?
UH, D-DID YOU WANT MORE TO DRINK?
...NO.
NO, I THINK I'M DONE HERE.

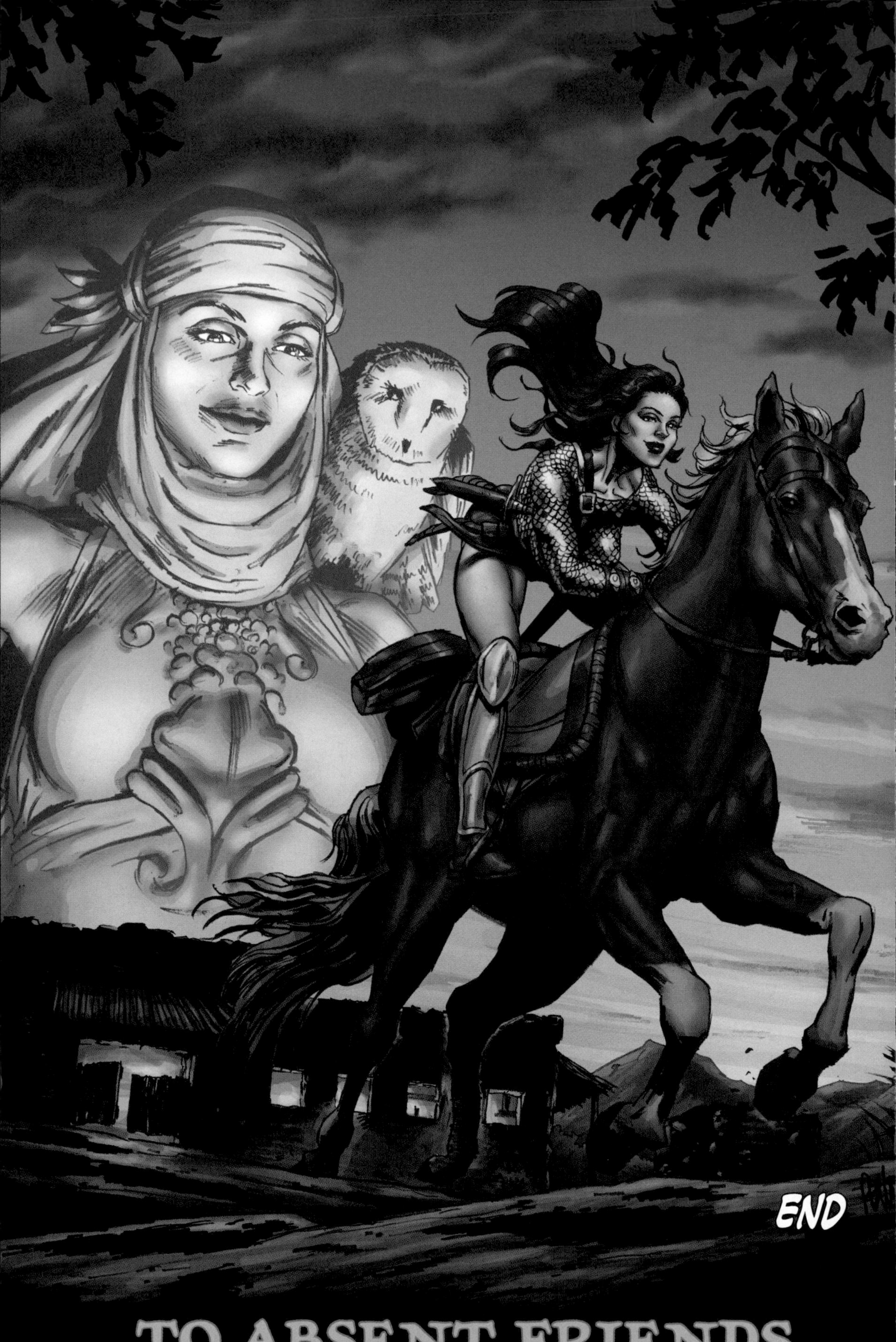
END

TO ABSENT FRIENDS

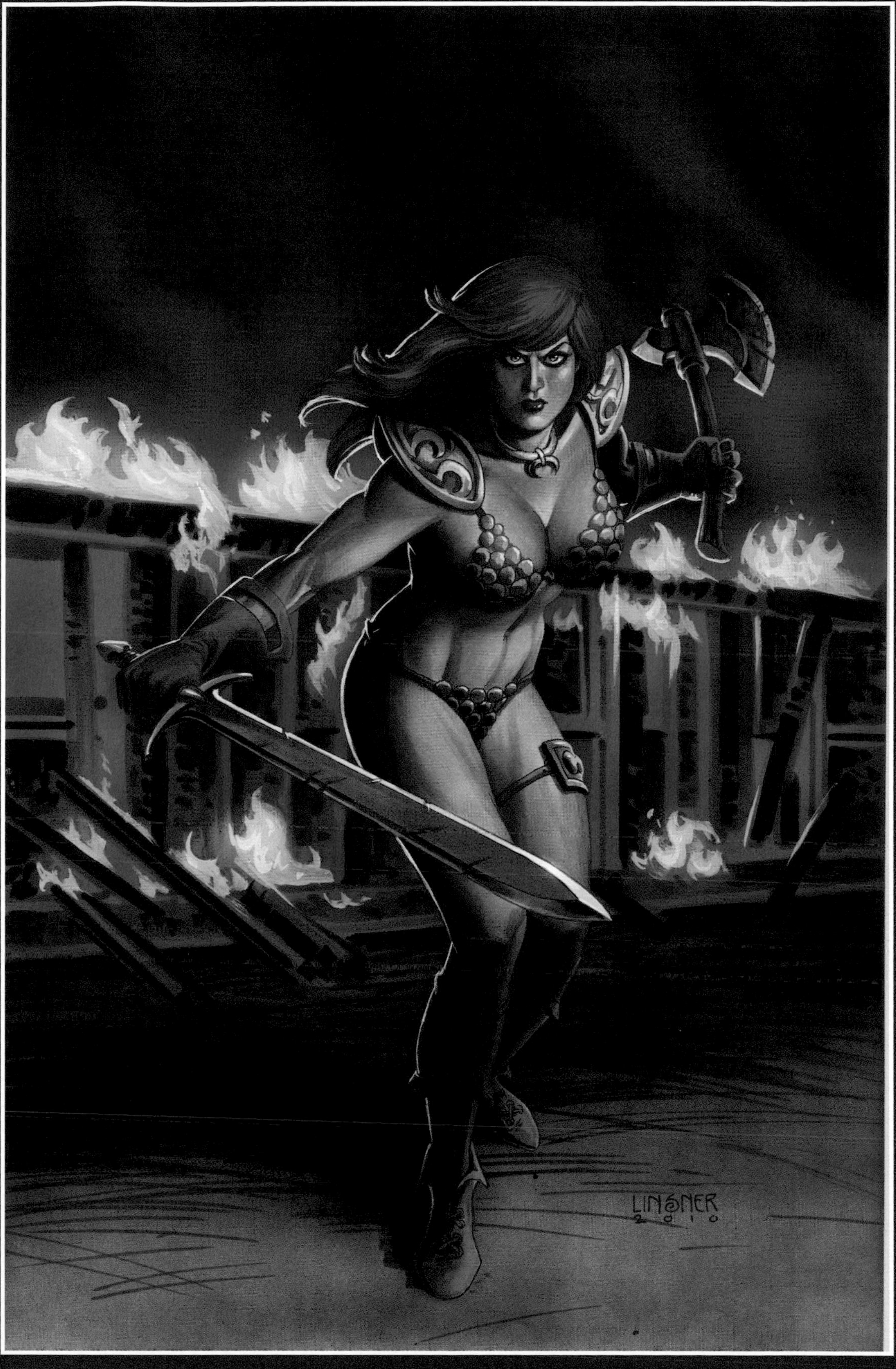
LINSNER
2010

ISSUE #51 COVER BY JOSEPH MICHAEL LINSNER

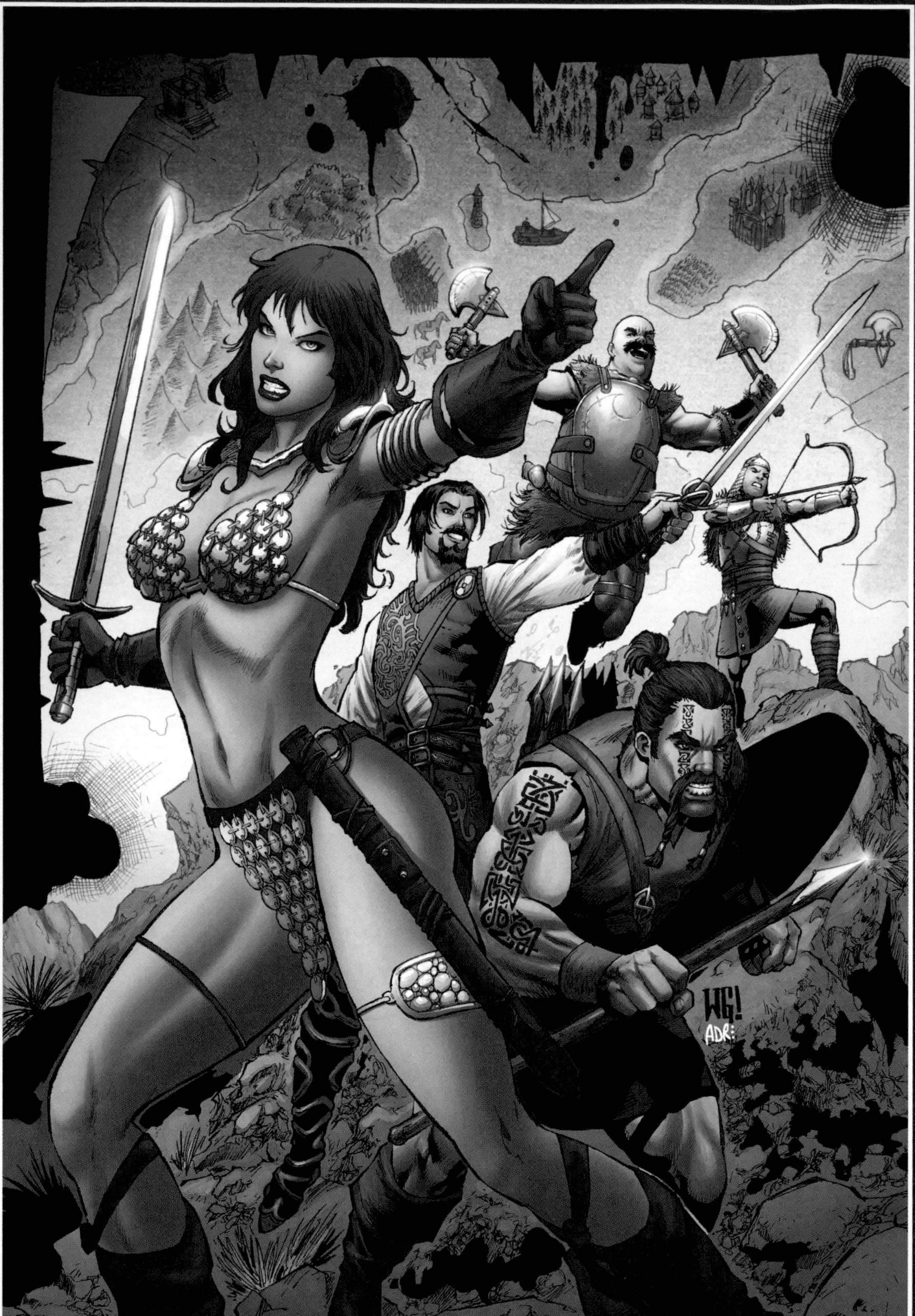
WG!
ADR

ISSUE #51 COVER BY WALTER GEOVANI

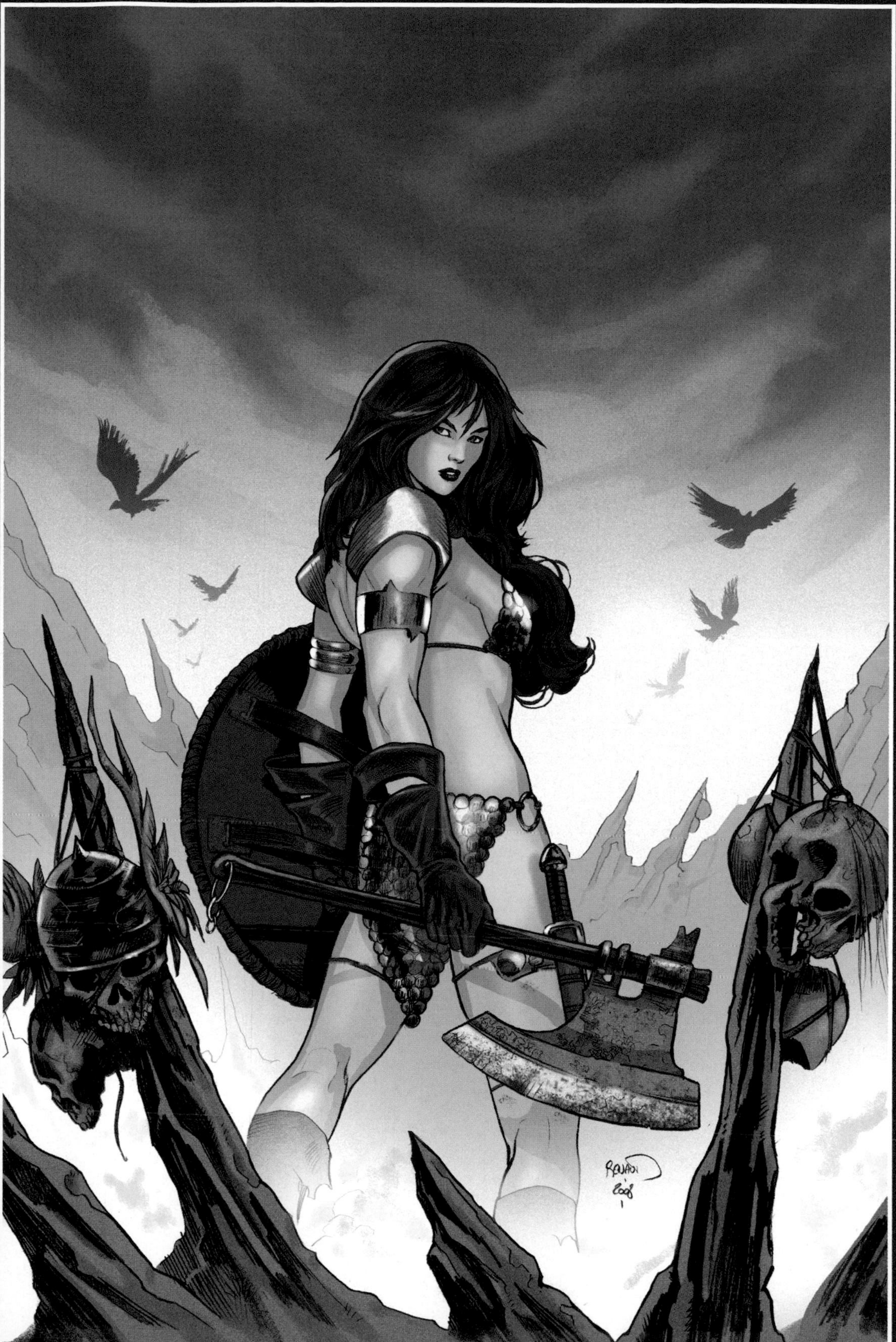

ISSUE #51 COVER BY PAUL RENAUD

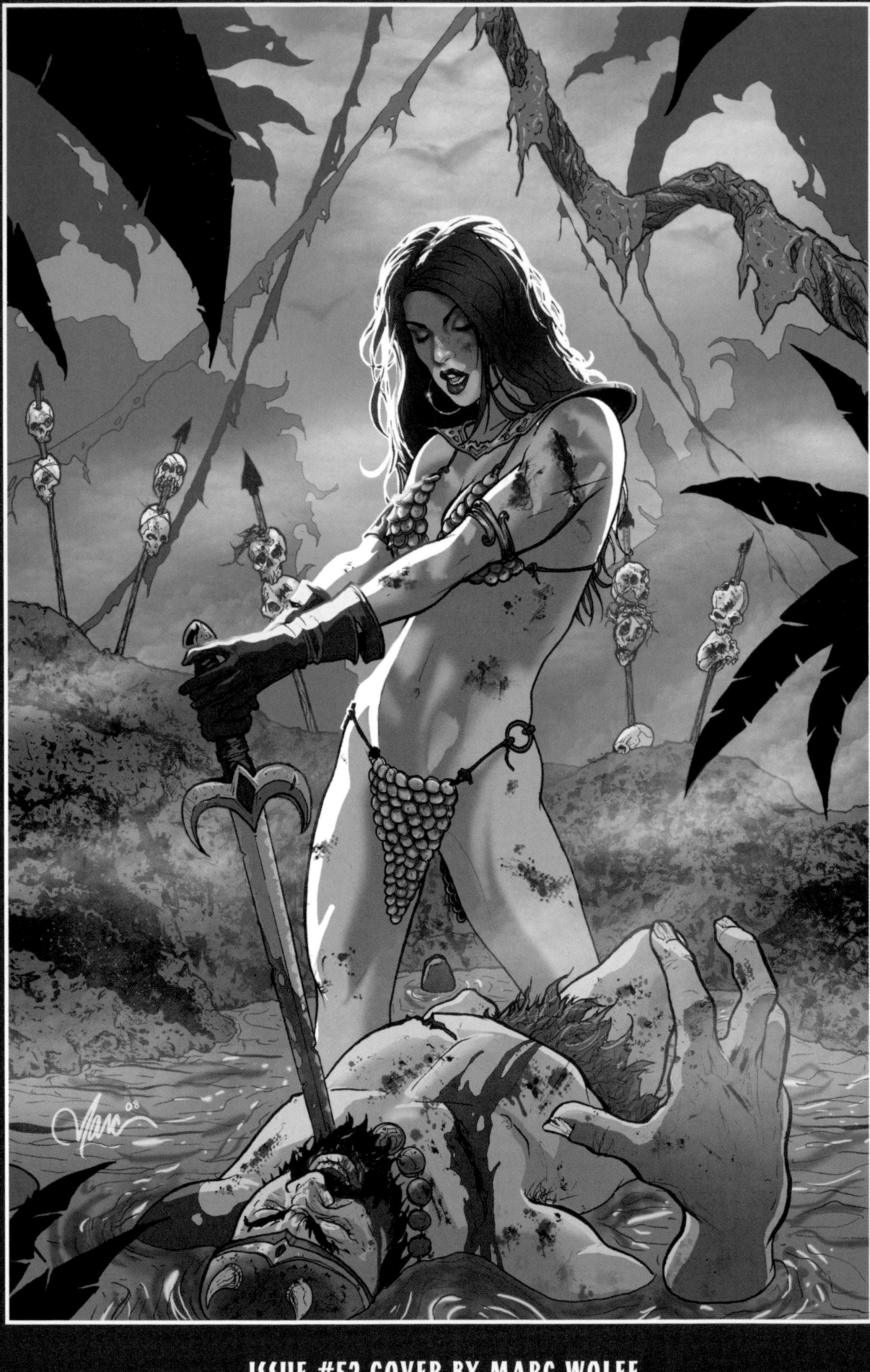

ISSUE #52 COVER BY MARC WOLFE

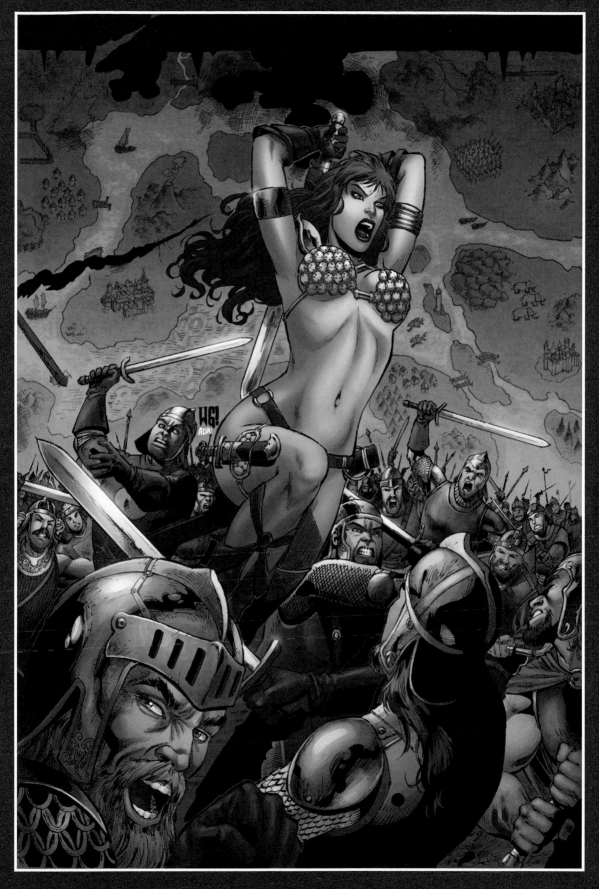

ISSUE #52 COVER BY WALTER GEOVANI

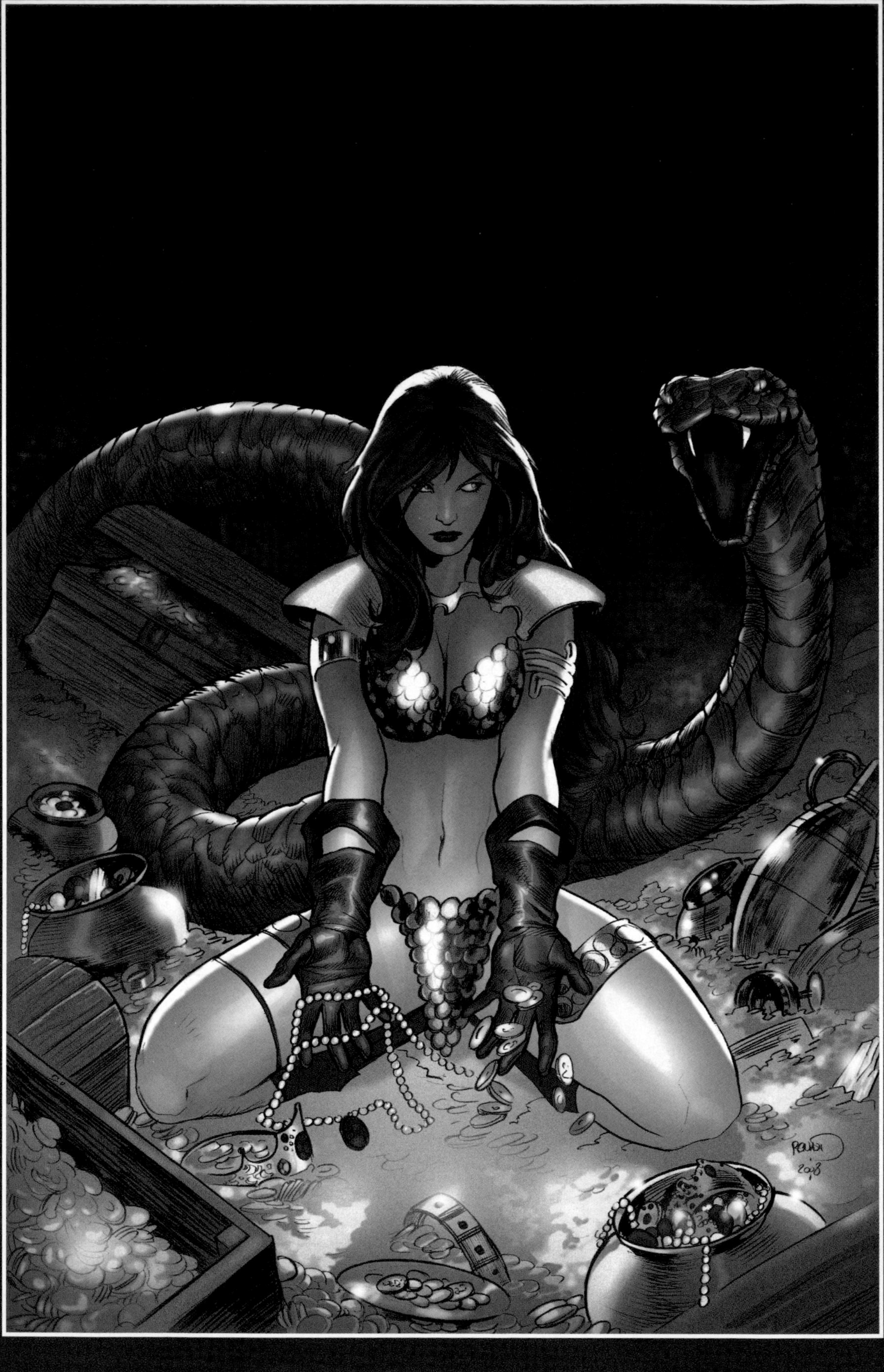

ISSUE #52 COVER BY PAUL RENAUD

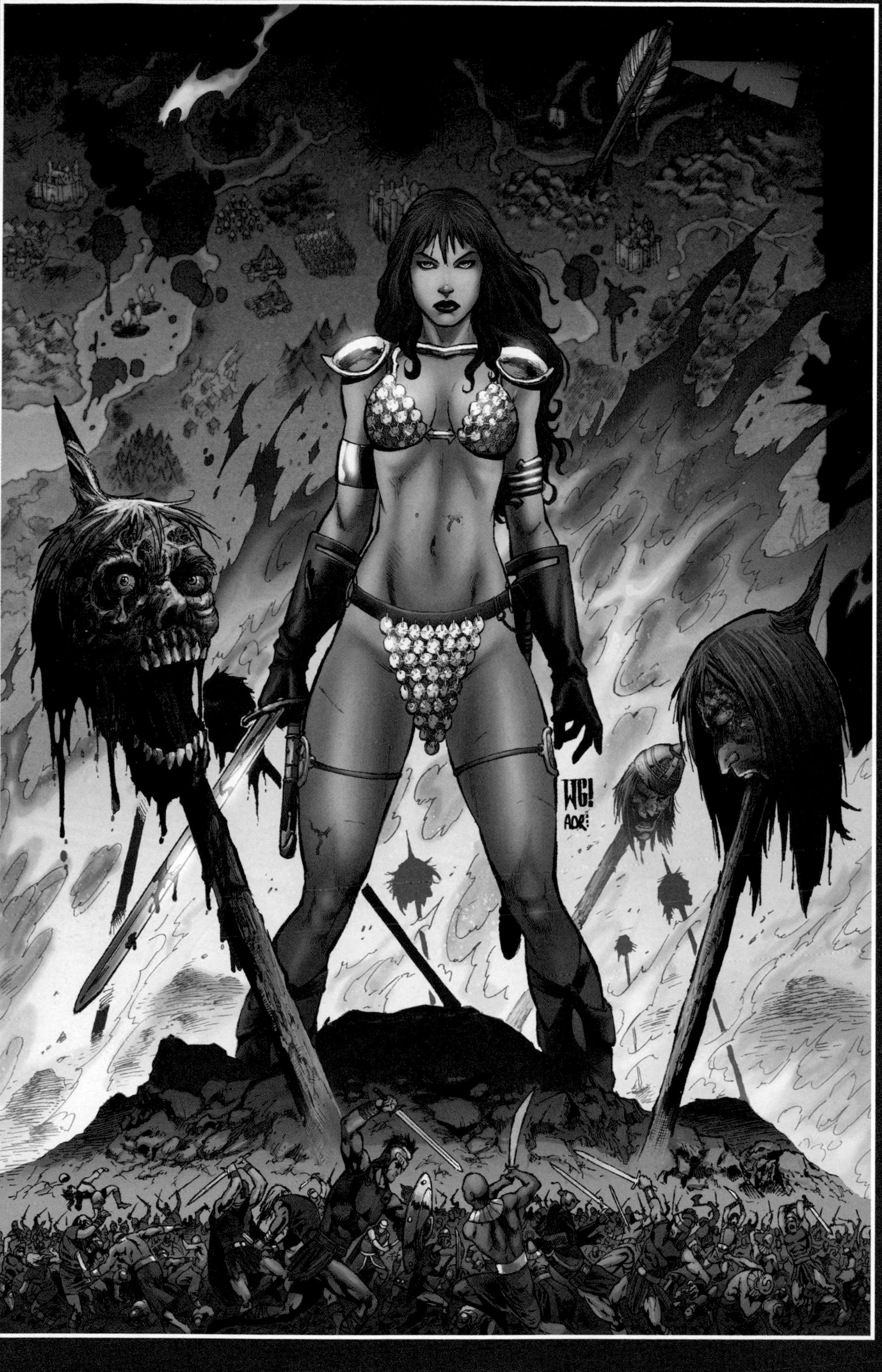

ISSUE #53 COVER BY WALTER GEOVANI

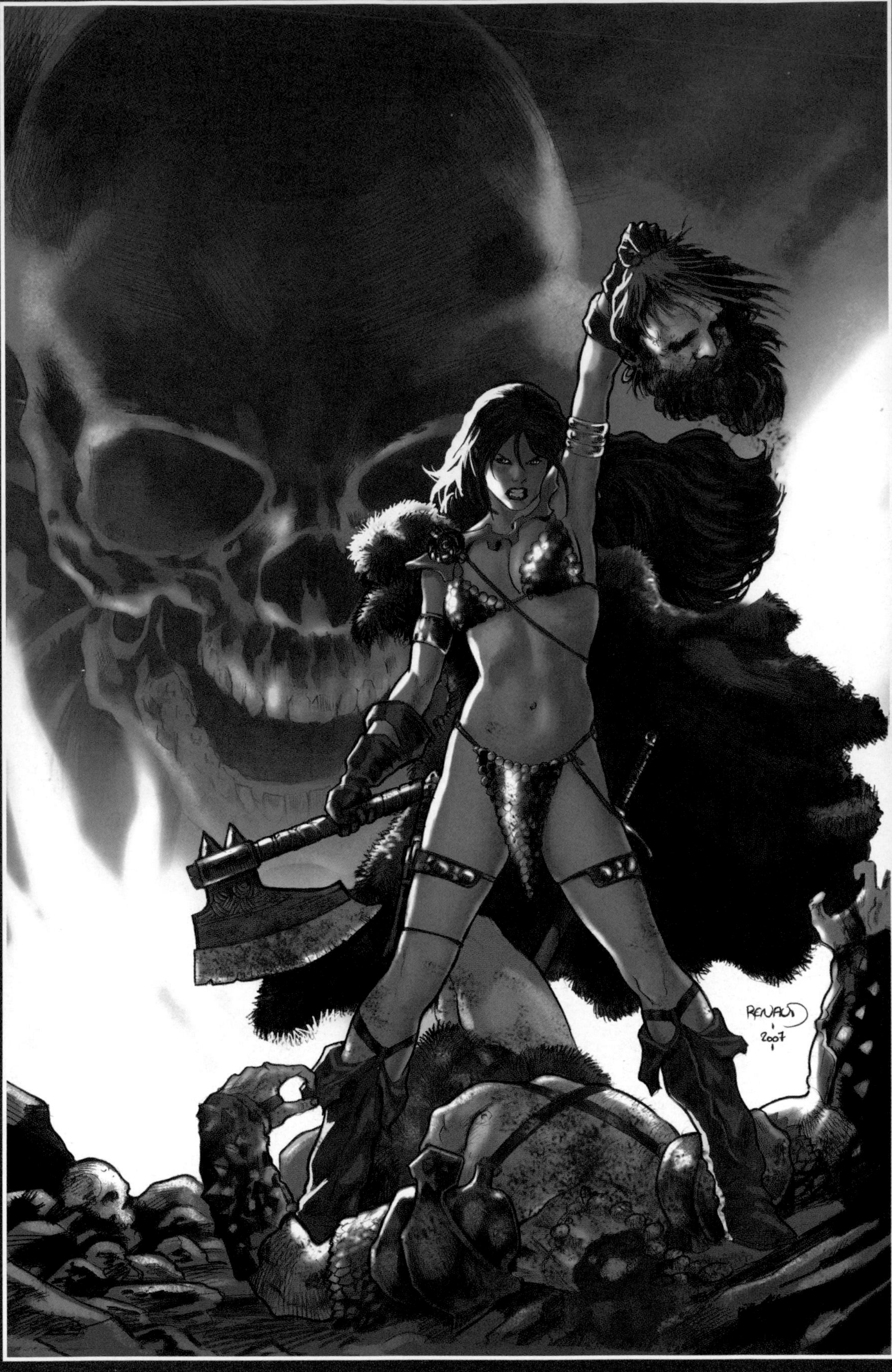
RENAUD
2007

ISSUE #53 COVER BY PAUL RENAUD

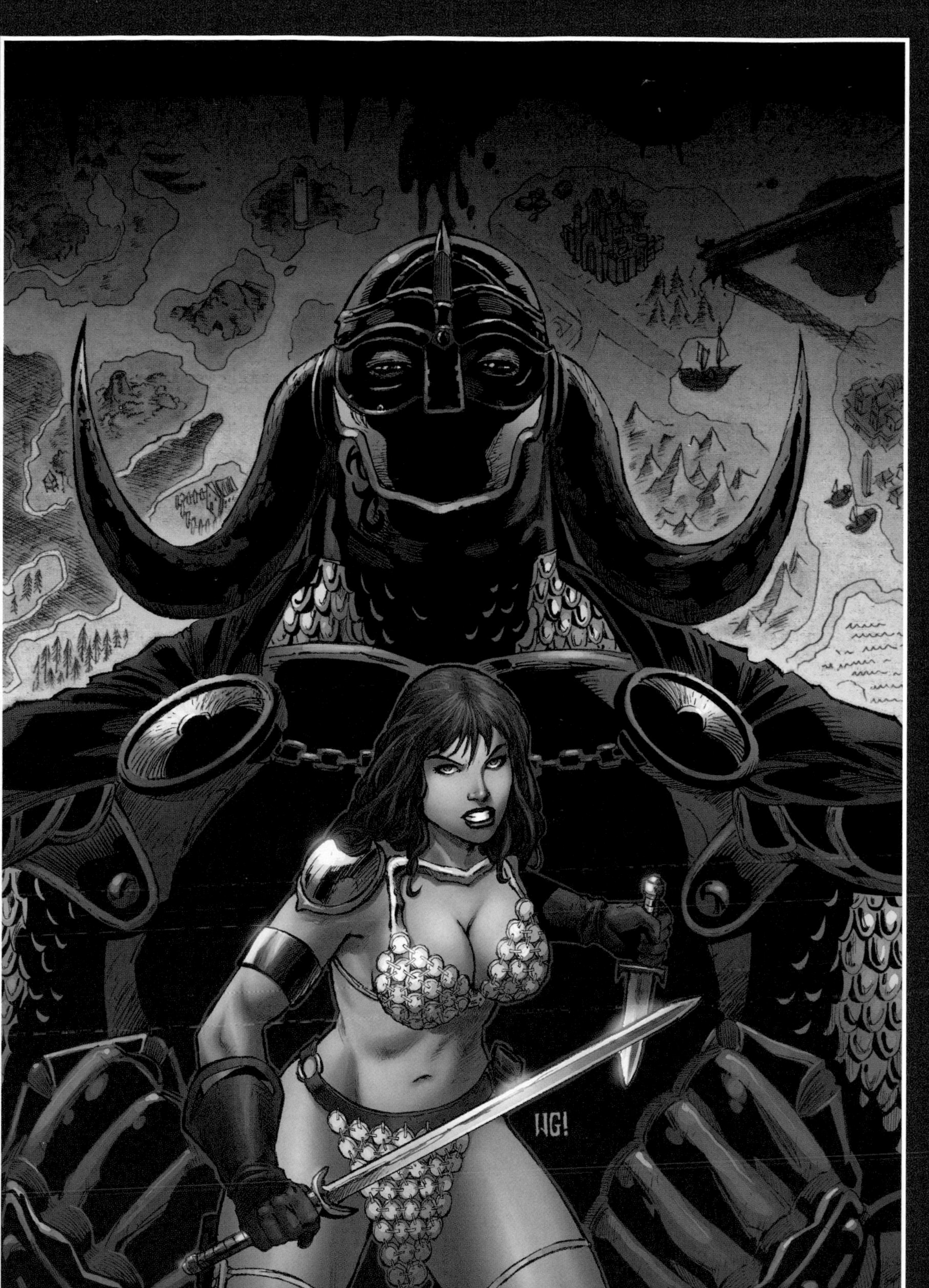
WG!

ISSUE #54 COVER BY WALTER GEOVANI

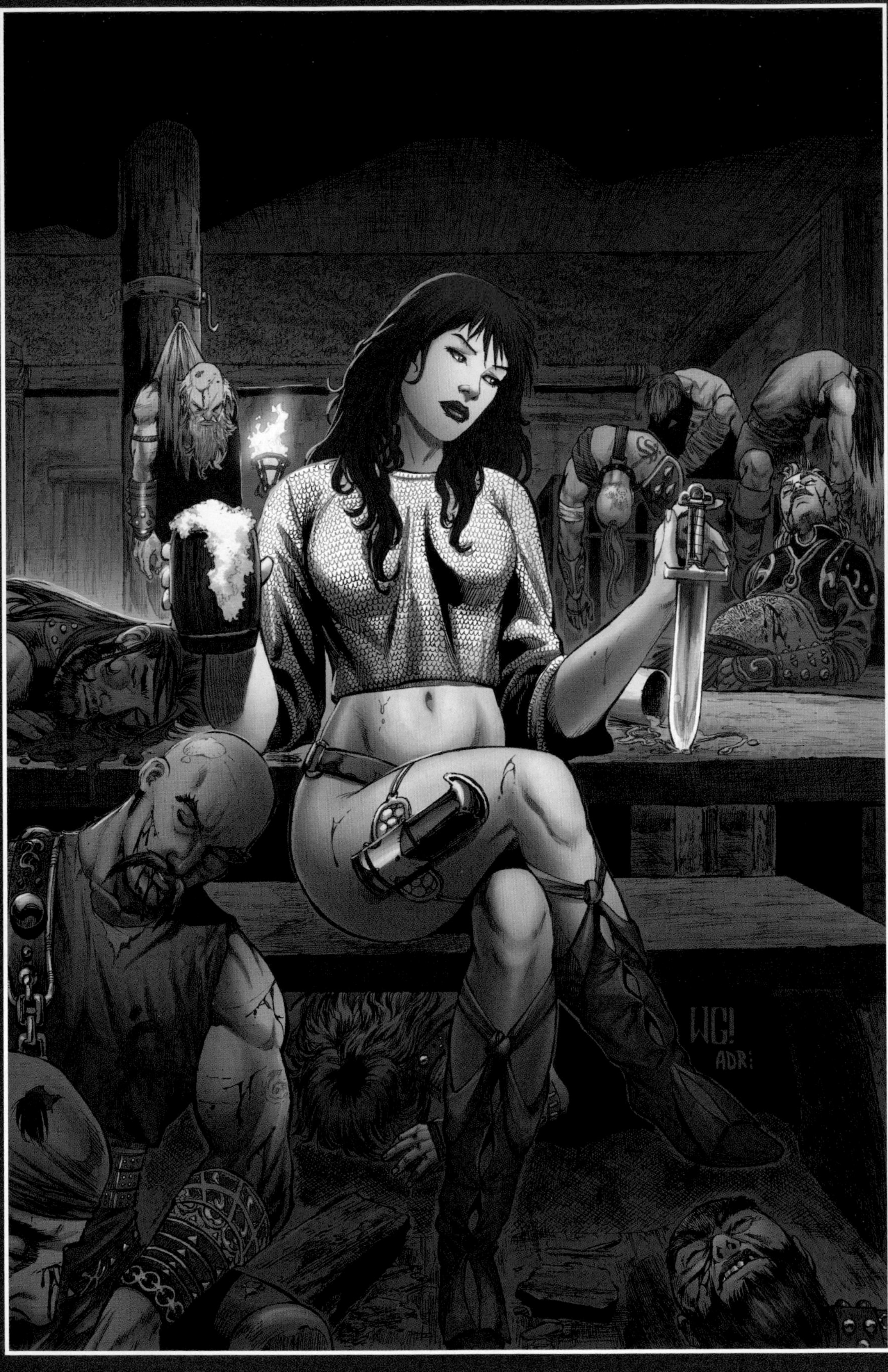
WG!
ADR

ISSUE #55 COVER BY WALTER GEOVANI

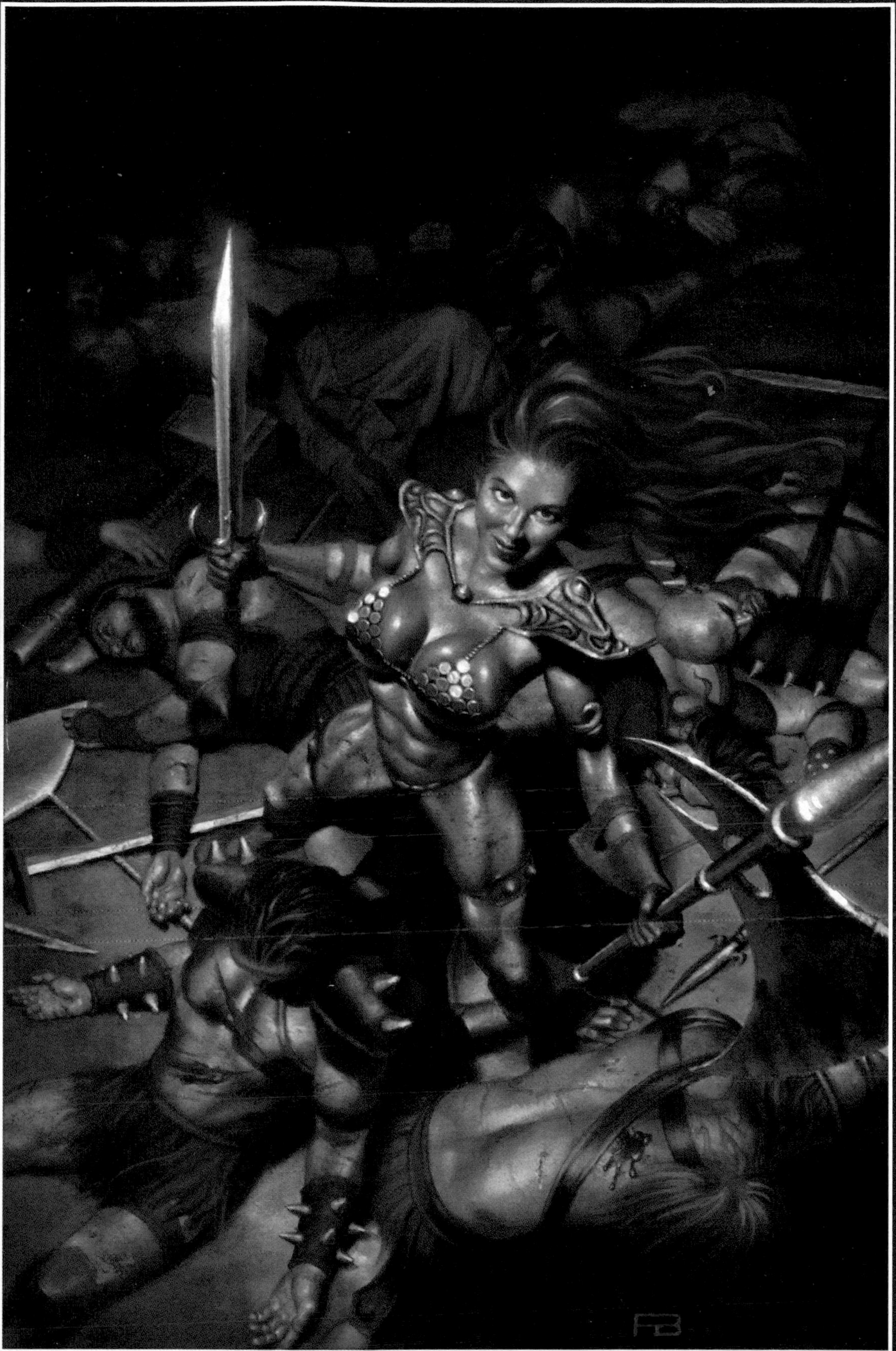

ISSUE #55 COVER BY PATRICK BERKENKOTTER

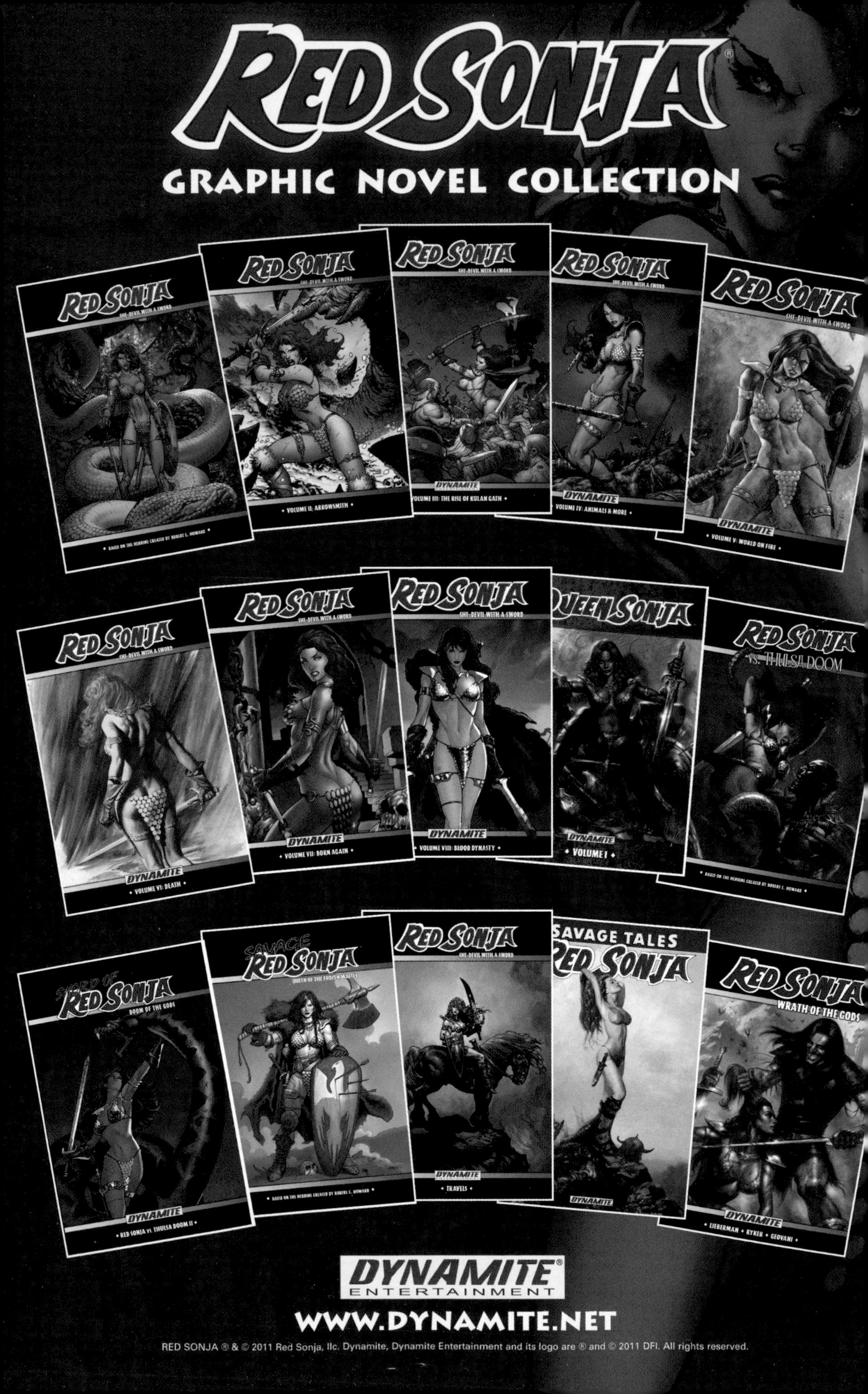
RED SONJA®
GRAPHIC NOVEL COLLECTION
RED SONJA
SHE-DEVIL WITH A SWORD
BASED ON THE HEROINE CREATED BY ROBERT E. HOWARD
RED SONJA
SHE-DEVIL WITH A SWORD
VOLUME II: ARROWSMITH
RED SONJA
SHE-DEVIL WITH A SWORD
DYNAMITE
VOLUME III: THE RISE OF KULAN GATH
RED SONJA
SHE-DEVIL WITH A SWORD
DYNAMITE
VOLUME IV: ANIMALS & MORE
RED SONJA
SHE-DEVIL WITH A SWORD
DYNAMITE
VOLUME V: WORLD ON FIRE
RED SONJA
SHE-DEVIL WITH A SWORD
DYNAMITE
VOLUME VI: DEATH
RED SONJA
SHE-DEVIL WITH A SWORD
DYNAMITE
VOLUME VII: BORN AGAIN
RED SONJA
SHE-DEVIL WITH A SWORD
DYNAMITE
VOLUME VIII: BLOOD DYNASTY
QUEEN SONJA
DYNAMITE
VOLUME I
RED SONJA
vs. THULSA DOOM
BASED ON THE HEROINE CREATED BY ROBERT E. HOWARD
SWORD OF RED SONJA
DOOM OF THE GODS
DYNAMITE
RED SONJA vs. THULSA DOOM II
SAVAGE RED SONJA
QUEEN OF THE FROZEN WASTES
BASED ON THE HEROINE CREATED BY ROBERT E. HOWARD
RED SONJA
SHE-DEVIL WITH A SWORD
DYNAMITE
TRAVELS
SAVAGE TALES
RED SONJA
DYNAMITE
RED SONJA
WRATH OF THE GODS
DYNAMITE
LIEBERMAN • RYKER • GEOVANI
DYNAMITE® ENTERTAINMENT
WWW.DYNAMITE.NET
RED SONJA ® & © 2011 Red Sonja, llc. Dynamite, Dynamite Entertainment and its logo are ® and © 2011 DFI. All rights reserved.